THE ROLE OF ROCK

Harmless Entertainment
or
Destructive Influence?

JOHN MUNCY

Daring Publishing Group, Inc.

DARING BOOKS • LIFE ENRICHMENT PUBLISHERS
CANTON • OHIO

Published by Daring Books
P.O. Box 20050, Canton, Ohio 44701

ISBN 0-938936-92-1

LCCN Pending

Printed in the United States of America.

1 2 3 4 5 6 7 8 9 10

Dedication

I want to dedicate this book to...

My lovely wife, Carolyn!
You are the greatest thing next to Jesus in my life!
The ultimate fulfillment of Proverbs 31!
Thank you, honey, for serving our Lord Jesus so willingly!!
Sorry for all the long hours while writing the book-
Thanks for putting up with me!
Carolyn, only God could have given me such a great wife,
I LOVE YOU!!!

My special sunshine, Bethany Grace!
You are such a wonderful daughter! My Miracle girl!
I will always love you!
You melted my heart from the day you were born!

To my main man, Titus Matthew!
"Nevertheless God, that comforteth those that are cast down,
comforted us by the coming of Titus" (2 Cor. 7:6)
I love you, son, I'm very proud of you!

To my Mom and Dad!
Thank you for allowing me to grow up in a home with my *real* parents
in an age of divorce! I love you both!

To my sister, Melissa, and brother-in-law, Chris!
How could I have such a good-looking sister?
Move to Ohio and I'll put you and Chris to work for Jesus!

*But most of all, I dedicate not only this book,
but everything I have to:*

THE ROCK...MY LORD AND MY GOD, JESUS CHRIST!
"For me to live is Christ, and to die is gain"
"He must increase, but I must decrease"
Lord, thank You for all You've done for me! I love You!!!

Acknowledgments

There is no way I could list all the many people who contributed to this book, but I would like to honour a few...

Thanks to all the precious young people I've met from coast to coast that have been such a source of information and challenge! I really love you young people!

Thanks to all the friends who have sent me clippings from the papers or the magazines to help keep me current!

Special acknowledgment goes to every **Pastor** and **Youth Pastor** who have opened their pulpits to Carolyn and me down through the years! Thanks to so many of my preacher buddies and their families who have shared their lives with ours! You all have truly been a blessing!

Thank you, **Pastor John Swint** for being a *spiritual* dad! We love you and **Alice** so much! You have done more for us than we could ever say! (**Gary**, **Brenda**, and **Karen**, too!)

Thank you, **Pastor Tim** and **Carol Sheets** and everyone at **The Living Word** for the many months of backing our ministry with your support! Thanks for giving me a home base to work from, with a nice office to be able to work from and for such a great staff to work with! Who knows where we would be today if you hadn't helped!!

Thanks to our special friends **Randy** and **Angie Grimes,** and their four precious children, **Lisa, Joshua, Jacob,** and **Luke** for their love and support! Thanks for helping us when we first started in the evangelistic work! Thanks for all the hilarious times and Alka-Seltzers!

Special thanks to **Beckie** and **Randy Cisler** and their two fantastic kids, **Allison** and **Brett**! Becky, this is the result of your encouragement! Thanks for believing in me!

Thanks to the whole **Bartow** family, our publishers, for the patient and professional way of handling things! Thanks for publishing my very first book!

Thanks to **Maggie Stewart**! A sister-in-law who didn't get alot of credit as a secretary, but was a good one anyway! Thank God for you and **Donald** and the unbeatable kids, **Donnie, Amy, Angel**, and **Jesse**! You guys are great, I love you all dearly!

Thanks to **Debbie Ratliff** for all the help with your computer knowledge and for being such a busy secretary!

To my special brother in Christ, **Joel Harris** for all the clippings and other info sent in those special envelopes!

Special thanks to **Tom** and **Stephanie Moore** and **Neil** and **Trudy Erisman** for their tremendous support down through the years!

Thanks to all my dear friends whom God has blessed me with! Especially **Mike Lindsey, Ron Henson, and Wayne Carter**...the "3 stooges"!!

Thanks to all the behind-the-scene prayer partners who have held us up before the Lord as we war against the powers of darkness, especially while we were dealing with Bethany's leukemia!

TABLE OF CONTENTS

Preface

This is a warning!!!

What you are about to read is a documented fact, so please read it very carefully...

> There is solid proof that there is a group of people coming into this country, entering in one at a time. They are becoming a large part of our communities. They are even now in the beginning stages to rule our financial institutions and are even in the process of taking them over completely. They will rule all our governmental institutions and eventually run the government itself. They are right now penetrating all our schools. They will eventually take over all our churches, all our social organizations, all communication systems including radio, television, and even the newspapers. They will take over all hospitals, all educational systems, all law enforcement agencies and virtually every leadership position in our city and nation. And there is absolutely NOTHING that we can do to stop it! They will take charge of us!!!

You may ask, "Who are these people? Where are they coming from? What can we do to stop them?" Well, we *wouldn't* want to stop them...because they are our CHILDREN!!!!!!!

That's right! Many of you thought I was referring to some terrible group of people from another country, some enemy of America. But the truth is that the ones who will soon be in control are now in *our* control as parents, entertainers, teachers, and ministers! And because of that fact, we need to be so careful to invest in them the best of everything we have!

With that purpose in mind, I have written this book. I want it
to be a challenge to the parents, the entertainers, the teachers,
the ministers, and most of all to the youth of this land to see
the importance of addressing a very powerful influence in the
lives of literally millions of young people, the future of this
land!

As we look at the "Role Of Rock", we are able to see how
many destructive elements are brought into acceptance merely
because it has a 'neat beat'! I hope that in these pages, I can
pull the facade off of much of today's music and hit the real
issue...the role that rock and roll is playing, bringing negative
results into the lives of our greatest heritage, our children! To
some people, the only problem they might see wrong in rock
music is the threat on the ear drums. I read where one group
has started HEAR (Hearing Education and Awareness for
Rockers) to help musicians and their fans to see the seriousness of the problem.[1] Others see the problem basically in the
rythmn or beat, claiming it runs against the natural rythmn of
the body, while others feel it calls forth some type of demon
power. However, I'm taking a different approach. I feel that
there is a 'message' in much of today's music that is being
presented with such wide acceptance, that millions of people
are swallowing it whole! And, in reality, I feel it is worse than
any physical problem presented!

It is not my intention to compete with the many great books
written on this subject but to simply share my own heart on a
vital part of our youth culture. Most of the material came from
digging into this thing head-on, with much prayer. No doubt
I will not have the applause of most rock fans, but if you will
read this book with an open heart I believe you'll see I'm not
knocking a certain style of music or picking on a particular
musical taste, but exposing the true **Role of Rock**...

---

[1]People, Jan. 23, 1989, pg. 95

The Role Of Rock

1

"Music is a vehicle for whatever you want..."[1]
-**Paul Stanley**, lead singer for **Kiss**

Rock and roll is more than a handful of musicians who play a guitar, a keyboard, a bass, and a set of drums...it is an avenue through which many concepts are being brought into the culture of millions of young people, either good or bad! It is a platform to preach almost anything, either true or false! It is much more than a musical style, it is a voice that is saying something...and it's being heard loud and clear!! Studies across our nation have revealed that the average teenager listens to rock music somewhere around 4 to 6 hours a day. Anything that has this type of daily influence on the youth culture will certainly leave its mark. Rock music definitely has!

It is easy to see the impact rock music has in the lives of young people. It's what most teenagers invest a greater part of their money in...the average record or tape sells for around $10.00, a normal rock T-shirt sells for $17.00, and a normal concert ticket will cost anywhere from $12.00 to $25.00 per person. Today, the rock industry has become a multi-billion dollar industry!! "Rock music is booming, and 1987 was certainly a banner year," declared Matthew Stuemky, spokesman for *Pollstar*, a music industry trade publication, "The top 40 money-grossing tours by rock musicians drummed up more than $503 million - a whopping $65 million more than 1986."[2] This goes to show that where your money is, there your heart will be also. *Forbes* magazine top forty in the entertainment industry for 1988 showed the following gross income...

Michael Jackson	$60 million
George Michael	$36 million
Bruce Springsteen	$34 million
Van Halen	$22 million
Madonna	$20 million
Prince	$16 million
Bon Jovi	$15 million
Pink Floyd	$15 million
Sting	$14 million
U2	$13 million
The Grateful Dead	$12 million
John Cougar	$12 million
Whitney Houston	$6 million
Billy Joel	$6 million
Tina Turner	$4 million

Everything from clothes to attitudes are being formulated by popular music. Kids hear it on their stereos at home, the radios in their cars. They hear it while riding the bus to school, and when they get to school, it's piped into the hallways and cafeteria throughout the day. It's played in the stores at the malls, the pizza palaces, the putt-putt golf courses, the video game rooms, the swimming pools, the amusement parks, the roller rinks, the ball games, it's found in most of the commercials on TV; rock music is virtually everywhere in today's society where young people are. Of course, if you say anything negative about it, you can get some pretty mean looks.

I remember as a young boy hearing the **Beatles**. I would listen to their records and watch them on TV, and like most other boys, I wanted to start my own rock and roll band. With a bunch of the neighborhood buddies, we would go downstairs with our makeshift band and "Twist and Shout". Of course, my mom thought it was cute. It was something that "everybody" was doing. I had my own little record player with a small collection of 45's. I dreamed of the day that I would get a real guitar and be like my rock and roll stars.

Then at the age of 12, a very important thing happened to my life...I gave my life to the *real* Rock...**Jesus Christ!** And shortly after receiving **Jesus** as Lord of my life, I felt the call of God to preach. I preached my very first sermon when I was 12, and by the time I turned 13, I was holding revivals. It didn't seem long until I began to feel uncomfortable listening to rock and roll. It wasn't that someone told me it was bad, it was as if I knew if I was going to become serious about serving Jesus, I was going to have to do something about my music. And after making that important decision, I remember almost overnight I began to really grow spiritually. I fell in love with the Bible, and would read it for hours at a time. I began to develop a prayer life and really grew in the Lord. Now looking back, I can see how important it was for me to allow Jesus to be Lord, even over my music.

Soon I became bold for Christ and began to carry my Bible to school. I would pass out tracts and witness to my fellow classmates. I had the privilege of leading many of them to Christ, some of whom are in full-time ministry today. I started a "Teens For Christ" club that grew from 5 to 60 in a short time. We would meet before school started every morning and prayed for revival. One thing I noticed in school, while many kids were into various things; drinking, drugs, parties, sex; one thing seem to span the whole school...rock music. No matter if they were 'jocks', 'heads', or 'wiz kids', they seem to all relate to rock and roll.

I maintained a preaching ministry throughout my high school years, and shortly after graduation, I became a full-time Youth Pastor. As a Youth Pastor, I was shocked to see how many parents would allow their kids to go to the dances and rock concerts, and then blame me because their kid didn't want to go to church. I began to preach heavily against dancing, rock music and other youth-related topics in our Thursday night youth service. I was even more shocked when I found out that one of the board members was thinking about not letting his teenage girl come back to youth service because I made her upset because I was preaching against kids going to the discos. (That was in the late 70's when *Saturday Night Fever* was hot!) I found out later, after he resigned, that he had become involved in homosexuality! To my knowledge, his daughter has never been back to church!

I got real training at that time, and even though I couldn't put my finger on it then, I have found this to be true, if you find a teenager who really loves **Jesus**; one who is "on fire" for God; one who has a prayer life; one who reads the Bible daily; and is a witness to the lost, you won't find them debating the rock music issue...they're not interested in it! They just want to be as much like **Jesus** as they can be! But the ones who want to fight over it, are the ones who have just enough religion to bug them instead of bless them! They're the up and down Christian, always struggling with their walk with the Lord. I've seen it time and time again!

After about a year and a half as Youth Pastor, my wife, Carolyn, and I took a step of faith and went "on the road" as Evangelists. This was my dream ever since I was a young teenager. And it didn't take long to realize what I faced as a Youth Pastor, almost every church was also facing...how to reach the youth.

I would notice as we traveled from church to church holding revival services, that if there were even a dozen teenagers in the church, that was almost a miracle! But most of the time, they were sitting in the back pew, passing notes, talking, or being completely bored. It hurt me so bad! I became so frustrated about it until I asked the Lord to give me direction so I could reach them. I began by having a special pre-service just for young people. I would talk to them about various issues and especially their music in a very straight but concerned way. The Lord blessed and we saw the teenagers wanting to know more. Soon I took one night out of the revival and shared my message with the whole church.

The response was great among the young people. They would come from the back pews all the way to the front pews and give me their undivided attention! When I gave the invitation for people to come and pray, the young people would flood the altars! But, sad to say, the adults were not so excited about the fact that I was bringing rock albums into the church! I remember one time while I was preaching against rock, I played a portion of a popular song to help make a point about what the song was saying...well, it didn't go ever too good with some of the people. Matter of fact, one family got up and literally stomped out of church and vowed that they were "not returning as long as John Muncy is here,"!! The sad part about it, the parents took their teenage boy who was really into the rock group I was playing! He needed to hear what I had to say! That's when I realized that this thing was not going to be easy to deal with, especially when parents would rather stick their heads in the sand, and try to just ignore it! That seems to be the normal response from many parents!

It's interesting that most parents fail to understand the fact that God can hear the music in their son's or daughter's bedroom as easy as He can hear it in the church building! Besides, the Bible says our bodies are the temple of the Holy Spirit, not some brick and mortar building!! (1 Cor. 6:19) So if it's wrong in church, it's wrong in your house! But in the minds of many people, it would be better to just be ignorant of the problem. But the verse rings loud and clear found in Hosea 4:6:

> *"My people are destroyed for lack of knowledge: because thou hast rejected knowledge, I will also reject thee, that thou shalt be no priest to me: seeing thou hast forgotten the law of thy God, **I will also forget thy children**."*

No, mom and dad, lacking knowledge about your teenagers music doesn't make you holy! Sticking your head in the sand will only aid to the destruction of your children! I think Satan has taken advantage of our ignorance to rob us of the greatest gifts God gives us parents! Paul even says in 2 Cor. 2:11:

> *"**Lest Satan should get an advantage of us: for we are not ignorant of his devices**."*

We need to know where our real enemy is and what devices he is using! Trying to ignore it only allows Satan free territory in our lives!

Before the popular MTV, VH-1, and other video rock programs, David Elkind, in his book, *The Hurried Child*, says,

> "Clearly, the most underestimated influence on young people today is the record business. Perhaps because most adults find the level of sound obnoxious, the harmonics jarring, and the lyrics incomprehensible, we prefer to ignore the impact of rock music on our offspring. As a culture, we are visually oriented, and this is why we are so concerned about the sex and violence presented on television and in films. But music can influence young people as much as any visual media. Philosophers and theologians have long been aware of the power of music: Plato in his *Republic* wanted music censored because he feared its citizens "would be tempted and corrupted by weak and voluptuous airs and led to indulge in demoralizing emotions."

I believe if we would all be honest with ourselves, we would admit that we have become comfortable as American Christians with things that should be alarming us!

Taking more and more of a stand against the messages in this music, I began to put together "rock seminars" during our revival meetings. Almost immediately I began to be attacked from Satan with everything from terrible nightmares to people who would come to the meetings with various threats if we didn't stop. It was also at this time that we even had our vehicle stolen and fire-bombed! As Carolyn and I continued to do what we felt the Lord had directed us to do, we saw just how serious this battle really was.

I'm aware there are some people who see our type of ministry as "flaky" or "silly" because we deal with this issue, but we are seeing thousands come to Christ every year. Tens of thousands of dollars of records, tapes, posters, occult books, etc. have been destroyed as a result of people getting their hearts right with God! I believe it's time to stand up for this generation and call it back to God! We desperately need a revival, and if we lose this generation, it will be because we are afraid to get involved, afraid we may get our hands dirty!!!

Satan knows as **Motley Crue** says in their song, "In The Beginning", that *"Those who have the youth, have the future"*! The devil is doing everything he can to raise up false teachers to lead the youth of this land to destruction. His prophets and teachers aren't always standing behind a pulpit, some are standing behind a guitar or microphone stand and like the Pied Piper, he has a large following of young people who will follow him anywhere.

"But are the kids *really* listening and understanding what is being talked about in the rock songs?", some have asked. Let's stop underestimating the power of young people! They aren't as dumb as some would think. **Ronnie James Dio,** former lead singer for **Black Sabbath,** now leader for the group named after himself says,

> "I'm slightly surprised that my form of writ-
> ing has been accepted as well as it has, but it
> only proves one point, people are not stupid.
> Kids absorb absolutely all of the lyrics.
> They're not dumb, mindless robots, they're
> smart kids. They're smarter now then they
> were five years ago."[3]

Many kids are looking for answers in a troubled world, but where do they turn? Most will turn to music as **Steven Tyler**, from the group **Aerosmith** says,

> "When people are really down in the mouth
> about things, hearing music gets you up. It's
> just the strongest drug in the world."[4]

I've talked to many young people who say music helps them get through the day, and it's the only thing that keeps them going. I had a girl come to me after one of our services recently with tears in her eyes, "John, I could never give up my music, it's the only thing I live for...I would commit suicide before I'd give up rock music."

But what exactly is being heard by all these faithful followers? Whatever the groups have enough guts to sing about, the kids are hearing what I believe to be the major themes of rock music; rebellion, sex, alcohol, drugs, false religions, violence, perversion, suicide, and the occult...all are preached freely in the name of rock and roll.

Quiet Riot, one of the few Heavy Metal bands to have a #1 hit, sings in their song "Scream and Shout",

> "You see that from the front row/we are shapes of things to come/You're handcuffed to your seats/there is no place to run/**Your brains are in our power/we conquer as we feed**/A healthy dose of metal/and that's all you'll ever need."

The Dayton Daily News carried a story about three teenage girls who drove two hours from Columbus, Ohio the night before **Quiet Riot's** December 30th concert. They spent the night in sleeping bags with the temperature dropping 9 degrees below zero because, "we love Quiet Riot"!!![5]

The University of Minnesota asked 3,600 teen-agers how they coped with problems. They were given 54 different options. "Kids in trouble turn to music, drugs, friends, and even video games before they talk to parents or other adults." Consulting with mother was thirty-first on the list and going to father ranked forty-eighth. **The poll revealed that listening to music was number one.** Who came in last? Teachers, counselors, and clergy![6]

Rock music has become the church of today's youth. It's

what gets their time, their money, their memory, their devotion. It's what they wear, sing, live, walk, talk, think, love, and what some would fight and kill and die for! You see, young people want to believe something! They want to give themselves to something! They want to be devoted! This is where I believe our churches have failed! Something needs to be their God! They want to look to someone who has the guts to say it! **Simon LeBon**, from **Duran Duran**, says he does just that,

> "Our songs really say something. I wouldn't feel comfortable if I had to sing mindless garbage! I'd feel quite embarrassed. So I take it upon myself to make sure I've got something to say...I work very hard on our lyrics."[7]

Of course, later in the book you'll see what he is saying to this generation. But what's the answer? Censorship? Well, unlike the motion picture industry, which rates about 325 films a year, the recording industry releases at least 25,000 songs annually.[8] Being next to impossible to try and rate each song, we are not solving the problem by labeling it, because it's going to take more than a sticker on the album to warn people of the danger and harm they are pumping into their lives daily!

One way to explain the draw and the appeal of most rock music is spiritual side of it. Some entertainers have an aura about them, a drawing power that almost puts the listeners in a spell. It gives a measure of spiritual high to the fans. Their performances are considered by some to be almost supernatural! This was true with **Elvis** and the **Beatles** and scores of others. **Michael Jackson** is one such figure. He is literally a god to some people! **Isiah Thomas**, the pro-basketball star says of **Jackson**,

> "When I see him dance and sing, it touches me, like a spirit; it moves me inside, sort of like the Holy Ghost. But it's more than singing and dancing; he manages to touch your soul."[9]

Jay, from the rapping group **RUN DMC** says,

> "I thought Michael Jackson would be a faggot, but he wasn't at all. He was cool, a cool person. He was like a godly figure; he had this sort of aura - as if when he's around, there's nothing wrong with the world."[10]

Even **Jackson** himself, who holds the record for the best selling album of all time, (over 38 million copies of *Thriller* sold) tells how his songs come to him,

> "I wake up from dreams and go 'Wow, put this down on paper', the whole thing is strange. You hear the words, everything is right there in front of your face. I feel that

> somewhere, someplace its been done and
> I'm just a courier bringing it into the world."[11]

Could that be true? Could **Michael Jackson** be a courier bringing a message to the world? And, *who* is giving the message to him? During his live performances, he claims,

> "When I hit the stage its all of a sudden a
> 'magic' from somewhere that comes and the
> spirit just hits you, and you just lose control
> of yourself."[12]

The question is, who *is* in control?

Even **John Lennon**, the former **Beatle** who was shot to death in 1980 said of himself,

> "I felt like a hollow temple filled with many
> spirits, each one passing through me, each
> inhabiting me for a little time and then leav-
> ing to be replaced by another."[13]

I believe that Satan would be an idiot if he passed up such a great opportunity to reach into the lives of millions of people via the music industry! It is one sure avenue that touches the lives of everyone of us directly or indirectly! Usually on any platform of rock music almost anything goes! As you'll see later, some messages are not a flat out "Hate God and Love Satan" message. But just as long as he can get you preoccupied with *anything* but **Jesus** is all that concerns him.

At the time of writing this chapter, we are coming into the fall season of the year. I have heard a number of times the last few days on T.V. and radio, warnings of frost..."Frost Warnings are out for tonight". Now, nobody gets mad at the announcer for saying that. As a matter of fact, they appreciate it, so they can cover their plants. If someone gives a tornado or a hurricane warning or if someone warns of the possibility of a snow storm, or an earthquake, it shouldn't cause people to get mad at the warning. They should take the necessary steps to prepare themselves! Well, why get mad when a preacher or someone else warns about the possible dangers coming from much of today's entertainment industry?

Starting with the next chapter, I want to give to you as I see it, ten good reasons I preach against much of today's rock music. Let me be quick to say that I'm not on an anti-drums campaign or such things as that. I am concerned with the *themes* that have become locked into the music. I'm not worried about somebody's guitar solo leading someone to hell, but I am concerned with the message that is getting preached loud and clear into the ears, the minds, and the hearts of precious souls!

---

[1]Hit Parader, Sept., 1987, pg.15
[2]Enquirer, May 31, 1988
[3]Rock Beat, Spring, 1987, pg.22
[4]Rock Beat, Spring, 1987, pg.23

[5]Dayton Daily News, Jan. 8, 1984
[6]Home School Helper, Ken Hay, pg.2, 1988
[7]Rock Fever, July, 1984
[8]People Weekly, Sept.16, 1985, pg.50
[9]People Weekly Extra, Nov./Dec., 1984, pg.78
[10]The Rock Yearbook, Vol.8, pg.56
[11]Rolling Stone, Feb.17, 1983
[12]Teen Beat-A Tribute to Michael Jackson, Summer, 1984, pg.27
[13]People, Aug. 22, 1988, pg.70

2
REBELLION

> **"...no self-respecting kid wants to listen to
> a band that his father approves of."**[1]
> **-Dee Snider**, lead singer for **Twisted Sister**

How many times do stories like the following repeat themselves...

*The teenager and the parent are at it again! Mom says, "You can't go out tonight because it's a school night and you have homework. Besides, you haven't cleaned your room this whole week." The reply comes from the once sweet, little, obedient child, "You're so unfair...Joey's mom lets him go out on school nights!" The mom then says, "Well, that's Joey's mom, I'm not Joey's mom." Then comes the reply that stabs her in the heart, "You and Dad never let me do anything, I can't wait till I turn eighteen, cause when I do, I'm leaving and I'll never come back!!!" He turns around and runs upstairs to his room, slams the door, and TURNS HIS STEREO ON FULL BLAST!!!

*The high school principal scratches his head after another teacher/student fight, wondering "why", as he signs the contract for the next assembly featuring a local rock band...

*The Pastor, seeking the Lord for his youth group, prays for wisdom on how to reach that one teenage girl who always sits in the back, dressed in the latest rock fashion with a heart as hard as a brick...

All these examples come from real life situations, and they all have one thing in common...REBELLION. Being rebellious isn't something you have to train a person to be. We are all born with a rebellious nature. If you doubt that, it's probably because you don't have children of your own. It seems to just come with the package! No matter how sweet they seem, all little babies learn to disobey. It's a part of that fallen nature in all descendents of Adam, and until we surrender our lives back into God's hands, rebellion will rule in us all. A fallen nature fights authority...

John Cougar Mellencamp puts it plainly with his single, "Authority Song" in which the chorus says,

> "I fight authority, authority always wins.
> I've been doing it since I was a young kid and
> I've come out grinning".

The dictionary defines rebellion as, **"defiance toward any ruling authority"**. It may be directed toward parents, teachers, a police officer, the government, but it's always directed against God, because *He* created authority. **Dave Mustaine,** from the group **Megadeth**, says, "I've always gotten a kick out of defying authority. Just wait, we want to name our next album, *The Second Coming Of Christ*."[2]

The Bible makes it clear that the very first sin was rebellion. Satan in his pride led a rebellion against God that got him kicked out of heaven. (see Ezekial 28 and Isaiah14) Ever since, Satan has used rebellion to destroy families, churches, and even nations. It was born in Satan's heart and it has nothing but destruction in it's path!! This is why the scriptures teach in 1 Sam. 15:23:

> **"For rebellion is as the sin of witchcraft,**
> and stubbornness is as iniquity and idolatry."

That's how serious rebellion is, it's on the level of the occult!!! You might not think you listen to a group that promotes the occult, but you might need to look again!

Wham has a song called "Bad Boys" which boldly proclaims,

> "Dear mommy, dear daddy, you had plans
> for me. I was your only son. When you tried
> to tell me what to do, I just shut my mouth
> and smiled at you. One thing that I know for
> sure, bad boys stick together never sad boys.
> Good guys, they made rules for fools, so get
> wise. Dear mommy, dear daddy, now I'm
> 19. As you see, I'm handsome, tall, and

25

> strong. So what the hell gives you the right
> to look at me as if to say, 'Hell, what went
> wrong?' But don't try to keep me in tonight
> because I'm big enough to break down the
> door."

But one thing for sure, rebellion is destructive! It is aimed at the destruction of homes. And what better means to preach rebellion than music. And rebellion is a major theme in the music industry! You can listen to **Johnny Paycheck** sing, "Take this job and shove it" and it's clear what the message is...REBELLION. It shows up in such rock videos as the group **Genesis** when they mocked President and Mrs. Reagan on their puppeteer video, "Land of Confusion", and it's clear what the message is...REBELLION. It can be seen in the groups **Venom** or **Bon Jovi** as they desecrate the American flag on their stages, and it's clear what the message is...REBELLION.

Authority is such a foundational teaching; upon it, everything else is built, and without it all things will collapse. Psa.11:3 says:

> *"If the foundations be destroyed, what can*
> *the righteous do?"*

Imagine the army, navy, air force, or marines without a system of authority. Why, it would be a joke in one month's time! One of the basic lessons taught to our service men and women is authority..."Yes, Sir!" is followed with a salute. Standing at attention, a certain time to get up, and a certain time to go to bed, clean, pressed clothes, spit-shined shoes. All these and other lessons teach a very vital part to running a nation...<u>Authority!!!</u> Without this training we would never be able to win a war. Jesus said in Mark 3:24:

> *"And if a kingdom be divided against itself,*
> *that kingdom **cannot** stand."*

Elton John shows how far it could go with his song, "Bennie and the Jets" which defiantly says,

> "We shall survive, let us take ourselves along,
> where we fight our parents out in the streets
> to find who's right and who's wrong."

Rebellion never causes strength, but is a destroyer of strength. Even though some may not like to hear it, we *all* must have an authority; someone we must submit to and if we don't, we are in serious trouble. Even when we get to heaven, we will find that authority still applies! Without it, everything would be chaotic!!!

Poison has a song entitled, "Let Me Go To The Show", which says,

> "Mamma, please let me go to the show, I dig
> those bad boys playing that rock 'n roll. No

> way, son, you can't go out tonight. So I got
> real upset and put up the biggest fight. Out
> the window shimmy down the tree, I take a
> look around, make sure no one's watching
> me. I steal the keys and take my old man's
> Chevrolet, I can hear my Mama scream from
> ten miles away"

Now, think for a minute; when was the last time you heard a rock song tell you to "love your parents" or "honor your father and mother" or "obey mom and dad" or "respect your elders" or "obey the law"? Some of you might see that as laughable, but let's be honest, *is* rock teaching children something about authority? Sure it is. **It's teaching them** *just the opposite* **of what God's Word teaches!** After Bono, lead singer for **U2** climbed San Francisco's Vaillancourt Fountain and spray-painted the words, "Stop the Traffic", and "Rock and Roll", Mayor Dianne Feinstein issued a statement that read, "I am very disappointed that a rock star who is supposed to be a role model for young people chose to vandalize the work of another artist...Defacing public property is malicious mischief under Section 594 of the state penal code, a misdemeanor punishable by a fine or jail or both."[3] This seems so very "innocent" when compared to some of the other things done on stage by rock idols, but the point made by Mayor Feinstein regarding "role model" rock stars shows that even adults realize the power one entertainer has, be it for good or for bad.

Grim Reaper advertised their album *Fear No Evil* by telling their fans that they don't have to fear "Ending up like your Mom and Dad...Don't worry. Grim Reaper will protect you. Their high-powered, kick-_ss, no-nonsense heavy metal will scare away <u>those demons</u> and let you 'Fear No Evil'." By referring to Mom and Dad as "those demons", one can see the plain anti-authority concept. **Niki Sixx** from **Motley Crue** defends their song "Shout at the Devil" by saying, "What we were telling the kids was to stand up and shout at whoever was putting them down - whether it was their parents, their teachers or their bosses. That's who the real devil is."[4] He further brags, "We're the American youth. And youth is about sex, drugs, pizza, and more sex. We're intellectuals on the crotch level. We're the guys your mother warned you to stay away from."[5] **Kevin DuBrow**, lead singer for **Quiet Riot** puts it plain when he says, "Kids love to have things their parents don't like."[6] **Paul Stanley**, guitarist for **KISS** shows his true colors to the parents as he defends heavy-metals reputation says, "If Elvis were playing through a stack of amplifiers today, he would probably be called a heavy-metal singer. The problem is some kids who grew up loving everything Elvis stood for are now journalists who have become what they feared most — parents."[7] **Madonna**, who is an idol to many young girls, reflecting life in the pop culture said, "I think your parents give you false expectations of life. All of us grow up completely misguided."[8]

One major rock group after another say such things as, "Rebellion is the basis for our group.", "We don't care what the parents think about us, the more they hate us, the more the kids love us." It really does seem the more rebellious they are, the more popular they become, but here is a warning from Psa. 66:7:

> *"He (God) ruleth by his power for ever; his eyes behold the nations: **let not the rebellious exalt themselves.**"*

I think of such groups as the Beastie Boys, the first group to be censored on *American Bandstand*, which is **Dick Clark's** weekly T.V. music/dance show. **Diamond** from the group says, "We're probably a parent's worst nightmare."[9] The Holiday Inn hotel chain has banned the **Beastie Boys** from all their hotels after they were found cutting a hole in the floor of their suite to serve as a passage way to the one directly below.[10] Their record *Licensed to Ill* was also banned by the BBC for its excessiveness.[11] All one must do is read an interview with these guys and you can understand their deception is deep. They appeared as the presenters of a '87 Grammy Awards, and they came leaping on stage, holding their crotches, screaming the "F" word on live nation-wide television.

Their smash hit "Fight for your Right" in which they talk about parents forcing their kids to go to school when they "don't wanna go", and then the teachers treating them "like some kind of jerk", then "that hypocrite" dad gets upset cause the kid is smoking, and "living at home is such a drag" cause mom threw away the kid's "best porno mag", then the song goes on to tell about how the parents are upset over the clothes they are wearing, and the long hair, and of course how they complain about "that noise" they're listening to. The video version makes the parents and the other kids look like a bunch of "nerds" and the **Beastie Boys** are a real cool group of guys who are just fighting for their "right to party"!! Add that concept with some rock and some rap, along with some pies thrown in the face and you've got a guaranteed hit!! And it was. But take a look at the alcohol and drug problem in our nation and see if kids should be encouraged to "fight for the right to party". All it is doing is encouraging young people to fight against rules, and in this case rules that could save lives. But as soon as I heard that song, it reminded me of the verses in 2 Pet.2:18-19:

> *"For when they speak great swelling words of vanity, they allure through the lusts of the flesh, through much wantonness, those that were clean escaped from them who live in error. While they promise them liberty, they themselves are the servants of corruption..."*

Punk music is probably best known for it's violence and rebellion. **Anarchy** is the title of one punk group and the theme of hundreds of other punk groups just like them. Anarchist even have their own symbol...a circled capital A. You'll see it on their posters, and albums declaring that they publicly support anarchy, which the dictionary defines as "the absence of government, a state of lawlessness; political disorder due to the absence of governmental authority; rebellion against authority". Titus 3:1-3 speaks to this generation plainly,

> *"Put them in mind to be subject* (obedient) *to principalities* (civil authorities) *and powers, to obey magistrates* (ones who are in authority), *to be ready to every good, To speak evil of no man, to be no brawlers* (rebellious to authority), *but gentle, shewing all meekness unto all men. For we ourselves also were sometimes foolish, disobedient, deceived, serving divers lusts and pleasures, living in malice and envy, hateful, and hating one another."*

Here is one example of how far many will go to disobey the commands of the Lord. It's by the group **Suicidal Tendencies** with their popular song, "I Saw Your Mommy",

> "I saw your mommy and your mommy's dead. I watch her as she bled. Chewed off toes on her chopped off feet. I took a picture cause I thought it looked neat. But the thing I like seeing the best, was the rodents using her hair as a nest. I saw your mommy and your mommy's dead. I saw her lying in a pool of red. I think it's the greatest thing I'll

ever see, your dead mommy lying in front of
me. I'll always remember her lying dead on
the floor, I hope she dies twenty times more."

How important is this issue? It is so important that God made
it one of the **Ten <u>Commandments</u>**!!!! Ex. 20:12,

> *"Honour thy father and thy mother: that thy
> days may be long upon the land which the
> Lord thy God giveth thee."*

Notice that there is a reward of long life for those who honor
their parents. Hundreds of times, God's Word refers to
obeying, honoring, and loving your parents. It is interesting
that the O.T. law stated that if a son or daughter struck his
parents they were to be stoned to death. (Deut. 21:18-21) It is
also interesting that in countries where elderly people are still
looked up to and respected, rock music is strongly opposed by
their society. It's because rock music is seen as destructive to
the home life. How sad that we as Americans can't be more
perceptive!! As one minister friend of mine put it, "We are
building our homes with one hand and tearing them down
with the other!"

Judas Priest sings in their song, "We don't need no Parental
Guidance here!",

> "Everyday you scream at me to turn the
> music low. Well if you keep on screaming,

> you'll make me deaf you know. You always
> chew me out, because I stay out late. Until
> your three-piece suit comes back in date, get
> one thing straight...We don't need, no, no no
> no parental guidance here!"

The video version of that song shows thousands of young people with fists raised high, singing a song that is against the very parents that brought them into this life.

The popular **David Crosby**, from the group **Crosby, Stills, and Nash** was quoted saying,

> "I figured the only thing to do was swipe
> their kids. I still think it's the only thing to do.
> By that, I'm not talking about kidnapping,
> I'm just talking about changing their value
> systems, which removes them from their
> parents world very effectively."[12]

It's very interesting to note that **David Crosby** just recently got out of prison. He was serving time for drug abuse and carrying a concealed weapon. Psa. 5:9-10 has a most fitting statement about **Crosby** and others like him,

> *"For there is no faithfulness in their mouth;*
> *their inward part is very wickedness; their*
> *throat is an open sepulchre; they flatter with*
> *their tongue. Destroy thou them, O God; let*

> *them fall by their own counsels; cast them*
> *out in the multitude of their trangressions;*
> *for they have **REBELLED** against thee..*

Another perfect example of out-right rebellion was a smash hit by a group called **Twisted Sister** (a very fitting name). The title of the song speaks for itself, "We're Not Going To Take It". The song plainly taught young people that no one has a right to tell you anything, no matter who they are. The video version of the song shows a family sitting around the supper table. The tension can be felt as the children sheepishly look at their hard nose dad. The oldest teenager asks to be dismissed, and goes up to his room to listen to his favorite group as he "plays" along on his guitar. Meanwhile the dad begins to question what his son is listening to and proceeds up to the son's room. When he enters the room, he begins to throw things around and complains about the boy's messy room. Then, acting like a real jerk, the dad begins to verbally abuse his son. Of course the producers of the video really center on the son's timid look as his dad makes all kinds of stupid remarks about his son's music. Finally, dad stops and says, "What are you going to do with your life?" The son, with a rebellious grin replies, "I wanna Rock" and with that, he strums his guitar and from its force, blows dad out the window of the two-story house to the driveway below. Then the young boy turns into **Dee Snider**, the leader of the band, and proceeds to get his dad back by throwing him down the stairs, pulling his hair, and knocking him out with the door. The sad thing about it was this song stayed at the top of the music charts for weeks!! Kids loved it!! Of course!! The real danger here is that young people aren't thinking about the results of such an idea, it's just "live for yourself, forget Mom and Dad". Isn't it sad that the older you get, the smarter Mom and Dad seem to get; and by the time you really begin to love them and want their advise, they're dead.

In an interview, **Snider** tells his teenage fans what real cool is,

> "I grew up with the attitude of 'F—that,' I'll be the way I want to be, the way I am, and I'll show people what's real cool...Real cool is not giving a sh-t what other people think. That's bottom line cool! When you say, 'I like how I am, F—them', that's bottom line cool."[13]

Prov.17:11 is a fitting verse for Snider,

> *"An evil man seeketh only **rebellion**: therefore a cruel messenger shall be sent against him."*

Another example was **Pink Floyd's** hit "Another brick in the wall". Here was a song that actually was banned in Africa due to riots that it caused in schools. A statement repeatedly used in the song was, "...teacher, leave those kids alone..." It is strange today that teachers and principles can't seem to figure out the cause of such rebellion in school, all the while rock 'n roll is blaring in the halls , on the buses, in the gym, and in the cafeteria! I've been to schools where they wouldn't let me share my seminar on rock 'n roll, but will let rock groups come in and do two hour concerts!

Now, wrapping up this chapter, here is a very important statement...Rock Music **DOES NOT** cause you to become rebellious! Rebellion was here a long time before rock music was ever heard of. So what's the connection? Rock music and rebellion are like gasoline and fire. Rock isn't the source, but it's like fuel on the flame. We read in 2 Tim. 3:1-2:

> *"This know also, that in the last days peril-*
> *ous times shall come. For men shall be lovers*
> *of their own selves, covetous, boasters, proud,*
> *blasphemers, disobedient to parents..."*

I personally believe that the Holy Spirit was showing Paul that our generation would be so unlike any other generation especially in this area that He emphasized on this point. The Holy Spirit was saying this would be a trademark for the last days... *"disobedient to parents"* !! What a description of our day! No doubt the very kids who screamed cheers to the **Beatles** never dreamed that they would grow up and have their kids screaming sneers at them!! But what is "permit-ted" in one generation is "fermented" in the next! And our children have become "intoxicated" with rebellion!

It is no longer even questioned if rock music has a message of rebellion, it's a fact! The problem is obvious...our culture has become so youth-centered! (I know some of you won't like this.) We have no time for the "old and feeble", we could care less about the unborn! Youth! Youth! Youth! Our society is built around them. Why, it has almost gotten to the point that if you aren't in the peak of health, and if you don't know how to ride a skateboard, or if your hair is turning grey; you have no value! It is sad but true! You know, even though I hate to say it, the Communists were really smarter than many Americans when it came to respecting the elderly. This is the main reason they are so against rock music in their country! At least they understood the damaging influence of rebellion! We are sometimes so naive! A culture that doesn't maintain respect and honor will always fall into <u>disrespect</u> and <u>dishonor</u>! The question is, what is a parent to do about it?

First of all, I think one thing that we better be careful *not* to do, is to cause our children to go into deeper rebellion by acting abruptly. In other words, don't run into your teenagers room and tear down all the posters, break all the records, and pull all the tape from their cassettes. This will probably cause them to go into deeper rebellion! Col. 3:21 says:

> *"Fathers, provoke not your children to anger,*
> *lest they be discouraged."*

If you've waited until your child has become a teenager to tell them what they can and cannot do, you've probably waited too long anyway. The truth is, unless that teenager gives it up himself, you won't stop him from listening to it!! He will find somewhere else to listen to it; either in his car, or his friend's house...if he must go behind your back to do what he wants, he will do it! What you need to instill in him or her is a deep love and fear for the Lord! If a teenager really gets their heart right with God, they will find they can no longer listen to that music! Rock music is just a symptom of an empty heart! Get that heart filled with **Jesus** and there's no need for junk!

If you have a rebellious teenager, you must develop a much needed relationship and try to share your concern in a loving, gentle way. In over a decade of dealing full-time with young people as a minister, I have found that teenagers will only really open up and respond to one thing from parents..."*speaking the truth in love*"! (Eph. 4:15)

I feel one of the reasons the message of rebellion is such an accepted theme in today's music is because of the lazy way we deal with problems in our homes. (And this is a spiritual problem) No doubt, one reason Dad doesn't get the respect he should have is because he is *not* the Priest in the home that God has called him to be! (Hosea 4:6) I could see how some young people have a hard time respecting their parents, some of whom act like a bunch of kids themselves! My prayer is that God will give us some Dads and Moms with some back-bone, who are not afraid to stand up for the Word of God, and will lovingly bring their children...

*"up in the nurture and admonition of the
Lord."* (Eph.6:4)

Mom and Dad, if your son or daughter had to describe your home, would they describe it as a place where you can feel the presence of God? Maybe if you would turn off the T.V. for awhile, or if you would leave the lawn alone for awhile, or plan your golf game for some other day and spend that time with your child, you might be able to wipe out that so-called "generation gap"! The home must be the most spiritual place on this planet, if it's not, we will lose this generation because "as the home goes, so goes the church"!!

Mom, when was the last time your son or daughter saw you praising the Lord with tears coming down your eyes at home? Dad, when was the last time your son or daughter walked in the family room and saw you on your knees praying, or sitting in your chair with the Word of God opened, studying it? That will say more to them than anything else you could do...set the example Dad! Set the example Mom!!!!!!!! I'm tired of parents who throw all the blame on music, school, church and ministers! Own up to the problem! Get on your face before God and ask Him to give you a love and concern for your children that will drive them to repentance!! Make yourself available to your children! Help them with their homework! Show up at their ball games! Do fun things together as parents! Ask them about their opinions instead of always giving yours!

Remember that they need most of all to know God's view! I was reading in my devotional time the other day from Judges 2:10 where it says,

> *"...and there arose another generation after*
> *them, which knew not the Lord..."*

To me, this seems to be one of the most tragic verses found in the Scriptures! A whole generation that doesn't know the Lord! I'm afraid that our generation could be described that same way! What bothers me more than the fact we have rock music in our generation, is that rock music in a generation that doesn't know the Lord!! This generation needs desperately to see revival! Mom and Dad, Grandpa and Grandma, what will happen to your children and grandchildren if we don't have one? Let's seek God for one!

And finally, to you young people, would you like to have a long and happy life? Well, if you would, then read this from Eph.6:1-3:

> *"Children, obey your parents in the Lord: for*
> *this is right. Honour thy father and mother;*
> *which is the first commandment with prom-*
> *ise; That it may be well with thee, and thou*
> *mayest live long on the earth."*

But understand this, God *did not* make this a suggestion, but a **COMMANDMENT**. Like it or not, for the rest of your life, you will have people telling you what you can and cannot do. Accept it. No matter how "big" you become, you still have others over you! Save yourselves alot of heartache and obey God's Word!!! Sure, Mom and Dad make mistakes, they are just as capable of missing the mark as anyone else, but God still says, "OBEY THEM!" You obey God's Word and you will be blessed! God PROMISES it! And He doesn't lie!!!

By the way, next time you listen to a song that puts down God, or Mom and Dad, or anything that should have our love and respect, remember the verse given earlier, *"For rebellion is as the sin of witchcraft..."* (1 Sam.15:23)

---

[1]Dayton Daily News, Oct.9, 1984
[2]Rock Scene Spotlights #3, pg.34
[3]People, 12-28-87, pg.66
[4]Heavy Metal Heroes, Summer, 1987
[5]Motley Crue, July, 1985, pg.34
[6]Rock Fever, July, 1984
[7]People, Oct. 31, 1988
[8]Spin, Feb., 1988, pg.48
[9]People, Feb.9, 1987, pg.93
[10]Creem, May, 1987, pg.7
[11]Metal Creem Close-up, Sept., 1987, pg.22
[12]"They're out to steal your children" Ray Allen
[13]Rockworld, May, 1985, pg.18

SEX WITHOUT MORALS

"Honestly, music is very sexual, that's why music is so special to me, because it's the closest thing to sex."[1]
- Neal Schon, from **Journey**

SEX SELLS! I'm sure you've heard that statement before, and I'm sure you know how true it is. If you do have any doubt, turn on your T.V. sometime and see how much emphasis is placed on sex when the commercials come on. Toothpaste, shaving cream, automobiles, pants, shoes, perfume, diet drinks, health spa's, etc., all are sold with an underlying theme of sex. Sex has been the seller of all kinds of things because sex gets our attention. Not only does sex sell products, but it also sells music. Turn on your radio to any local rock, soul, or country station and listen for only about 15 minutes and see if you hear any references to "making love", or "I want to love you all over", or "let's spend the night together", or "I want to feel your body", or "let's do it in the back seat" or a million other ways to describe sex. Turn on a video rock station, such as MTV, and observe the sexual overtones constantly showing up, not to mention the very obvious!

One rock magazine asked **Paul Stanley** and **Gene Simmons** of the popular group **Kiss**, "Does sex sell rock and roll?"

Paul Stanley said,

> "Rock 'n roll is sex. Real rock 'n roll isn't based on cerebral thoughts, it's based on one's lower nature."

Gene Simmons said,

> "The term rock 'n roll comes from an old Leadbelly song called "Let Me Rock and Roll You All Night Long." And he's not talking about, 'Let me read you a book.' Rock 'n roll *means* sex. So does it sell? You'd better believe it!"[2]

Bananarama had a very successful remake of the old 1970 **Shocking Blue** hit tune entitled, "Venus", which talked about a "goddess on the mountain top". Historians tell us that *Venus* was the Roman goddess of sensuality and was identified with the Greek goddess, *Aphrodite*. They would actually worship sex! Many times their rituals would include sex orgies where temple prostitutes would be used to seduce men in the worship of their pagan gods! This, of course, led to the eventual destruction and fall of Rome, and, may I add, is leading to the destruction and fall of this great nation of ours!!!! But what happens when we treat such an important and sacred thing as sex this way? What happens when we put sex at this level?

Because sex is such a fundamental issue, your view of sex will be the way you will view many other things!! A nation which lowers it's morals is open to anything destructive. The Playboy philosophy will never build a great nation, for the Word of God says,

> *"Righteousness exalteth a nation: but sin is*
> *a reproach to any people."*   (Prov.14:34)

In 1969, a nationwide survey asked the question, "Is premarital sex acceptable?"...

68% said, "No"
21% said, "Yes"

The same survey was asked again in 1985, "Is premarital sex acceptable?" and the results were very revealing...

39% said, "No"
52% answered, "Yes"[3]

What happened between '69 and '85 to bring about such a huge change in our thinking? And, what has been the results of this "new morality"? It's important to also notice that during those same years, we saw...

*the divorce rate increased...
*the suicide rate soared...
*illegitimate births sky-rocketed...
*juvenile crime intensified...
*venereal disease multiplied....
*abortion mushroomed....

Why?...<u>because sex is such a fundamental issue</u>!!! **When sex is placed on a level of deity, it will turn into a cruel god, damning us rather then blessing us!**

Some might say, "What's so bad about sex?" And obviously the answer would be, "Nothing", for *God created sex* and He created all things good. If it wasn't for sex, you and I wouldn't be here. God created sex to be enjoyable and fun. As a matter of fact, the very first recorded words of God talking to mankind was when He told man and his wife to *"be fruitful and multiply"*...God was talking about sex! He is the designer of our sex organs. He was the One Who made the male body and the female body in such a way that men and women could have intimate sexual relationships. This all started in the mind of God! He made sex to feel good and to bring pleasure! He isn't embarrassed about it, in fact, only after He made man and woman in His creation did He say it was, *"very good"* (see Gen. 1:31)

Well, then what's the problem? The problem is clear!! Notice again the title of this chapter, "Sex *without* Morals". That's the whole point! There is nothing wrong with sex, but there *is* something wrong with what mankind has done to it!

Like anything else God created, Satan would love to pervert it. Satan is not a creator, he's a perverter!! And sex is not exempt. He would love to destroy sex because it is so dear to God's heart!! And when sex has been lowered down to such a degree as it is today, it has no resemblance to what God intended sex to be.

Sex is being preached today by most rock stars without any morals; but the truth is, sex and morality have to go together to get the full benefit from this God-given gift to mankind!!

All one must do is look at the Top 40 charts and you can see how the rock industry continues to produce "sensuality in stereo"! The young people of this and other nations have been bombarded with a bunch of fleshly entertainers who have been able to use young people's interest in sexual matters as a chance to make big bucks! It might be a soft rock group like Chicago as they sing, "Stay the Night", about a guy who wants his girl to spend the night and he "won't take no for an answer", or lovely **Whitney Houston** singing, "Saving all my Love" to a married man she's got her eyes on, who she ends up "making love all night long" with. Or, others like **Phil Collins,** who sings about one night stands in his hits, "Take Me Home" and "One More Night".

It's interesting that most people would feel uncomfortable having some of these songs sung in a church setting, but fail to realize that God is no more *inside* a church building than He is *outside* one. If it would be wrong in a church, then it would be wrong in you, because the Bible clearly teaches in 1 Cor. 6:19:

> *"...that your body is the temple of the Holy Ghost..."*

God can hear the music in your bedroom or your car just as well as he can anywhere else. Oh, but John, you say, these are all such beautiful songs. Last time I remember, those things were called, Fornication and Adultery!!! Eph. 5:5-7 says:

> *"For this ye know , that no whoremonger, nor unclean person, nor covetous man, who is an idolater, hath any inheritance in the kingdom of Christ and of God. LET NO MAN DECEIVE YOU WITH VAIN WORDS; for because OF THESE THINGS cometh the wrath of God upon the children of disobedience. Be not ye therefore partakers with them."*

Notice the phrase, "vain words". That's all rock and roll really is, **vain words put to an attractive sound.** Satan knows how to wrap his gifts! It may seem to come in a very beautiful package, but trash is still trash no matter how much you try to package it, and sin is sin no matter how you try to gloss over it!!

For example, isn't it interesting how we have been able to change terminology to make our sins sound better!! We want to get the hiss of the serpent out of sssSin!! We want to pull the stinger out. We don't like sin to sound sinful!!! Look how we have done it in our terminology of sexual sins...

Old Terminology	New Terminology
Fornication	"Premarital Sex"
Adultery	"Extramarital Sex"
Orgy	"Group Sex" or "Sharing"
Perversion	"Sexual Variation"
Promiscuous	"Sexually Active"
Sodomites	"Homosexual" or "Gays"
Pornography	"Erotica"
Masturbation	"Self-Help"
Loose	"Liberated"

Lust   "Searching"

Prostitute   "Party Girl" or "Escort"

By changing the terminology, it eases our conscience some-what, but way down deep inside we all know the real truth. Sexual sin is unlike any other type of sin, this is one reason we try and cover it up because it has a way of coming back and haunting us! Today we have been sold a lie. We are told that we are in a "new age" and that we have a "new morality", but the truth is that we are doing nothing new. Man has been sinning in this area for as long as history records. No, it's not a "new morality", but the same **"old immorality"!!**

It would be so easy for us to put our heads in the sand and try to ignore the issue of sexual sins. But now we are finding the same sins in the world can be found in the church. One reason is because we don't want to deal with issues! I believe that many ministers have added to the problem simply by the fact that they have kept silent!! **Jesus** prayed in John 17:15:

> *"I pray not that thou shouldest take them out*
> *of the world, but that thou shouldest keep*
> *them from the evil."*

The Lord made it plain that we can be *IN* the world and not be *OF* it! We don't have to stick our heads in the sand and pretend it doesn't exist! **Jesus** said in Matt. 5:13 that we, as Christians, are the *"salt of the earth"*. Salt is a preservative!!

This is what God has called us to be...**a preservative to this world.** We are to be that which holds back corruption! Sad to say we have done a very lousy job so far! By remaining silent we have allowed the humanist, the liberal, the entertainment world and many other ungodly influences to move in and give our teenagers destructive teaching on sex. Phil. 2:15 tells us:

> *"That ye may be blameless and harmless, the*
> *sons of God, without rebuke, in the midst of*
> *a crooked and perverse nation, among whom*
> *ye shine as lights in the world."*

We must "shine as lights" in this dark society!! We must bring light to a world that is stumbling in darkness!! Again, the reason we have failed is because we find it more convenient to stick our heads in the sand and pretend that this evil thing will just disappear. And nothing is further from the truth! While we ignore it, the problem grows!

A look at a recent line-up of rock stars shows the message hasn't changed. You have **Bon Jovi** singing the mellow tune, "Never Say Good-bye" in which he says,

> "Remember when we used to park on Butler
> Street out in the dark. Remember when we
> lost the keys and you lost more than that in
> my backseat, baby."

And sad to say, many girls and guys have "lost" something that they will later wish they still had. The truth is, you have one thing, that you can give or lose to just one person, just one time...and that's your virginity! But, of course, terminology puts it like this song by **Bon Jovi**, "Wild in the Streets", the chorus says,

> "We were cruising to the backbeat. Oh, yeah,
> making love in the backseat..."

More recently, **Bon Jovi** made it back to the top with the hit song, "Living In Sin", which says,

> **"I don't need no license to sign on no line,** and I don't need no preacher, to tell me your mine. I don't need no diamond, I don't need no new bride. I just need you baby, to look me in the eye. I know they have a hard time, and your daddy don't approve, but I don't need your daddy telling us what we should do...Is it right for both our parents who fight it out most nights, then pray for God's forgiveness when they both turn out the lights...Or is it right to hold you and kiss your lips goodnight, **they say the promise is forever, if you sign it on the dotted line.** Baby, can you tell me just where we fit in, I call it love, they call it living in sin..."

You know, I find it rather interesting that **Bon Jovi** gives the message that getting married is nothing more than just "signing on the dotted line", so therefore, it isn't really that important, and mocks the fact that others call this "living in sin". I'm sure that **Bon Jovi** would not be willing to tour the country doing concerts for just six months without a contract, and I'm sure he wouldn't even cut another album without "signing on the dotted line", well, then why believe marriage is any less important? Why has this "back seat love" mentallity swept our nation? It certainly has been a main topic in rock and roll...

Gene Simmons, bass player for **Kiss**, says concerning the main message of the songs on their 21st album, *Crazy Nights*, "What they express is promiscuity. It's sex with a backbeat."[4] **Bruce Springsteen** sings about the many different girls he has had in the backseat of various cars, but claims that the girl with the "Pink Cadillac" is the best, since her backseat is much larger. Then of course you have **Prince** singing about his quick ride with the girl in the "Little Red Corvette" who has a "...pocket full of horses, Trojans, some of them used..." Or it could be a hard rock group like **Motley Crue** with "Ten Seconds To Love" singing about group sex in an elevator. Or **Judas Priest's** song "Eat Me Alive", a song about forced oral sex at gun point. Of course the list is endless. By the time this book is in print, these songs will probably seem mild in comparison! But the point is this...once you start this thing rolling it's like the snowball effect...it just keeps getting bigger! Let me show you what I mean...

The very term, "Rock and Roll" was coined by a D.J. from Cleveland, Ohio. **Alan Freed** borrowed the term from the ghettos for having sex in an automobile..."rock and roll". "That's it!", Freed thought, "That's what I'll call this new music...'Rock and Roll Music'!" For you see, from the very start it was music with a message of sex. **Alan Freed** was one of the first to promote this new type of music. **Buddy Holly, The Platters, Fats Domino, Elvis, Little Richard, Jerry Lee Lewis, Bill Haley and the Comets, Chuck Berry, The Everly Brothers** were just a few of the beginners that **Freed** would play on his radio show and, boy, did it get the young people's attention! Of course, Mom and Dad objected to it...that made it grow even stronger.

Even the **T.V.** industry had a hard time with some of it, for when **Elvis Presley** appeared on one of **Ed Sullivan's** show's, they decided that the way he was shaking his hips to be much too vulgar for television...thus, "Elvis the pelvis".

But as the 50's were quickly passing by, Americans were getting accustomed to this new form of "art" and the young people were talking about it all the time. Dances became common place for teenagers. Weekends were for cruising the hotdog stands with the radio's blaring "rock and roll". Soon the 60's were here, and as always, we had to have something different to keep up with our fast paced lives...

Then came **Brenda Lee, Connie Francis, The Four Seasons, Dion, The Supremes, Four Tops, The Beach Boys,**

Donovan, The Temptations, James Brown, Marvin Gaye, The Beatles, The Rolling Stones, more and more groups were coming out and in no time "rock and roll" became one of the most powerful forms of entertainment this nation had ever seen. It was then that rock music became the "lover" that America married! And the messages were slowly becoming the philosophies of a new generation!

During the 60's, they began to call it, "free love". The idea was, "forget marriage, forget morals, forget what some old, out-dated Bible says...live it up! No one has a right to force their opinions on you! If it feels good, do it!" And from that point until now we have seen a steady decline in morals. (By the way, there is no such thing as "free love"...true love, like anything of real value, costs!) By the time the 60's were over, we had seen a nation which had once maintained a pretty moral standard fall to a new, all time low. And "rock and roll" had a very powerful influence on it! It was changing a whole generation...

Then came the 70's bringing us **Elton John, David Bowie, Janis Joplin, Jimi Hendrix, The Doors, Led Zeppelin, Badfinger, Three Dog Night, Climax, Grand Funk, Cher, Eagles, Doobie Brothers, Ohio Players, Linda Ronstadt, Ted Nugent, Alice Cooper, Rod Stewart, Wild Cherry, Chicago, Donna Summer, Chic, Queen, Blondie,** and the spearhead of the sexual revolution. From that decade came the homosexuals, the lesbians, the bi-sexuals and others, out of their closets. One thing leads to another...soon not only marriages among homosexuals were being preformed, but these perversions were looked favorably upon by leading churches and denominations. Porno became "big business". Nude beaches, gay churches, massage parlors, XXX rated peep shows, sado-masochism, bestiality, child-porn, all became common. Nothing was sacred, even so-called ministers were preaching on the sex life of Christ, going as far as to say that Jesus was involved with, not only his women followers, but also some of his disciples!!! But then came the 80's...

Prince, The J. Geils Band, Devo, Go-Go's, Cars, Eurythmics, Stray Cats, Van Halen, Heart, Janet Jackson, Madonna, Cindi Lauper, Bruce Springsteen, Twisted Sister, Pointer Sisters, Michael Jackson, Billy Idol, John Cougar, Poison, Duran Duran, Culture Club, Run DMC, Sheena Easton, Pat Benatar, Whitesnake, Beastie Boys, Motley Crue, Cinderella, Bon Jovi, Guns 'N Roses, and hundreds more who began to freely sing out about immorality, as if it is acceptable. Now we are slowly beginning to see the long term effects of our "new morality". Broken homes, broken lives, suicide, alcoholism, abortion, drugs, incest, rape, VD, herpes, AIDS, lawlessness, and just a whole generation without direction! All stemming from our immoral sex life, our so-called "freedom"!

The very reason AIDS is such a huge problem to deal with is because it is a sexual disease! If it was only an I.V. drug user's disease and wasn't transmitted sexually, we would have had no problems dealing with it! We would declare war on it. But our problem now is we're having a hard time trying to tell people not to do "whatever feels good" after years of telling them they could!!

Immorality is so ingrained into our fabric, we don't know how to handle it's results! We wanted kids to stop producing babies out of wedlock, so instead of telling them to be sexually pure, we invented birth control for "safe sex". Then abortion, in case they have a "mistake"...now we have to deal with a whole generation with messed up minds, full of guilt and shame from killing babies!! We're just getting ourselves deeper and deeper! We should have obeyed God's Word a long time ago!

I thought it was interesting to see **George Michael**, one of the guys from the now disbanded group **Wham**, sing "I Want Your Sex", and then say he was trying to promote monogamy, "...sex is best when it's one on one" the song says. The video version ends with the words, "Explore Monogamy" written with a tube of lip-stick on a half-naked girl laying in bed with **Michael.**

The dictionary tells us that *monogamy* is "having only one husband or wife", but also defines *explore* as "to examine, or to have a close search". May I say that from those two definitions, you don't "explore monogamy", but you "**live** monogamy"!!! We've got alot of people who are exploring the laws of God, while God says that we are to live them! It's rather strange that the video shows a number of seductive "below the belt" shots of a well-built woman walking in her underwear and repeated shots of both of them in bed nude, neither one having a wedding ring on. If, as the song says, "sex is best when it's one on one"... why bring the whole TV audience in on it? Seems to me if it is one on one it should be private, and that's the whole point! So much of today's sexuality it based on **voyeurism** and **exhibitionism**...we'll deal with those more in a later chapter.

Sexual sin is unlike any other sin in the Bible. We read in 1 Cor.6:18:

> *"Flee fornication. Every sin that a man doeth is without the body; but he that committeth fornication sinneth against his own body."*

It's interesting to note here that this is the only time in the Word that we are told to "flee" or *run* from sin. There are literally millions of ruined lives to back up the fact that this sin is unlike any other sin. Ask any Pastor or Counsellor who deals with the young and old alike, and they will tell you some heartbreaking stories of people who are burned out because of immorality!! I've heard hundreds of different testimonies in my life from every kind of background you could name and I've found it rather interesting that people talked freely of their life before Christ...

"Before I came to Christ, I was a drug user...I

> was a pusher...I was a robber...I drank all the
> time...I was a member of a gang...I spent time
> in prison...I stole cars...I murdered a man..."

...and they go on and on, but very rarely have I ever heard someone talk about their sexual sins before they came to Christ. You know why? Because sexual sins are unlike any other sins you can name. It's embarrassing. There is something about "used" merchandise...it doesn't seem to hold its value. It's not something you can brag about. It does something to you personally because sex is more than an "animalistic urge". Sex is more than hopping in a bed, it's a whole being action. It encompasses your whole being...spirit, soul, and body!! Yet it seems that the secular music industry wants to ignore the spiritual side altogether, but can it be done?

Listen to how some of these groups tell just one side of the story. It's all rosy for awhile, but what about the fears, the guilt, the shame that follows?

•They'll never tell you of the lonely feeling of the boy who is afraid he may have V.D., or herpes!
•They don't talk about the fear the girl has that her boyfriend may tell his friends, and it gets around!
•No one tells about the feelings the teenage girl has when she finds out that she's going to have a baby, but her boyfriend says she must get an abortion!
•They never talk about the hospital beds where men and

women are dying from AIDS because they never learned to say, "NO" to their sexual desires.

Some people see this type of preaching as censorship. To them anyone should be able to do anything he or she wants. Could you imagine what this country would be like if we did just that..."just do whatever you what, no rules, nobody can tell you anything, you just do what your little heart desires". Let me illustrate it like this...what would it be like if we just took all the stop signs and red lights down, and just told people to drive as you please, no speed limits, no rules, just drive how you want to drive. If you like driving on the other side, fine. Just, **what ever feels good, do it!** Sounds good, but it wouldn't work, my friend. I saw a nice red Corvette pass by me the other day with a bumper sticker saying, "WHAT-EVER FEELS GOOD, DO IT!" and I thought to myself, *'wonder what he would say if I just rammed him right now with my car...boy, that would feel GOOD for me, that would really be fun'* ...of course, I didn't do it, but it just shows you how dumb some of these sayings really are!

At the time of this writing, my wife, Carolyn, and I have two small children who, if we would let them, would eat only candy. But because we love them and are very concerned for their well-being, we have to give them some guidelines when they can and cannot have candy. Now some believe we ought to just let them do what they want, but any dummy knows that kids would choose candy any day over green beans! And I want my kids to still have teeth by the time they turn 10! The point is this, God in the same way must set some rules and guidelines concerning sex. Since He owns the blue-prints and copyrights on our bodies, and since He took the time to design them the way He did, surely He knows what He is talking about when He says, *"Thou shalt not..."*!! He is not a cruel, mean, old man who doesn't want anyone to enjoy sex. He is looking after us. He wants the best for us! He wants sex to be not only fun but fulfilling, and a source of added love in a husband and wife relationship!

But if you disobey His rules (written in His Word) you will find sex not doing what it was intended to do. It simply loses it's ability to satisfy under normal conditions. This is why, after awhile, a person who is living in immorality begins to look for "other ways" to fulfill their desires, i.e. masturbation, pornography, other partners, homosexuality, and all types of perversions, etc. They need a new thrill because each perversion grows dull and more is needed to excite!

Janet Jackson made a big impression with her album *Control*. Starting off the title cut she says,

> "This is a story about control. My control.
> Control of what I say, control of what I do
> and this time I'm gonna do it my way...got
> my own mind, I want to make my own
> decision, when it has to do with my life, I
> want to be the one in control..."

The only problem is the scripture says in 1 Cor.6:19-20:

> *"What? know ye not that your body is the temple of the Holy Ghost which is in you, which ye have of God, and YE ARE NOT YOUR OWN? For ye are BOUGHT WITH A PRICE: therefore glorify God in your body, and in your spirit, which are God's."*

As a Christian you and I are to satisfy God's desires, not ours! We have been bought with the blood of **Jesus Christ** and since we are NOT our own, and since we are to glorify Him in our bodies, we can't be in "Control".

I remember one time a mother came over to me after one of our services and told me she had bought her 14 year-old daughter the *Control* album, and wanted my opinion. I asked her, "Have you ever heard the album yet?" As I expected, her answer was, "No." I told her, "Go home tonight, and listen to just the last song on the album, and you'll know what to do with that album." The last song on the album has **Janet** telling her boyfriend that she has to go, but he keeps forcing her to do it "one more time"...finally, she gives in, and as the song fades out with groans, you find she is no longer in "control"!!

I'm sure you've heard this excuse..."But we're in love". Why is it 6 months later they "love" somebody else? I wonder if we really know what love is? What some call love would be much better defined, "lust"!! People throw the word love around like it's nothing. We use the word so loosely today. We talk about love in so many different ways. I've heard people say they loved someone, two weeks later, they say they hate them. I'll never forget one day as we were driving to our next meeting, I happened to notice that someone had painted on the bridge we were driving under, "Frank loves Mary FOREVER!" but later, with a different color paint, they had tried to cross out Mary and put, Beth. I guess it would be funny if it wasn't so sad!

Think of the many young people who jump from one person to another, trying to find love. Many of them try to find it in some sexual thrill, but keep coming up empty. Then they go to another partner, again finding emptiness and even less sure of what love really is. Even **Lionel Richie**, with all his "love songs" and interviews endorsing marital fidelity, shows it takes more than a song to keep a happy marriage. His wife, **Brenda** was charged with assault, resisting arrest, trespassing, battery, disturbing the peace and vandalism after breaking into the apartment of **Diane Alexander - Richie's** girlfriend - and attacking her and **Lionel** himself.

What about the many lonely people who thought they had found their dream girl or dream guy, as the songs so sweetly sing about, and then realize that love cannot be found in sexy bodies, but only in the heart. **You can truely love someone and never have sex with them, and you can have sex with someone and never love them. <u>So it's plain that love and sex</u>**

<u>don't mean the same thing.</u> But how often have you heard singers talk about *"making love"* when they were just referring to the *act of fornication*. If you want to know what true love is read 1 Cor.13, the love chapter!

Often, people mistake the sex drive with lust. We hear some say that the sex drive is the strongest drive of the human being. "I have to have sex!", they say. But is it really the normal sex drive or is this LUST? Now, from the way some people talk, sex is a must. But this is just another over-emphasis that has been swallowed by millions of people. Sex **IS NOT** the strongest desire in the body...*breathing is*! If you don't believe me, try not breathing for about 90 seconds and see what your body is craving for! The next strongest craving or desire in the human body is *"to go to the bathroom"*! Try not going for about 18-20 hours! The next strongest is *sleep*. You can only go so long without sleep and your body would start craving sleep. Next in line is *water,* you can only go three or four days without water and you would die, so you must have water, but you can go four days without sex and still live! (HA!) Then next would be *food*. You could go about 40-50 days without food and you would begin to die of starvation. Now, you could go 40-50 days without sex and be perfectly normal, you wouldn't die, you wouldn't even be sick because you DON'T HAVE TO HAVE SEX!! Now let me say here again that *sex* is not a sin, but at the same time it is what life is all about in it's *proper* perpective.

Paul hit this thing right on the head in Romans 1, when he said starting at verse 18:

> *"For the wrath of God is revealed from heaven against all ungodliness and unrighteousness of men, who hold the truth in unrighteousness; Because that which may be known of God is manifest in them; for God hath shewed it unto them. For the invisible things of him from the creation of the world are clearly seen, being understood by the things that are made, even his eternal power and Godhead; SO THAT THEY ARE WITHOUT EXCUSE; Because that, when they knew God, they glorified him not as God, neither were thankful; but became vain in their imaginations, and their foolish heart was darkened. Professing themselves to be wise, they became fools, and changed the glory of the uncorruptible God into an image made like to corruptible man, and to birds, and fourfooted beasts, and creeping things. WHERFORE GOD ALSO GAVE THEM UP TO UNCLEANNESS THROUGH THE LUSTS OF THEIR OWN HEARTS, TO DISHONOUR THEIR OWN BODIES BETWEEN THEMSELVES...BURNED IN THEIR LUST ONE TOWARD ANOTHER..."*

Notice the progress of this...

1) They didn't give God the glory
2) They became vain in their imaginations
3) Their foolish hearts were darkened
4) They professed themselves to be wise
5) They became fools
6) They changed the glory of God to flesh glory
7) God gives them up to uncleanness
8) They dishonor their own bodies

We've done just that as a Nation; we failed to glorify the Lord, and have became full of vanity, while our hearts became deeply stained by sin. We think we are so wise*, but we act and talk like fools. We pulled down the glory of a Holy God into a fleshly comprehension, so God gives us over to the lustful desires we so willingly go after, but we have dishonored ourselves!

> (*since when do we think just because someone calls themselves a "doctor" they are so wise?...the Bible speaks of those who are *"Ever learning, and never able to come to the knowledge of the truth."* 2 Tim. 3:7 We need to stop hearing "Dr. Ruth" and start reading the "Book of Ruth"!!)

Let me conclude this chapter by saying this, God made sex. He made sex to feel good and to bring intense pleasure, but He also knows what makes sex fulfilling. But by not obeying the rules, you'll lose in the end. The world says, "I want ME to have pleasure NOW!!!" with no thought of the consequences. God wants you to have the ultimate in pleasure with no guilt, fear, or hurts. God places emphasis on companionship, but the world centers on selfishness! **Sly Fox** had a big hit called, "Let's Go All The Way", as if to say that wanting to have sex with someone means that you want to "go all the way" with them. But listen to me my friend, that's not going all the way with someone, that's just going part of the way!!! When you commit yourself for life to that one you love, get a job, work hard, save your money, buy a nice ring, get married, raise a family, remember the birthdays and anniversaries, serve God and live faithfully in love together till death; **that, my friend, is going ALL THE WAY!!!** But does that sound too old fashion? Does that sound out of date with our new ways of looking at things? The world doesn't want to hear that! They want to live in some pleasure palace of sin and have an ungodly lifestyle and then have all the security and peace and love of a godly home. Friend, it can't happen any other way, either go "all the way" with God or you'll end up losing in the end! Choose one way or the other! <u>Either God is *all right* or He is *all wrong*!!!</u>

---

[1]Circus, Dec.31, 1983, pg.72
[2]RIP, October, 1987, pg.43
[3]The Plain Truth Magazine
[4]RIP, October, 1987, pg.43

ALCOHOL

"Rock 'n roll will last as long as people drink and f—."[1]
- David Coverdale, Whitesnake

An estimated 100 million persons in the United States consume alcoholic beverages. [2] The average American will spend $570 on alcohol this year.[3] But alcohol is a killer, for it has killed more people than all the wars America has been involved in, combined. It is responsible for 50% of all automobile fatalities, 80% of all home violence, and 60% of all child abuse.[4] It is responsible for 70% of murders, 55% of arrests, 41% of assaults, 53% of fire deaths, 50% of rapes, 37% of suicides.[5]

At least **50,000 people will die** from alcohol-related accidents in the United States **this year**. The suicide rate among alcoholics is **58 times** that of the general population. In all, there are **200,000 premature deaths** annually attributed to alcohol abuse, 200,000 deaths by accidents, suicide and premature physical deterioration.[6] **ALCOHOL IS A KILLER!!!!!!**

There are an estimated 12 to 15 million alcoholics in America, 3.5 million of whom are adolescents.[7] Today alcohol-inflicted deaths are the *number one* reason for deaths of young people!! More than 8,000 teenagers and young adults are killed annually in the U.S. in drunk-driving accidents!![8] According to a recent survey, 93% of teenagers have tried alcohol by 12th grade.[9] Last year, Parent Resource Institute for Drug Education (PRIDE) did a study with 6,155 seventh graders. The study showed that 43% were already experimenting with beer and wine and 23% with hard liquor.

And it's getting worse...

In 1974, *one in eight* families reported an alcohol problem affecting it directly...

In 1978, *one in four* families reported an alcohol problem affecting it directly...

In 1982, *one in three* families reported an alcohol problem affecting it directly...[10]

And it's starting younger...

In 1977, 92% of *college students* reported they drank alcoholic beverages regularly.

In 1981, 80% of the *12-18 year olds* surveyed in Midwest schools reported they used or abused alcohol.

In 1982, a California survey revealed 47% of the *sixth graders* got drunk once a week.[11]

Now the question I would like to bring up is...Does rock music have any part in this problem? "NO WAY!!", says most of the rock producers, (as they drink their wine coolers). I find it rather strange that these guys say that the mention of alcohol in their songs have absolutely **no effect** on the listeners, but will turn around and brag about how great it is of them to have songs that put down drinking! For example...when **Stevie Wonder** released his song and hit video called, "Don't Drive Drunk", the rock crowd were patting themselves on the back because they were "fighting against drinking and driving"!! Of course, they claimed it would have a **real effect** on the listeners. To claim that when some rock artist glorifies alcohol in his song, it has "no effect" on young people at all, but then if he is fighting the drinking problem, he's a hero, IS PURE HYPOCRISY!

David Roth can stand on stage with his *Jack Daniels* bottle in hand and claim that it has no effect on his audience at all. Bologna!!! Every time he takes a drink, the kids cheer! He is setting an image for literally thousands of impressionable young men and women that "this is fun". I remember speaking at a high school, and one on the teachers said that maybe the Jack Daniels might just be colored water. Well, here is how **Roth** bragged about it in *Hit Parader Magazine*, "The Jack Daniels I drink on stage is real!"[12]

The Beastie Boys bragged about their drinking lifestyle in a number of their songs. **Mike D**, from the group says, "Our lyrics are about girls, drinking, getting drunk with girls, and hanging out with girls. Basically, we make fairly sexist drunk records."[13] *Heublin Inc.*, an American liquor firm, boast a 200% increase in sales of their "Brass Monkey" ready-mixed cocktail. The falling-over qualities of the blended vodka, rum and citrus juices were glorified in their song of the same name.[14]

On one of their live albums, **Kiss** performs "Cold Gin", a song which glorifies alcohol. Right before they start the song, you can hear the young people scream as **Paul Stanley** questions his admirers...

> "I wanna know, how many of you people
> here like to take a taste of alcohol?...(screams,
> cheers)...I tell you something, when you're
> down in the dumps and you need something
> to bring you up, there's only one thing that's
> goin' to do it the way you want it...COLD
> GIN!!!!...cold gin...cold gin..."

Ace Frehley, former lead guitartist for **Kiss** said concerning his days with the band, "I was abusing myself by over-indulging in alcohol and chemicals."[15] In May 1984, **Frehley** was sentenced to five years' probation, fined $500 and had his New York driver's license suspended six months after pleading guilty to drunken driving.[16]

George Thorogood and The Destroyers (a fitting name) had a hit song, "I Drink Alone" in which he talks about his "good Buddy, Weiser", his "pal, Jack Daniels, and his "partner, Jimmy Bean" as if they were his best friends...and of course 12-15 million alcoholics feel the same way.

Journey brags in their song "Lay It Down", that "Whiskey, wine and women, they get me through the night..."

The group **Los Lobos**, a popular band among college students with a recent #1 hit "La Bamba", had a song entitled "I Got Loaded" in which they brag,

> "Last night I got loaded on a bottle of gin...but I feel alright...night before last I got loaded on a bottle of whiskey...but I feel alright...tonight, I might get loaded on a bottle of wine...gonna feel alright"

Another way rock promotes alcohol is in their publicity. Almost without fail every rock magazine I pick up will have a picture of some band member holding his favorite can of beer or bottle of wine with that certain smile saying, "Hey man, this is what it's all about...let's PARTY!!!" And there are literally thousands of kids who idolize these guys so much that they even go as far as to buy the same brand of brew!! I know this for a fact! I've seen it firsthand!

But let me say it again, **"ALCOHOL IS A KILLER!!!"**

*Alcohol was responsible for the death of...
Hank Williams, the popular country and western artist, died in the back seat of his chauffeur driven car at the young age of 29. One of the many songs he wrote was entitled "I Saw The Light", which oddly enough is a "religious" song. Sad to say, the light wasn't bright enough for him. How true is the statement found in Job 12:25:

> *"They grope in the dark without light, and*
> *he maketh them to stagger like a drunken*
> *man."*

While I'm on this particular point, I think it is important to mention the Country and Western's glorification of beer, wine, whiskey, etc.!!! No doubt C.&W. music talks more about alcohol than Rock and Roll does!!! **By the way Mom and Dad, it is hypocritical to tell your kids to stop listening to rock and roll because it glorifies booze and sex while you keep listening to Merle, George, Tammy, Larry, Dolly, Willie, Waylon, Johnny, Kenny, Barbara, and Hank as they sing about the very same things!!**

*Alcohol was responsible for the death of...
John Bonham, the drummer for **Led Zeppelin**, who was found dead in bed after a night of partying. The coroner's report claimed he had the equivalent of 40 measures of vodka

in his system at the time of his death.[17] Oh, if he would have only heard the message found in Joel 1:5...

> *"Awake, ye drunkards, and weep; and howl, all ye drinkers of wine..."*

<u>*Alcohol was responsible for the death of...</u>
Bon Scott, lead singer for **AC/DC** who sang,

> "No stop signs, no speed limits, nobody gonna slow me down, Hey, momma, look at me, I'm on my way to the promised land, I'm on the Highway to Hell."

He was found dead in the back seat of a car. He had swallowed his own vomit after throwing up and choked to death. And no doubt he got his wish and he's in hell tonight, for the Bible says,

> *"Know ye not that the unrighteous shall not inherit the kingdom of God? Be not deceived: neither fornicators, nor idolaters, nor adulterers, nor effeminate, nor abusers of themselves with mankind, nor thieves, nor **DRUNKARDS**, nor revilers, nor extortioners, <u>shall inherit the kingdom of God.</u>"* (1 Cor.6:9-10)

<u>*Alcohol was responsible for the death of...</u>

Dennis Wilson, drummer for the famous **Beach Boys**, who drowned in the ocean after a drinking party. A doctor who was trying to help **Dennis** overcome his addiction claimed he was "drinking about a fifth of vodka a day and doing a little coke (cocaine)"[18]

> *"But they also have **erred through wine, and through strong drink are** <u>out of the way</u>..."*
> (Isa.28:7)

I bet if **Dennis** would have it to do over again, he'd get his alcohol "out of the way"!!

<u>*Alcohol was responsible for the death of...</u>
Nick Dingley, the drummer for the band **Hanoi Rocks**, who was killed in a head-on collision. **Motley Crue's** lead singer, **Vince Neil** was responsible for **Nick's** death because he was drunk while he drove his car into oncoming traffic, killing **Nick** and seriously and permanently injuring the passengers in the other car. Just as Psalm 107:27 says:

> *"They **reel to and fro, and stagger like a drunken man**, and are at their wit's end."*

"Live fast, die young" is the **Motley Crue** motto, and singer **Vince Neil** backed up that belief with actually being convicted of vehicular manslaughter for the death of **Nick Dingley**. **Vince** spent a month in prison in the spring of '86, made several million dollars in restitution to the injured parties, and received five years probation. Did it stop him? Nope! He still brags "that he might put away a case of beer and half a fifth of gin on a day off."[19] It's rather interesting that on the record sleeve of the "Shout At The Devil" album, the Crue boasts that their album was...

> "...recorded on Foster's Lager, Budweiser, Bombay Gin, lots of Jack Daniels, Kalua, and Brandy..."

Not long after the death of **Nick Dingley, Motely Crue** released the "Theatre Of Pain" album with this vulgar filled statement on the record sleeve...

> "To all Crue Fans: If and/or when you drink
> - Don't take the wheel. Live and learn - so we
> can all f—king rock our a—es off together
> for a long, long time to come."

Real strong stand, huh? What about Isa. 5:22-23, which says:

> *"Woe unto them that are mighty to drink*
> *wine, and men of strength to mingle strong*
> *drink: Which justify the wicked for reward,*
> *and take away the righteousness of the right-*
> *eous from him!"*

***Alcohol was responsible for the death of...**
Ray "Pablo" Falconer, the sound engineer and co-producer

of most of **UB40** records. His brother **Earl Falconer**, the bass player for **UB40**, was sent to prison for 6 months, with a further 12 suspended, after admitting to causing his brother's death because of his drunken driving which resulted in the car crashing into a wall. Imagine having to live with that the rest of your life! All for just a few drinks of alcohol!

It's important to note here that over 25,000 people die every year because of drunk drivers!! That is about 1 person every 23 minutes!!! With over 1 million arrested annually for driving while under the influence, insurance companies consider there to be over 20 million drivers with drinking problems!!![20]

In 1948, only 17% of traffic fatalities in the U.S. were caused by alcohol. By 1956 that percentage had risen to 30%. In 1980, 50% of those killed in auto accidents died because of alcohol! And in 1986, 52% of all traffic fatalities were because of alcohol![21] That's more than the totals for all those who died from drowning, burns, poisons, suffocation, firearms and airplane crashes all put together!

Less than 8% of the licensed drivers in the U.S. are under the age of twenty. But almost 17% of all automobile accidents in 1980 involved a teenager behind the wheel. Alcohol was found in the blood of 58% of teenage drivers killed, with 43% of those kids legally drunk.

Believe it or not, despite all those facts, auto homicide is still considered a misdemeanor in most states.[22] Think about that next time you're driving behind some beer truck!   We just recently held a meeting where a family lost their 7 year-old daughter as the result of a collision with a drunken driver. It was his *third* time for a D.W.I. arrest!!! God help us!!!

Alcohol was responsible for the death of...
Wells Kelly, the drummer for **Meat Loaf**. After returning home from a party, he never made it up the steps, collapsed under his intoxication and choked to death on his own vomit, his body being found the next morning. He was as Isa.19:14 desribes:

> *"...as a drunken man staggereth in his vomit."*

The following artists all died of complications believed to be brought about because of their drinking problem...

- **Florance Ballard**, one of the original **Supremes**
- **Allen Freed**, the famous DJ, who coined the phrase "rock and roll"
- **Ron McKernan**, a former drummer for **The Greatful Dead**
- **Clyde McPhatter** of **The Dominoes**
- **Jim Morrison**, the lead singer of the **Doors**
- **Gene Vincent**, writer of the '56 hit "Be Bob a LuLu"

Read carefully these verses found in Prov.23:29-32, the end of some "leading rockers" should be enough to prove these verses!

> *"Who hath woe? Who hath sorrow? Who hath contentions? Who hath babbling? Who hath wounds without cause? Who hath redness of eyes? They that tarry long at the wine; they that go to seek mixed wine. Look not thou upon the wine when it is red, when it giveth his colour in the cup, when it moveth itself aright. At the last it biteth like a serpent, and stingeth like an adder."*

Alcohol was responsible for the near death and the loss of an arm of **Rick Allen**, the drummer for **Def Leppard**, again after a night of "boozing it up". Being so drunk, he lost control of his sports car and crashed and forever lost his arm. Before the accident, **Allen** thought himself almost unstoppable. As one rock magazine observed,

> "Drummer Rick Allen has considered the possible existence of *a guardian angel* keeping the band safe and warding off ill-luck. 'There's definitely someone looking over us,' he laughs, 'Whatever we do lately is right, and I know we aren't doing it all ourselves!'"[23]

Maybe his guardian angel wouldn't ride with him while he was drunk or pehaps his "guardian" wasn't an angel at all, and "it" really was seeking to lead him on to destruction. As Peter said,

> *"Be sober, be vigilant; because your adver-*
> *sary the devil, as a roaring lion, walketh*
> *about, seeking whom he may devour."*
> 1 Pet. 5:8

Joe Elliott, bragging on the fact that "being sober isn't a favorite state for any of the Leppard members" claimed that when they recorded the *Pyromania* album, "We tried to get ourselves as drunk as possible, then we turned the amps up as high as they'd go and let loose."[24] Of course, *High and Dry*, which was the title of their second album and also the title of one of their songs says, "I've been drinking all day...I got my whiskey, got my wine...Saturday night...I'm high." It is interesting that Prov. 20:1 says:

> *"Wine is a mocker, strong drink is raging:*
> *and whosoever is deceived thereby is not*
> *wise."*

It certainly has proven to be a mocker of **Rick Allen.** Next time you see a picture of him, remember that verse! Not only did it mock him, look how it has mocked our nation!!!

Alice Cooper in 1977 committed himself to a sanatorium to help him "dry out" after he began to throw up blood! He claimed he was drinking two quarts of whisky and 40 cans of beer every day! He boasted that his group was spending over

$250,000 a year on booze.[25]

But sad to say, alcohol has become one of those "acceptable" sins, and today it isn't shocking to find even ministers promoting the advantages of "social drinking". With alcohol listed as a number one killer of teenagers, one wonders where the voices are who really care for the youth of America. This <u>one thing</u> has destroyed more homes, deformed more bodies, defeated more men, degraded more women, demolished more lives, deluded more minds, deceived more young people, deviated more morals, defamed more leaders, defrauded more families, defiled more marriages, degenerated more successes, dejected more souls, demoralized more nations, denied more hopes, denounced more truth, debased more integrity, depraved more devotion, depressed more joy, deprived more children, despised more love, devised more wickedness, and decreed more deaths than any other single vice on this planet!

According to the *Journal of Studies on Alcohol*, 78% of all prime time entertainment episodes contain references to the use of alcohol. 60% show characters drinking alcohol. The average hourly number of drinking acts or drinking-related acts on prime time television is 11. The ranking of the comsuming of all beverages on television is alcohol first, then coffee and tea, soft drinks and water.[26] A child will see alcohol consumed an average of 75,000 times on TV before he or she is of legal drinking age![27]

Genesis, a group that boasts that they are members of **R.A.D.,** (Rockers Against Drugs), are giving a perfect example of the hypocritical, inconsistent stand against drug abuse in our nation. Their tours are sponsored by **Michelob Beer!** And the Michelob T.V. commercials, using hits from Genesis, paint a picture of fun and excitement with the nations **#1** abused drug...ALCOHOL!!!!!! According to recent statistics, $39 billion is spent alone on beer in America![28]

I thought it was a rather intesting article that my local paper had, when Tom Hopkins, Televison Editor wrote,

"Fonzie applied for a library card on *Happy Days*, and the episode set off an unprecedented flurry of interest in books as libraries around the country reported a 500% increase in registrations.

"After watching a TV showing of *The Deer Hunter*, a film featuring scenes of Russian roulette, more than 30 persons have shot themselves in the head — 27 of them fatally — according to the National Coalition on Television Violence.

"Johnny Carson held up a roll of toilet tissue on his show one night and joked about a shortage of the item. The next day (and this is no joke, folks), many stores reported a run on toilet paper.

"There's no question about the ability of a television program to influence the real-life behavior of viewers. It's a powerful medium. Plant the seeds of an interesting idea in the minds of 40 million Americans, and you're bound to harvest some kind of a crop."[29]

But for some reason the media seems to be more concerned over such things as the threat of nuclear power plants...consider this...

1. What if 40 or 50 people were killed everyday by malfunctioning nuclear power plants?
2. What if such malfunctions seriously injured 1,500 more every day?
3. What if the presence and influence of nuclear plants caused eight to twenty people per day to commit suicide?
4. What if the secondary effects of nuclear power caused 200 broken homes every day?
5. What if it caused 250 people to suffer permanent brain damage daily?
6. What if it caused from 1,000 to 3,000 parents to abuse their children or to assault loved ones every day?
7. What if it caused $27 billion a year in direct damages, and an inestimable amount in indirect damages every year?

Awesome and disturbing statistics? Well, if you will *double* every figure I just cited, you will have a fragmented picture of the effects of alcohol on American society today. In view of the fact that after decades of use there hasn't been a *single* case of a person in the public sector being injured by a nuclear power plant, one would have to question why the media remains silent on alcohol's effects while carrying on a scathing campaign of induced terror against the nuclear power industry.[30]

Of course the statistics could go on and on with the line of tragedies in its path. **Ozzy Osborne** is a perfect example of how alcohol finds it way into the lives of rockers and how it can get the best of someone. Because of his inability to get free, he admitted himself into Betty Ford's Hospital to try and help break the bondage of the "bottled killer". But sad to say, **Ozzy** like millions of others, find that its grip is stronger than man's power to help. And at the time of this writing, **Ozzy Osborne** is still a slave to alcohol!! In his song, "Demon Alcohol", Ozzy sings,

> I'm sick and tired of your excuses, can't deal with living anymore. I'll give you reasons to continue while you lie writhing on the floor. I'll wash away your lies and have you hypnotized. There'll be no compromise today, I'll share your life of shame, I think you know my name, I'll introduce myself today, I'm the demon alcohol, demon alcohol, I'll get you."

One reason today that the world has such a hard time freeing people from the binding hands of alcohol is because of the way it is viewed...many see it as a disease!! People don't want to call it 'SIN' cause that sounds too much like something that we might be responsible for. But if we call it a disease or a sickness then we can blame it on our society or our family or some other scape-goat. It is interesting that we call it a disease because if alcoholism is a disease, it is the only disease:

1. That is contracted by an act of will.
2. That requires a license for its distribution.
3. That is bottled and sold.
4. That requires outlets for its sale.
5. That produces revenue for the government.
6. That promotes crime.
7. That is habit-forming.
8. That is spread by advertising.
9. For which we are fined and imprisoned when we exhibit its symptoms.
10. Which brings death on the highway.
11. Without a bacterial or viral cause, and for which there is no corrective medicine.
12. Last but not least, it is only disease that bars the patient from heaven. For the Bible clearly states in 1 Cor.6:10 that no drunkard shall inherit the kingdom of God. (And I hasten to point out that while no drunkard will inherit the kingdom of God, **the power of God can set the drunkard free** and make him a fit subject for the portals of glory...just as it can for anyone else.)[31]

As long as we make excuses for this "destroyer of lives" we will never get free from it's destruction. It's time that we speak out against the #1 abused drug in our nation!!! Sad to say, many do not realize the true harm that comes from alcohol. As I mentioned earlier, even some churches and ministers promote drinking alcohol beverages, but let's look at more important facts about the harmful effects of alcohol...

*It causes birth defects. Babies of mothers who drink during pregnancy are likely to be small and have facial deformities; those babies of fathers who drink heavily during the six months prior to conception are likely to be small.

*It causes liver damage.

*It changes the metabolism of some heart cells, which can cause fibrillation (uncontrolled fluttering of the heart), arrhythmias (disturbances in the heart's rhythm), and possibly heart attack.

*It damages the pancreas, which hinders digestion and upsets blood-sugar balance.

*It impairs absorption of nutrients in the intestine, causing malnutrition. Deficiency of vitamin B1 resulting from poor absorption can cause neurological damage to the brain. The liver's failure to absorb vitamin A causes night blindness.

*It impairs the immune system through its interference with the production of white blood cells.

*It enlarges red blood cells, causing high blood pressure.

*It alters the hormone balance so that the body is in a state of permanent stress.

*It disrupts menstrual cycle.

*It interferes with sexual performance in males by interfering with the production of the hormone testosterone. It shrinks the testicles and decreases fertility by lowering the sperm count.

*It causes slurred speech, disorientation, lack of coordination and impaired memory, perception and judgment.[32]

After sharing these facts concerning the destructive power in alcohol, I find it amazing that even Christians are swallowing a lie about alcoholic beverages! Today, more than ever, we are seeing a compromise among some Christians who try and justify drinking. All one must do is sit down and read his Bible and you will find many, many references to the negative influence of wine and other strong drinks. Someone told me one time while dealing with this issue that I ought to mind my own business...well, my friend, this is my business...to preach <u>the truth in love</u>. And if the Bible speaks out against it, then I better NOT keep silent!!! I would encourage you to get your Bible and look up the following verses and see what God's Word says about alcohol and then compare what others are saying and make up your mind who you will obey...

•Gen. 9:20-26 This is the first time drunkenness is mentioned in the Bible. Notice the tendency toward the sin of homosexuality which accompanied this case.

•Gen. 19:30-38 In this instance, drinking resulted in Lot

committing incest with his two daughters.

•Gen. 27:25-29 Isaac was deceived after drinking wine.

•Lev. 10:9 An express command not to drink wine or strong drink given.

•Num. 6:3 A Nazarite was never to drink wine or liquor.

•Deut. 21:20 Here drinking is associated with stubbornness, rebellion, and disobedience in young men; and brings dishonor to parents.

•Deut. 29:2-6 Abstinence assures a better knowledge of God.

•Jud. 13:4,7,14 Samson's mother; an example to all womanhood, was commanded to drink neither wine nor liquor.

•1 Sam. 1:14-15 Samuel's mother, Hannah, a great example to all mothers, practiced total abstinence.

•1 Sam. 25:36-38 Nabal, a rich man, died at the end of a drunken spree.

•2 Sam. 11:13 David used strong drink to try and lure Uriah into a trap after he had committed adultery with Uriah's wife.

•2 Sam. 13:28-29 Amnon, while in a drunken brawl, was murdered by his own brother Absalom.

•1 Ki. 16:8-10 While King Elah was "drinking himself drunk", one of his captains conspired against him and killed him.

•1 Ki. 20:13-21 No drinking army can hope to win battles. While Ben-hadad and 32 other kings were drinking and getting drunk, a small band of Israel's men attacked the Syrians and slew a large number of their men.

•Esther 1:5-22 Drinking wrecks homes and separates husbands and wives. At a drinking party, King Ahasuerus tried to subject his wife to the lustful eyes of his drunk friends, which brought about the separation of the royal husband and wife.

•Job 1:13-19 Job's children were drinking wine when the hurricane hit and took their lives.

•Prov. 4:17 Violence is associated with drinking.

•Prov. 20:1 Wine is a mocker of people.

•Prov. 20:1 Liquor is a great commotion maker.

•Prov. 20:1 No wise man will ever drink wine or liquor.

•Prov. 21:17 Wine leads to poverty.

•Prov. 23:19-20 Young men should avoid the company of drunks.

•Prov. 23:21 Drinking leads to poverty.

•Prov. 23:20-30 Wine and mixed drinks produces woe, sorrow, contentions, babbling, wounds without cause, and redness of eyes.

•Prov. 23:31 We are told not to even look upon intoxicants.

•Prov. 23:32 Drinking ends up hurting one as the bite of a snake and the sting of an adder.

•Prov. 23:33 Alcohol leads to sexual sins.

•Prov. 23:33 Alcohol causes one to utter indecent words from his heart.

•Prov. 23:34 Alcohol causes one to be unbalanced in his life.

•Prov. 23:35 Alcohol causes one to become insensitive.

•Prov. 23:35 Alcohol becomes habit-forming and brings one into constant bondage.

•Prov. 31:4-5 Kings, Presidents, nor any Governing Official are to drink wine or strong drink.

•Prov. 31:6-7 The only Old Testament sanction on wine or liquor...to be given as a form of anesthesia for those about to die. We now have far better medicines and anesthetics than whiskey, wine, or beer.

•Eccl. 2:3,11 Solomon shares how strong drink brought only vanity into his life.

•Eccl. 10:17 A blessing promised to those nations who have leaders who will turn away from drunkenness.

•Isa. 5:11 A woe placed upon those who drink and become drunk.

•Isa. 5:22 A woe placed upon those who boast in their drinking and mixed drinks.

•Isa. 22:13 Drinking develops fatalism.

•Isa. 24:9 Drinking causes depression and bitterness.

•Isa. 28:1 A woe placed on drunkards and those who are overcome with wine.

•Isa. 28:3 The drunkards in their pride will be trodden down.

•Isa. 28:7 Preachers have erred because of wine.

•Isa. 28:7 Preachers have gone out of the way because of

strong drink.

•Isa. 28:7 Preachers finally become swallowed up by wine.

•Isa. 28:7 Drinking brings preachers into spiritual blindness.

•Isa. 28:7 Drinking causes preachers to stumble in judgement.

•Isa. 56:10-12 A strong rebuke to pastors and spiritual leaders for drinking.

•Jer. 35:5-8,14 Total abstinence of a family is commended.

•Ezek. 44:21 Priest are forbidden to drink wine.

•Dan. 1:5,8,16 Daniel determined not to defile himself by drinking wine.

•Dan. 5:1-4 King Belshazzar drinks before hundreds of people setting a terrible example for others men and women to follow.

•Dan. 5:2-4 Belshazzar becomes bold in his blasphemous action toward the things of God while under the influence of alcohol.

•Dan. 5:4 The people who drank wine began to praise false gods.

•Hosea 3:1 The adulteress was a lover of wine.

•Hosea 4:11 Immorality and wine go hand in hand, for they take away the heart.

•Hosea 7:5 A king and the people are reproved because of their drinking.

•Joel 1:5 Drunkards and those drinking are told to awake and weep and howl because of their wine.

•Joel 3:3 People who would sell children for wine, so that they might be able to drink.

•Amos 2:8 Drinking the wine of the condemned.

•Amos 2:12 A condemnation to those who give wine to ones dedicated to God.

•Amos 4:1 Those who drink had oppressed and crushed the poor and needy.

•Amos 6:1,6 A woe placed on those who drink wine in abundance and are not concerned for the things of God.

•Nah. 1:10 The sudden destruction of drunkards.

•Hab. 2:5-8 The one who sins with wine is a proud man, a

destroyer of his home, and will have unsatisfied desires. A whole nation will be heaped up against him with violence and blood.

•Hab. 2:15 A serious woe is placed on anyone who gives his neighbor strong drink.

•Hab. 2:15-16 A person who gets someone drunk to shame them, God will see to it that they also will be put to shame.

•Matt. 24:49-51 Drunkards are warned about the coming of Christ and their appointment in hell.

•Luke 1:15 John the Baptist's greatness is linked with his total abstinence.

•Luke 12:45-46 Warnings to the drinking crowd and drunkard that they will be cut off and sent to hell.

•Luke 21:34-35 A warning given to the drunkard that the coming of Christ will catch them unaware and will be a snare to them.

•Rom. 13:13-14 A command to walk honestly and not in drunkenness, but to put on Christ.

•Rom. 14:21 Drinking wine will cause others to stumble, be offended, and made weak.

•1 Cor. 5:11 Christians are not to even eat with someone who claims Christ and is a drunkard.

•1 Cor. 6:10 No drunkard shall inherit the Kingdom of God.

•1 Cor. 11:20-22, 27-28 Being drunk has no place in the Lord's Supper but causes people to despise the church of God.

•Gal. 5:19-21 Drunkenness is a work of the flesh and will keep one from inheriting the kingdom of God.

•Eph. 5:18 A direct command not to be intoxicated.

•1 Thess. 5:6-8 A command to be sober at all times and not drunk.

•1 Tim. 3:1-3, Titus 1:7 A pastor is not to drink wine.

•1 Tim. 5:23 Even when used as a medicine, Paul told Timothy to use only "a little" amount of wine.

•1 Pet. 4:3-4 Excess of wine goes hand in hand with lasciviousness, lusts, wild parties, and abominable idolatries.

No one can be honest and study these verses without seeing that the Bible preaches against alcohol! As we have tried to show through the example of its destructive nature and ability, I believe that alcohol is one major reason why much of today's rock music is destroying this generation.

The whole "party mentality" has flooded the rock music industry. In Galatians 5:19-21, Paul lists 17 "works of the flesh" that will keep a person from the kingdom of God. The last one mentioned is "revellings". The definition of revellings is, "lustful and boisterous feastings, with obscene music and other sinful activities". It was during this feasting that the Greeks would honor **Dionysus**, the god of wine and fertility. The feast would include orgiastic rites, but the major part of the "party" was the drinking!

Actually, rock music didn't invent the problem of alcohol, it simply has glorified alcohol! The promotion and glorification of alcohol in this generation will lead to a sure "hell on earth" for millions of precious lives.

And in closing, 1 Cor.10:31 tells us:

> *"Whether therefore ye eat, or drink, or whatsoever ye do, do all to the glory of God."*

So think the next time you are going to take a drink, or go to a party or a rock concert; will *this* give glory to God?! If not, think twice!!!

[1]The Rock Yearbook 1984, pg.203
[2]"Drug Abuse...What can we do?" Loyde V. Allen, Jr. pg.18
[3]USA Today, Dec.31, 1987

[4]"Living with Jellinek's Disease" Newsweek, Oct.17, 1983
[5]U.S. Department of Health and Human Services
[6]"National Institute on Alcohol Abuse and Alcoholism"
[7]"National Institute on Alcohol Abuse and Alcoholism"
[8]"Listen", July, 1985
[9]USA Today, Nov. 16, 1987, pg.1
[10]Gallup Poll
[11]"National Institue on Alcohol Abuse and Alcoholism"
[12]"Hit Parader", July, 1984, pg.33
[13]The Rock Yearbook, Vol.8, pg.59
[14]The Rock Yearbook, 1989, pg..6
[15]Blast, Aug.8, 1987, pg.19
[16]Dayton Daily News, May 13, 1985
[17]"Rock and Roll Babylon" Gary Herman, pg.55
[18]People, Jan.16, 1984
[19]Circus, Dec.31, 1986, pg.56-57
[20]Good Housekeeping, April, 1986, pg.56
[21]USA Today, Dec.21, 1987, pg.1
[22]"Temptation", John C. Souter, pg.41
[23]Tiger Beat Rock, Feb., 1984, pg.30
[24]Cream, Apr.30, 1983
[25]Rock and Roll Babylon, pg.71
[26]NFD Journal, Aug. 1987, pg.16
[27]The National Council on Alcoholism
[28]USA Today, Dec.31, 1987
[29]The Journal Herald, Sept.25, 1984
[30]"Alcohol: America's Greatest Problem", The Evangelist
[31]Ibid.
[32]USA Today, Sept.16, 1986, pg.4-D

5

DRUGS

> "Do you wanna know how I keep this tired
> and battered body in shape folks...I'll tell
> you how...the same way we're going to keep
> the whole Godd—world into shape...drugs,
> sex, and rock and roll...drugs, sex, rock and
> roll...drugs, sex, and rock and roll...!!!"

So goes the chant lead by **Bette Midler** on the live *Rose* album. It seems to be the adopted triplets of the youth culture in our land today...Drugs, Sex and Rock n' Roll!! And sad to say, it has literally destroyed millions of young lives!

Most groups don't try to hide their feelings about drugs any more. It seems to be an accepted fact that drugs are a part of this "high" society. What was shocking in rock and roll 20 years ago, is expected today. A recent hit by **Lita Ford,** called "Kiss Me Deadly" shows the casual attitude today,

> "Had a few beers, gettin' high. Sittin',
> watchin' the time go by, Uh Huh, It ain't no
> big thing"

Lita gives her philosophy on the back of her album...

> "People are always gonna try 'n' tell ya how
> to run your life, but...what you have to do
> is...make up your own mind. Who do you
> live for? Do you live for yourself, or do you
> live for what other people are trying to make
> you out to be? Great!!! So listen to what they
> say, that's OK! Just learn from it. But do it
> your own way. Follow your heart and you
> will last forever...Lita"

In a concert in Detroit, Mich., **David Roth**, then with the group **Van Halen**, yelled out to his young audience, "We are gathered together in celebration of drugs, sex and rock and roll!!!" To that came a burst of cheer! Later in an interview with *USA Today*, **Roth** was asked what he thought of the use of drugs and alcohol in the entertainment industry. **Roth** confessed, "If you took away every musician...who drank or did drugs, you wouldn't have anybody left."[1]

Circus Magazine, a popular rock-fan magazine, records a manager of a popular rock group saying, "No matter what anyone tells you, drugs will always be a part of the rock scene."[2] Rock critic, **Robert Forbes** says, "Drugs are a necessary ingredient for many rock musicians. It is almost impossible to sustain the frantic pace, ungodly hours and inhuman energy without resorting to some kind of drug. The rock musician thrives on the periphery of that high, and uses it as a crutch to hold his position, audience and individuality."[3] **John Cougar** told *Creem magazine* that he wasn't going to judge people for taking drugs "in the music business, because everyone's blowing cocaine."[4] **Billy Idol,** contesting the anti-drug movement says, "I never found that not taking drugs did anything for me."[5] and "Drugs don't really alter your perception or anything that much. I mean they do, but I think if you feel pretty much in control of who you are, then drugs aren't really a problem."[6] **Mike Levine** from **Triumph** says, "The bottom line is, there's nothing like going to a hockey arena with a bunch of friends, getting drunk, getting stoned and watching a great rock and roll band perform live. I don't think that's ever going to change."[7] **Nikki Sixx** from **Motley Crue** says concerning him and the band, "We were always rowdy - we can't lie to you. We're not faking, we're just us. We drink and f— and do drugs. Doesn't everybody? The only difference now is we can afford better drugs!"[8] "Sex and Drugs and Rock and Roll...that's our cup of tea." sings the group, **Krokus.** I wonder what their song will be when their cup is empty?

"Are drugs still a problem in our society?", some may ask. Many have erroneously believed that the problem was just a '60's problem. The fact is, drug abuse is at an alarming level today...

•500,000 estimated hard-core heroin addicts[9]
•20-24 million Americans have tried cocaine
•5 million regular cocaine users
•30% of all college students will have tried cocaine
•16% of all high-school seniors have used cocaine at least once
•more than 500,000 high schoolers use cocaine regularly.
•20% of high school students use "uppers" or "downers"
•LSD is making a comeback, with 10% of high school students who have tried it
•more than 300,000 high school students use LSD-type drugs at least once a week.[10]
•more than half of all teenage deaths are drug-related.[11]

Government studies have revealed some very scary facts concerning our drug problem in the United States, while adding that after years of educational programs and literally millions of dollars being spent to try and combat the problem, <u>no real progress has been made</u>!! According to a congressional report, the illegal drug sales in 1985 amounted to 50 Billion Dollars!

But of all drugs, none seem to have the appeal that marijuana does...

•According to recent studies, Marijuana is now the number one selling crop in our nation! According to The National Organization for the Reform of Marijuana Laws, the total U.S. crop in 1986 had an estimated street value of $26.7 billion, while in comparison, the combined value of the U.S. corn, soybean, and wheat crops was 26.6 billion.[12]

•America has over 31 million people who have tried marijuana within the last year, and currently has 20 million users of marijuana.[13]

•Approximately 6.2 million young people ages 12-17 have used marijuana at some time during their lives.

•15% of kids ages 9-12 say marijuana is very easy to get.

•2.7 million have used marijuana in the last month. 4.8 million have used marijuana in the past year.[14]

•25% of high school students smoke marijuana. 10% smoke at least once a week. 5% smoke it daily.

•Marijuana use is on the increase among sixth, seventh, and eighth-graders. Studies show that 2% of this age group smoke pot at least once a week.[15]

•42% of all college students have tried marijuana.[16]

•Many studies have shown that those who are on "harder drugs" got their start by smoking marijuana.

But before you think that marijuana is just a mild drug, read this...

Dr. Robert DuPont, former director of the *National Institute on Drug Abuse* said, "I believe marijuana to be our most dangerous drug because the psychological as well as the physical effects are insidious and ultimately devastating."[17]

The American Medical Association,-"There is now no doubt at all that marijuana is a dangerous drug, with great potential for serious harm to young American users...Marijuana is by no means the harmless amusement many believe it to be..."[18]

Here are some of the facts about Marijuana...

•The marijuana plant contains 421 chemicals, the smoke contains over 2000.

•Marijuana impairs psychomotor function, such as driving a car or piloting a plane.

•Marijuana impairs short-term memory and learning ability.[19]

•The psychoactive chemicals in marijuana are *not* water soluble, which means they accumulate in your system. It takes about one month for all the THC[20] in *one joint* to leave your body. No other drug used or abused by man has such harmful staying power.

•Marijuana use increases the heart rate by as much as 50%, depending on the amount of THC in the joint.

•Two joints (Marijuana cigarette) can reduce lung capacity more than one pack of tobacco cigarettes.

•Marijuana smoke increases airway resistance at least 25% under laboratory conditions in which a similar amount of tobacco smoke produces no significant increase in airway resistance.

•Marijuana may cause the deadly disease emphysema *20 times faster* than regular tobacco cigarettes.

•Marijuana smoke has 50% more tar than regular tobacco cigarettes.

•In laboratory tests, the tars from Marijuana smoke have

produced tumors when applied to animal skin. These studies suggest it is likely that marijuana may cause cancer if used for a number of years.[21]

•Marijuana smoke has been found to contain more cancer-causing agents than is found in tobacco smoke. For example, marijuana tar contains 70% more benzopyrene, a major cancer-causing chemical.

•Examination of human lung tissue that has been exposed to marijuana smoke over a long period of time showed cellular changes called metaplasia, which are considered precancerous. Marijuana smoke produces greater cellular changes in the lungs than does tobacco smoke.

•Marijuana appears to lower the normal testosterone levels in boys. Testosterone is the major male sex hormone responsible for the physical changes that take place at puberty and for normal adult male sexual functioning. In girls, there are also disruptions of normal hormone levels, with possible accumulation of marijuana's chemicals in the ovaries.[22]

•Marijuana weakens the immune system. Researchers are now investigating whether those who smoke marijuana may be more vulnerable to AIDS if exposed to the virus.

Now with all that in mind, let's see if rock music has anything to say about Marijuana...

The group, **Journey**, who have had a number of successful years in rock ' roll, are a very large financial supporter of N.O.R.M.L. (The National Organization For Reform Of Marijuana Laws).[23] This organization is trying to reverse the marijuana laws in our country, making marijuana as easy to buy as a pack of cigarettes.

Head East has an album entitled, *Get Yourself Up*, which shows a truck overloaded with a huge mound of marijuana.

Legalize It , is the title of an album by **Peter Tosh**. The cover depicts Tosh smoking a joint while sitting in a field of marijuana.

Rick James has many songs dedicated to marijuana. Matter of fact, he has often "lit up" right on stage in front of thousands. "I smoke a joint on stage because I wanna get high at that particular time."[24] He also has a back-up group of girls called, **Mary Jane Girls**, which, of course, is a street term for marijuana.

Ambrosia's album, *Road Island*, shows a huge marijuana plant on the cover with a guitarist pictured craving it.

Black Sabbath sings about marijuana in their song, "Sweet Leaf" and encourages their audience to "Come on now, try it out. Straight people don't know what you're about. They put you down and shut you out. You gave to me a new belief, and soon the world will love you, sweet leaf".

Styx, from their *Equinox* album encourages their listeners to "Light Up"..."All I need is just one 'hit'* to get me by...light up everybody, join us in this celebration, light up and be happy, sweet, sweet sounds will fill the air" (I might note here that in the background of the last chorus you can faintly hear the group repeatedly saying "smoke it", using a popular form of subliminal persuasion, which we will be dealing with in a later chapter.)

Boston in their song, "Party" says, "Yea, get down and party, if you need a cue, you're sure to find one in the crowd. Just meet some friends and have a 'toke'* or two, in a place where they can never play the music too loud." (*terms used for smoking marijuana)

The Doobie Brothers got their name from the street term for a marijuana cigarette, a 'doobie'., and inside their *Minute by Minute* album, the record sleeve exhibits just that, a half-smoked doobie.

Rush is another group who borrowed their name from the drug culture. Those who use drugs refer to the "rush" or the "high" they experience while taking them.

ZZ Top also got their name from the drug culture, naming themselves after two popular brands of "marijuana papers"...Zig-Zag and Top's. They have many different examples of boasting their pro-drug lifestyle. On the cover of their album entitled, *El Loco*, (marijuana is sometimes called, 'loco-weed') the group is being caught with four huge sacks full of marijuana. Their song, "Under Pressure" speaks of a girl who's got them under pressure, saying, "She don't like other women, she likes whips and chains, she likes cocaine..."

Paul McCartney, who has been arrested a number of times for drug possession, shows off his love for smoking dope on the *Pipes of Peace* album.

Black Flag has an album entitled, *Annihilate This Week*, which shows their fans how to do just that...blow your week away on dope. The album cover depicts a young man with his "artillery" of beer, rolled joints, a pipe and along with a "nickle bag" of pot.

"Smokin' In The Boy's Room" was a hit by **Motley Crue,** a song that speaks of smoking more than just cigarettes. **Nikki Sixx** says, "I use to smoke "Angel Dust" in school in my math class. I'd sit in the back. I had this pipe that looked like a pen and no smoke ever came out of it."[25]

It is most surprising to me that more people can't see the obvious problem. I believe we are being hypocritical!! With the exposure of drug abuse in the entertainment industry, including many popular T.V. personalities and various movie stars, along with the drug problem among many sports figures, it doesn't take a genius to understand why many teenagers are having a hard time living "straight" as they follow these role models!

If we want to deal with the problem, let's get to the root!!! Today we are struggling with a problem that goes much deeper than what doctors, teachers, psychologists, health groups, and even governmental organizations can handle...because drug abuse is a spiritual problem!!! That may sound silly, but it is true!! And the Bible is not silent about it...

We read in Rev.9:20-21, referring to the days during the great tribulation,

> *"And the rest of the men which were not killed by these plagues yet repented not of the works of their hands, that they should not worship devils, and idols of gold, and silver, and brass, and stone, and of wood; which neither can see, nor hear, nor walk: Neither repented they of their murders, nor of their *sorceries, nor of their fornication, nor of their thefts."*

It is very interesting to note that the word, "sorceries", found in this verse is from the Greek word, *"pharmakia"*, which is where we get our word, "pharmacy", meaning medication or drugs. Here, and also in Rev.18:23; 21:8; 22:15; the word, "sorcery", along with the word, "witchcraft", found in Gal.5:20, all come from the same Greek root word, and refer to *"coming under spells or magic induced by medication or drugs"*.

This is very significant when you hear of some of the "spiritual feelings" and "visions" many people have had while under the influence of mind-altering drugs. Isn't it also interesting that the teachings of eastern cults and mysticisms, along with the occult, began to be very popular in rock music during the drug explosion in the '60's and early '70's!! One such example is **Nina Hagen,** the bizzare female rocker known for her blasphcmous music, claimed at the age of 17, she had an "out of body" experience during an LSD trip.[26]

It seemed to some that drugs got people's minds "opened", so they could get some "real truth". It was called "acid rock" because young people were encouraged to take some "acid" (LSD) while listening to the music. During this time, many young people spoke of "tripping out on acid" and having visions of angels, demons, satan and even God. Some of "trips" were so bad, many committed suicide. Again, let me say, I believe from scripture that we can say beyond doubt that experimenting with drugs is trafficking with demonic powers!!! This is why I say that drug abuse is a spiritual problem. It goes much further than just getting "high"; it is messing with the powers of darkness!!

> "Staring blindly into space/Getting up to
> splash my face/Wanting just to stay awake/
> Wondering how much I can take/Should I try
> to do some more/25 or 6 to 4"

Those were the words to the song "25 or 6 to 4", sung by **Chicago.** The song rose to No. 4 on the *Billboard* charts in 1970, while the song's subject—25 or LSD—has risen to No.

2 on the Drug Enforcement Administration's charts in 1988. LSD (lysergic acid diethylamide 25) has made a "marked and sudden advance" on the American drug scene according to Michael A. Pavlick, of the DEA's Dangerous Drugs division in Washington, D.C.[27]

I believe we can trace the current drug problem in our nation directly to the rock/drug culture of the '60's and '70's!!! But, despite the history of what drugs have done to others, today many groups are learning the hard way that drugs still kill! All one must do is take a look at the tragic end of many rock stars.

R.A.D. (Rockers Against Drugs) was formed to help fight the problem. But I fear the damage is too deep and the grip is too strong for mere warnings to turn the drug problem around. The damage is already done. Attend a rock concert one time and you'll be shocked into reality. Open drug abuse!!! To see just how hypocritical this organization has been thus far, listen to this. **Doc McGhee**, the manager for **Bon Jovi, Motley Crue,** and **Pat Travers** was ordered to produce anti-drug concerts and spend time in a treatment facility for his role in an international drug smuggling ring which authorities contend had ties to Panamanian strongman, **Gen. Manuel Noriega.** One report said he was responsible for smuggling 20 tons of marijuana (street value $10 million) into the US.[28] **McGhee** was also fined $15,000 and placed on probation for five years for supplying a smuggling ring with a new source of marijuana in Colombia after a boat the operation was using was seized with 29,000 pounds of the substance off the coast of North Carolina.[29] It is common information that many rock producers and promoters also have close contacts with the "drug world", and hardly anything is done about it. As **Elvis Costello** said concerning drugs in the music industry, "In my line of work, if you drank all the drinks, and took all the drugs you were offered, you would die. Simple as that."[30] The monster they helped to create has come back to destroy...and look at its path of destruction...(* denotes death)

In '43, **Lysergic acid diethylamide (LSD)** is first synthesized by **Albert Hofmann** in a laboratory in Switzerland. LSD is later to play a major role in the evolution of music and culture in the '60's.

*In '53, **Hank Williams** died in the back seat of his car from drugs and alcohol while going to his next performance.

*In '59, **Billie Holiday**, considered by many to have been the best blues singer, died from an overdose of heroin.

In '60, **Freddy Fender**, writer of "Wasted Days and Wasted Nights", began his three year prison term for a drug-related conviction. He certainly wasted alot of days and nights.

In '61, the popular blind pianist, **Ray Charles** was arrested twice for possession of drugs and drug paraphernalia.

*In '63, **Dinah Washington**, a jazz singer with **Lionel Hampton's** band, died from an overdose of sleeping pills.

112

In '64, **Ray Charles** was busted at Logan Airport in Boston for heroin and marijuana possession. After this third drug charge, he decided to give up his 17 year heroin habit.

In '65, **Dr. Timothy Leary**, of Harvard University claimed the **Beatles** as his helpers in promoting the 'golden age' through LSD.

In '65, **Ken Kesey**, novelist who wrote, *One Flew Over The Cuckoo's Nest*, and his band of **Merry Prankster**, held their first public LSD-taking test while listening to the **Grateful Dead.**

In '66, **Bill Graham**, considered to be most important rock promoter ever, helped **Ken Kesey** stage a three-day "Trips Festival", a sort of extended LSD-taking test.

In '66, LSD finally became illegal in California where most of the early "Acid Rock" groups gathered. Groups like **The Grateful Dead, Jefferson Airplane, Moby Grape, Big Brother and the Holding Company,** and **Quicksilver** were started from that area of the country.

In '66, **Donovan**, with the hit tune, "Mellow Yellow" was fined 250 English pounds for possession of marijuana.

In '67, **Brian Jones** of the **Rolling Stones** was sentenced to nine months in jail on drug charges, but was released on bail. Of course, he never learned his lesson, as you'll see later.

In '67, **Keith Richards** of the **Rolling Stones** was found guilty of allowing his home to be used for drug use and was sentenced to one year in jail and was fined 500 pounds.

In '67, **Mick Jagger** of the **Rolling Stones** was found guilty of illegal possession of pep pills and was sentenced to three months in jail and fined 300 pounds.

In '67, **John Sinclair**, manager of the **MC5** was arrested along with 57 other people at his Artist's and Writers' Workshop in Detroit and was charged with possession of marijuana.

In '67, all six members of **The Grateful Dead** were busted for possession of marijuana.

In '67, **Rolling Stone Magazine** put out it's first issue, which included a free "roach clip" (A device used to hold a marijuana cigarette).

*In '67, **Brian Epstein**, manager for the **Beatles**, died from an overdose of sleeping pills. By this time, all four Beatles were experimenting with various drugs including LSD. That same year, **Paul McCartney** told *Life magazine* that he was "deeply committed to the possibilities of LSD as a universal cure-all". He went on to say, "After I took it, it opened my eyes. We only use one-tenth of our brain. Just think what all we could accomplish if we could only tap that hidden part. It would mean a whole new world. If politicians would use

LSD, there would be no more war, poverty or famine."[31]

In '67, *Time magazine* reported that **Sgt. Pepper's Lonely Hearts' Club Band** album was "drenched in drugs".[32]

In '68, **Brian Jones** was fined $150 plus court costs after a judge finds him guilty of possession of marijuana.

In '68, **Larry Graham** of **Sly and the Family Stone**, was arrested in London for possession of marijuana.

In '68, **Frank Weber**, manager of **The Kingston Trio** was arrested along with 5 others, when 400 pounds of marijuana were found in their possession.

In '68, **John Lennon** and **Yoko Ono** were busted for marijuana possession in the home of **Ringo Starr**.

In '68, **Bob Weir** and **Ron McKernan** of **The Grateful Dead** were busted on a variety of drug charges after a police raid at their San Francisco home. **Ron** later died in '73 because of his alcohol problem.

In '68, **Eric Clapton**, and three members of **The Buffalo Springield—Neil Young**, **Richie Furay** and **Jim Messina** were arrested on marijuana charges. About this same time, **Clapton** claimed that "Acid was conducive to exploring music."[33]

In '68, **Syd Barrett,** founder of **Pink Floyd** left the group, suffering from psychiatric disorders brought about by his drug abuse. **Roger Waters** from the group said, "There was so much dope and acid around in those days that I don't think anyone can remember anything about anything."[34]

*In '68, **Frankie Lymon,** writer of, "Why do fools fall in love", died from an overdose of heroin.

In '69, **Etta James,** the 50's R & B singer, with the hit song, "The Wallflower", tried to kick her heroin habit with the aid of methadone, but it turned out to be "the most horrible thing I've ever experienced. It sets up a blockage against heroin, but creates a stomach habit. Then the blockage wears off, and you have a double craving; your stomach craves methadone and your veins crave heroin." (Rock 'n Roll Confidential, Penny Stallings, pg.231)

In '69, **Paul Kantner,** of **Jefferson Airplane,** was busted in Honolulu for possession of marijuana. An earlier hit by the group entitled, "White Rabbit" caused much controversy because of its obvious reference to drug use.

In '69, **Jack Casady,** also of **Jefferson Airplane,** was arrested for possession of marijuana in his hotel room in New Orleans and received a two-and-a-half year suspended sentence. **Grace Slick,** the lead singer for the group, also known as the "Acid Queen", told *Cavalier,* "We all use drugs and we condone the judicious use of drugs by everyone. Kids are going to blow their minds somehow, and this is a better way to do it than racking up their car against the wall."[35] She also claimed she had planned spiking President Nixon's tea with 600 micromilligrams of LSD at a White House Party.[36]

In '69, **Mick Jagger** was busted in London for possession of marijuana. And what's his stand on drug enforcement today? "It still seems absurd to me now that anybody can actually be put in jail for smoking marijuana or even selling it. It's absurd...You can't just pass laws and enforce them, as far as drugs are concerned. It doesn't work. It didn't work during Prohibition, and it doesn't work with cocaine."[37]

In '69, **Marianne Faithful**, girlfriend of **Mick Jagger**, nearly died from an overdose of barbiturates. Two days later she entered a hospital for treatment of heroin addiction.

In '69, **George Harrison** and his wife, **Patti**, were arrested at their home and charged with possession of 120 joints of marijuana.

In '69, **Jimi Hendrix** is busted in the Toronto International Airport for possession of several ounces of heroin in a travel bag. Hendrix is quoted saying, "Knowing me, I'll probably get busted at my own funeral."[38] Sad to say, he was dead one year later.

*In '69, **Brian Jones**, the guitarist for **The Rolling Stones**, died from drowning, too high on barbiturates and alcohol to help himself.

In '70, **Steve Stills**, of **Crosby, Stills, Nash** and **Young** was arrested in his motel for possession of cocaine and barbiturates.

In '70, **Marty Balin**, singer for **Jefferson Starship**, was busted for marijuana possession and for contributing to the delinquency of minors. Police found Balin and friends with several girls aged 12 to 17. He was fined only $100.

In '70, **Chubby Checker** and three others were arrested at Niagara Falls after marijuana, hashish, and unidentified drug capsules were found in his car.

*In '70, **Jimi Hendrix**, died from inhalation of vomit after his body rejected an overdose of sleeping pills.

*In '70, **Janis Joplin**, died from an overdose of heroin. *Time Magazine* quoted her a year before saying, "I wanted to smoke dope, take dope, lick dope, anything I could get my hands on I wanted to do."[39] Her body was cremated and thrown in the ocean.

*In '70, **Jim Morrison**, singer/songwriter for **The Doors**, died of heart failure due to his lifestyle, full of drugs and alcohol.

*In '70, **Al Wilson**, Singer/Guitarist for **Canned Heat**, died from an overdose of barbiturates.

In '71, *Illinois Crime Commission* issued a list of "drug-oriented rock records". Included were: "Let's Go Get Stoned", "A Whiter Shade Of Pale", "Hi-De-Ho (That Old Sweet Roll)", White Rabbit", "With A Little Help From My Friends", "Yellow Submarine", "Lucy In The Sky With Diamonds", and "Puff, The Magic Dragon".

In '71, members of **The Grateful Dead** were accused of distributing LSD-laced apple juice to an unwitting audience. Police shut down the concert and rushed 36 people to a nearby Crisis Clinic for treatment.

In '71, **John Lennon** admitted he and **Yoko Ono** had taken heroin and LSD. He told *Time magazine*, "I must have had a thousand trips. I used to eat it all the time."[40]

In '72, **Joe Cocker** and six members of his band, along with his road crew were busted for drug possession after a concert in Australia. Police had confiscated marijuana, heroin and hypodermic syringes. He was forced to leave the country.

In '72, **Paul McCartney** and his wife, **Linda**, along with drummer **Denny Seiwell** were arrested for drug possession in Sweden.

*In '72, **Miss Christine**, a member of **Frank Zappa's GTO's**, died from overdose of heroin. Zappa once said,

"Society's major hang-ups could be cured by a drug and sexual openness."[41]

*In '72, **Billy Murcia**, drummer for **New York Dolls**, accidentally choked to death during a drug-induced stupor.

*In '72, **Rory Storme**, of **The Hurricanes**, died from an overdose of sleeping pills.

*In '72, **Brian Cole**, bass player for **The Association**, died from an overdose of heroin.

*In '72, **Danny Whitten**, singer for **Neil Young's Crazy Horse**, died from overdose of heroin.

In '73, **Phil Lesh**, bassist of **The Grateful Dead** was busted for possession of drugs in Marin County, California.

In '73, **Jerry Garcia**, lead guitarist for **The Grateful Dead** was busted after being pulled over for speeding. The police found pot, cocaine and LSD. He was released on $2,000 bail. Referring to their style of music, Garcia once said, "Acid rock is music you listen to when you are high on acid. (LSD)"[42]

In '73, **Paul McCartney** was busted for growing pot on his farm in Scotland.

In '73, **Buddy Rich** was busted for possession of marijuana while touring Australia, the second bust for the 56-year-old

Jazz drummer.

In '73, **Tom Johnston** of **The Doobie Brothers** was arrested on charges of marijuana possession. Johnston told *Rolling Stone magazine*, "We were sitting, passing around a joint — a doobie — so we called ourselves the 'Doobie Brothers'."[43] Oddly, about the same time of his hearing, the Dobbie Brothers album, *What Were Once Vices Are Now Habits* was released.

In '73, **Keith Richards** of **The Rolling Stones** and **Anita Pallenberg** were busted in France for drug possession.

*In '73, **Gram Parsons**, once of **The Byrds** and **The Flying Burrito Brothers**, died from an overdose of multiple drugs.

In '74, **Vinnie Taylor**, guitarist for **Sha, Na, Na**, died from an overdose of heroin.

*In '74, **Pamela Morrison**, wife of **Jim Morrison**, died from an overdose of heroin.

*In '74, **Nick Drake**, singer/songwriter, died from an overdose of pills.

*In '74, **Robbie McIntosh**, drummer for **Average White Band**, died from an overdose of heroin.

In '75, **Chuck Negron**, lead singer of **Three Dog Night**, was busted in Louisville, Ky., after police found two grams of heroin and a gram of cocaine in his hotel room.

In '75, **Chad Mitchell**, leader of the folk trio named after him was sentenced to five years in prison for possession of over 400 pounds of marijuana.

In '75, **Linda McCartney** was busted for possession by a Los Angeles police officer. She was carrying 8 ounces of pot in her purse.

In '75, 511 people were busted at a series of concerts being performed by **Pink Floyd** at the sports arena in Los Angeles, for possession of drugs.

In '75, members of **Dr. Hook** were busted after marijuana was found in one of their hotel rooms. One of their songs entitled, 'Get My Rocks Off' says, "Some men need some killer weed, (pot) And some men need cocaine, Some men need some cactus juice (peyote) to purify their brains. Some men need two women, And some need alcohol; Everybody needs a little something, But, Lord, I need it all...to get my rocks off."

*In '75, **Tim Buckley**, popular Sixties folk-rock singer died from an overdose of heroin/morphine.

In '76, **Eric Faulkner**, singer for **Bay City Rollers** nearly died after swallowing Seconal and Valium tablets.

In '76, 188 were arrested for drug possession at a **Jethro Tull** concert in Los Angeles.

In '76, **Allman Brother Band** roadie, **Scooter Herring**, was sentenced to 75 years in prison for distributing cocaine and other drugs to **Gregg Allman**. Gregg was granted immunity in exchange for his testimony.

In '76, **Keith Richards** of **The Rolling Stones** was busted after he had lost control of his car, slamming into a center divider on the highway. The Police discovered a silver cylinder containing cocaine.

In '76, **David Bowie** and **Iggy Pop** were busted in their hotel room in Rochester, NY, and charged with possession of six ounces of pot.

In '76, **Neil Diamond** was busted in his home for possession of marijuana.

*In '76, **Paul Kossoff,** leader of **Free**, died from an overdose of heroin.

*In '76, **Tommy Bolin**, guitarist for **James Gang** and **Deep Purple,** died from an overdose of heroin.

*In '76, **Scott Quick**, guitarist for **Sammy Hagar Band**, died from an overdose of drugs.

*In '76, **Gary Thain**, **Urian Heep** bassist, died from an overdose of heroin.

In '76, **Bette Midler** bails out seven members of her entourage following a bust for possession of cocaine and marijuana.

In '77, **Rock Scully**, manager for **The Grateful Dead**, was jailed for four months for conspiracy to smuggle marijuana.

In '77, **Keith Richards** of **The Rolling Stones** was arrested and fined a mere $1,300 for possession of heroin, 130 grams of cocaine and other narcotic paraphernalia.

*In '77, **Elvis Presley** dies of heart failure due to multiple abuse of drugs. In the last 18 months of his life, Elvis took literally thousands of drugs including **Amytal** (a sedative, used to relieve insomnia), **Biphetamine** (a stimulant, given to control hyperactivity in children), **Butabarbital** (a sedative, reduces anxiety), **Carbrital** (a seditive, reduces nervous tension), **Codeine** (a narcotic, a pain reliever), **Demerol** (a narcotic, relieves pain), **Dexamyl** (a barbiturate, to help reduce tension), **Dexedrine** (an amphetamine, given to prevent narcolepsy; attacks of uncontrollable sleepiness), **Dilaudid** (a narcotic, prescribed to suppresses cough), **Hycomine** (a antihistamine, given to reduce allergic symptoms), **Ionamin** (an appetite suppressant), **Leritine, Lomotil** (an antidiarrheal, relieves intestinal cramps), **Morphine** (a narcotic, a very strong pain reliever), **Nembutal** (a seditive, reduces nevous tension), **Pentobarbital** (a barbiturate, reduces anxiety), **Percodan** (a stimulant, used to treat drowsiness and fatigue), **Phenobarbital** (an anticonvulsant, used to prevent convulsions or seizures such as epilepsy), **Placidyl** (a sleep inducer), **Quaalude** (a hypnotic, decreases anxiety, tension or insomnia), **Tuinal** (a sedative, relieves insomnia), **Valium** (a tranquilizer, used for treatment for nervousness, tension, muscle spasms and convulsive disorders), **Valmid**, and others. It's rather interesting that the "King of Rock and Roll" died a victim of a concept that he helped get started! Elvis, "...be sure your sin will find you out!" (Num.32:23)

In '77, **Keith Richards** of **The Rolling Stones** was busted in Toronto for possession of heroin. His sentence included a benefit Rolling Stone concert.

*In '78, **Rich Evers, Carol King's** songwriter, died from an overdose of cocaine.

*In '78, **Greg Herbert**, saxophonist for **Blood, Sweat, and Tears**, died from an overdose of drugs.

*In '78, **Pete Meaden**, manager for **The Who**, died from an overdose of barbiturates, later ruled a suicide.

*In '78, **Keith Moon**, drummer for **The Who**, died from an overdose of drugs.

*In '79, **Philip Hale**, a photographer friend of **Jimmy Page**, died in the home of Page from an overdose of morphine, cocaine and alcohol.

In '79, **Marianne Faithful** was arrested at Oslo Airport in Norway for possession of marijuana. After signing a full confession, she was set free to resume her concert tour.

*In '79, **Sid Vicious**, bassist for **The Sex Pistols**, died from an overdose of heroin.

*In '79, **Lowell George**, singer/songwriter for **Frank Zappa's, Mother of Invention** and also **Little Feet**, died of heart failure due to overdose of drugs.

*In '79, **Jimmy McCulloch**, guitarist for **Paul McCartney's** band, **Wings**, died from an overdose of heroin.

In '80, **Ron Wood**, guitarist for **The Rolling Stones**, and his girlfriend were arrested for possession of 5 grams of cocaine.

In '80, **Paul McCartney** was busted by customs officials at Tokyo International Airport when nearly a half-pound of pot was discovered in his suitcase. He was kicked out of Japan after being detained for nine days. Later McCartney told reporters, "Marijuana isn't as dangerous as some people make it."[44]

In '80, **John McVie** from **Fleetwood Mac** and his wife, **Julie** were busted in their resort home in Honolulu and charged with possession of cocaine when a drug-sniffing dog found the contents in a package addressed to the McVie's.

In '80, **John Phillips of The Mamas and the Papas,** known to have been a long-time cocaine addict was arrested and found guilty for his involvement in a major drug ring. He admitted squandering as much as a million dollars a year on his and his third wife, **Genevieve Waite's** coke and smak habits. **Mama Cass Elliott,** also a member of the group, died in '74 of a heart attack while eating. She said of drugs, "Pop music is just hard work, long hours, and a lot of drugs."[45]

In '80, **Don Henley,** drummer for **The Eagles** was arrested at his home in Los Angeles when a 16-year old girl was found nude and overdosed on drugs. Henley was charged with possession of various drugs including marijuana, cocaine, Quaaludes and contributing to the delinquency of a minor. **Glenn Fry,** also from the group, told *People magazine,* "I'm in the music business for the sex and the narcotics."[46]

In '80, **Hugh Cornwell,** singer/guitarist for **The Stranglers** was sentenced to two months in a London jail for possession of marijuana, cocaine, and heroin. He claimed he used heroin for a couple of years[47] and is quoted saying, "The greatest thing I discovered at the university was marijuana."[48]

*In '80, **Malcolm Owen,** singer for punk group, **The Ruts,** died from an overdose of heroin

*In '80, **Tim Harden**, writer of "If I Were A Carpenter", died from an overdose of heroin.

*In '80, **Carl Radle**, bassist for **Derek and the Dominoes, Leon Russell** and **Eric Clapton**, died of a chronic kidney disease, complicated by his heroin addiction.

*In '81, **Darby Crash**, lead singer for **The Germs**, died from an overdose of heroin.

In '81, **Robert Kimball**, lead singer for **Toto**, was arrested for selling four ounces of cocaine to an undercover officer.

*In '81, **Bob Hite**, vocalist for **Canned Heat** died of heart failure believed to have been brought on by drug abuse.

*In '81, **Mike Bloomfield**, guitarist for **The Paul Butterfield Blues Band,** died from an overdose of drugs.

*In '81, **Bob Marley**, a popular reggae artist, lost his life to brain and lung cancer, most probably brought about because of his constant devotion to marijuana, a part of his religious belief called, **Rastafarianism**, believing that marijuana is a form of communion with God.

In '81, **Ozzy Osbourne** told *People magazine*, "I took LSD everyday for years. I was spending about $1,000 a week on drugs. I went through cocaine by the bagful...I OD'd about a dozen times...sampled heroin..." all before he committed himself to a mental hospital.[49] "I'm the same guy now that I was when I started and that's the thing that kept me alive. I get drunk. I get stoned and have a good time. I lay a few chicks. I was baptised a Christian."[50]

In '82, **David Crosby** was busted for possession of Qualludes and drug paraphernalia, driving under the influence of cocaine and for carrying a concealed .45 caliber pistol. Two weeks later he was arrested again for possession of cocaine and a concealed weapon. He said about his drug problem, "I was stoned for every bit of music I've ever played. Every record, every performance - I was stoned halfway out of my gourd."[51]

*In '82, **John Belushi**, comedian for Saturday Night Live and a member of **The Blues Brothers** died from an overdose of cocaine and heroin.

*In '82, **James Honeyman-Scott**, guitarist for **Pretenders**, died from an overdose of cocaine/valium.

In '82, former lead guitarist for **Led Zepplin**, **Jimmy Page** was arrested and charged for possessing 198 milligrammes of cocaine.

*In '83, **Pete Farndon**, bassist for **Pretenders**, died from an overdose of drugs, found dead in his bathtub.

In '83, **Sting**, lead singer with **Police**, told newspaper reporters that he had been taking drugs since he was 12. He said he decided he was quiting because they're "not even that much fun."[52]

*In '83, **Gary Thain**, bassist for **Uriah Heep**, died of a drug overdose.

In '83, **Sly Stone**, leader of **Sly and the Family Stone** was arrested for possession of cocaine and drug paraphernalia in Fort Myers, Florida. Shortly after his divorce in '74, **Stone** was busted for possession and possession for sale of marijuana, cocaine, and other dangerous drugs. Later, taking up freebasing cocaine for months, he again was arrested along with **George Clinton** for possession of narcotics in L.A.

In '83, police arrested 60 youths and adults for drinking and drugs at a **Def Leppard** concert in Columbus, Ohio.

In '83, **B.J. Thomas** was arrested and fined for possession of marijuana.

In '84, **Paul McCartney** and his wife **Linda** were fined 70 pounds by Barbados magistrates for possession of marijuana. A few days later, Linda is charged again, this time for importing cannabis at Heathrow, and is subsequently fined 75 pounds. Paul said about it, "I'm telling you, this substance, cannabis, is a whole lot less harmful than rum punch, whisky, nicotine or glue - all of which are perfectly legal. I would like to see it decriminalized."[53]

In '85, **Ike Turner**, ex-husband of **Tina Turner** was arrested along with three others for conspiracy to sell $16,000 worth of cocaine.

In '85, **Ace Frehley**, former lead guitarist for **Kiss**, was arrested and charged for trying to buy drugs with a forged prescription.

In '85, **Jerry Garcia**, guitarist for **The Grateful Dead**, was arrested and charged with possession of narcotics. Among his 23 bags of drugs, cocaine and heroin were found.

*In '85, **Gary Horton**, vocalist for **Heavy Metal Kids**, died as a result of drug overdose.

*In '85, **Ricky Nelson**, veteran rock star, with such hits as 'Hello, Mary Lou', 'Poor Little Fool', and 'Travelin' Man', was killed, along with 6 others when his private plane crashed. Investigation showed that freebassing cocaine was considered the probable cause of the crash.

In '86, **Culture Club's**, **Boy George** was arrested and charged with possession of an undisclosed amount of heroin. His brother claimed Boy George had a $1,200 a day habit.[54]

In '86, **Marilyn**, boy-friend of **Boy George** was arrested for possession of heroin.

*In '86, **Michael Rudetsky**, another friend of **Boy George**, who had flown to London to help **George** record a solo album, was found dead of a heroin overdose in the home of **Boy George.**

*In '86, **Phil Lynott,** leader of **Thin Lizzy,** died of heart disease and pneumonia, but this was brought about because of his drug problem.[55]

In '86, **Boy George** and his friend, **Mark Golding** were arrested for possession of marijuana and held in jail for 12 hours. The next day, **Golding** was found dead from an overdose of heroin and methadone, a heroin substitute, in one of the homes of George.

In '86, **Howard Hewett,** former lead singer of the group, **Shalamar,** along with his wife were arrested for selling a kilo of cocaine to an undercover officer.

In '87, **Sly Stone** is charged with possesion of cocaine twice. The second time the drug was found on him when police entered his house to arrest him for non-payment of child support and found him "incoherent and violent".

In '87, **Ike Turner** was arrested after police found 6 grams of a crystalline form of the drug known as rock cocaine in his car after being pulled over for "erratic driving".

In '87, **Boy George** checks into the *Betty Ford Hospital* to obtain help in kicking the drug habit.

In '87, Former **Clash** drummer, **Topper Headon** is jailed for 15 months at Maidstone Crown Court for suppling heroin to a man who later died.

*In '87, **Paul Butterfield** of *The Paul Butterfield Blues Band* died as a result of drug abuse.

*In '88, **Andy Gibb**, called the "baby Bee Gee", died of "inflammation of the heart" believed to have been brought on by long-term cocaine use.

In '88, **James Brown** and his wife, **Adrienne** were arrested for possession of PCP (also know as Angel Dust).

*In '88, **Jesse Ed Davis**, guitarist, who worked with The Monkees, Jackson Browne, Rod Stewart, George Harrison, Bob Dylan and an host of others, died as a result of drug overdose.

*In '88, **Hillel Slovak**, lead guitarist and founder member of the **Red Hot Chilli Peppers**, died as a result of drug overdose.

Others whose drug problem went public include...

Natalie Cole...daughter of the late **Nat King Cole**,
Johnnie Taylor, soul singer, 'Disco Lady'
Debbie Harry, former singer for **Blondie**
Lou Reed, former vocalist for **The Velvet Underground**
James Taylor, singer/songwriter

Belinda Carlisle...former member of **The Go-Go's,**
Lenny Breau...jazz guitarist,
Frank Beard...drummer for **ZZ Top,**
Johnny Winter, singer
Johnny Thunders, former guitarist for **New York Dolls**
Linda Ronstadt, one of the '70's premier women vocalists
Stephen Stills, guitarist and vocalist for **Buffalo Springield**
Leon Russell, singer/songwriter

Rod Stewart claims his way of "letting off steam" is "...drinking, taking drugs, and picking up groupies and generally raising hell..."[56]

Joe Strummer from **The Clash** said, "I've smoked so much pot, I'm surprised I haven't turned into a bush."[57]

Paul Walthall, from the punk group **The Butthole Surfers** brags, "It used to be that we'd put LSD on our tongues when we started playing, and we'd swallow the hit after the first number. Really though, it's best taken half an hour before a gig so the furze and lights are all revolving when you pick up your instrument."[58]

William Reid, from **The Jesus and Mary Chain** group, mockingly said, "Sometimes speed makes me feel like I could walk on water."

Ian 'Lemmy' Kilmister, from the group **Motorhead** claims his teeth rotted out because of him taking so much speed, because it takes the calcium out of your blood.[60]

Aerosmith's guitarist, **Joe Perry** acknowleged that drugs nearly killed him and vocalist **Steven Tyler**, "We had to get together and clear up residual habits. Chemical dependencies in particular. Doctors told us it's amazing we're alive...I spent so many years sedated. We were all addicted, some more than others. Everyone in the band has been through an up and down thing — whether it's alcohol or cocaine, I guess Steven and I have been the worst as far as that goes. We've been junkies, heroin addicts, and we thought it worked really well in the early years..."[61]

I think it is very obvious from the things you've just read, that drugs have a very prominent place in rock history; much of its disaster and most of its problems stem from drug abuse. Is there an answer? Yes! But first, what is the real reason people take drugs? The Bible gives the problem and the solution in this one verse, Prov.17:22:

"A merry heart doeth good like a medicine..."

Today, we seem to have a whole generation that turns to "medicine" or drugs to help them escape because they have no real joy in their heart!! The saddest people I know are those who must depend on booze or drugs to keep them happy!!!

As mentioned earlier, the drug problem is a spiritual problem. The only way to take care of the "real cause" of drug abuse is to offer people the "real cure"...**Jesus Christ.** Friend, what you are looking for can't be found in a pill, a needle, or a plant...it can only be found in **Christ!**

I remember reading as a teenager the following version of the 23rd Psalm written by a young heroin addict. Before taking her own life through asphyxiating herself in her car, she wrote...

"King Heroin is my shepherd, I shall always want. He maketh me to lie down in the gutters. He leadeth me beside the troubled waters. He destroyeth my soul. He leadeth me in the paths of wickedness. Yea, I shall walk through the valley of poverty and will fear all evil for thou, Heroin, art with me. Thy needle and capsule comfort me. Thou strippest the table of groceries in the presence of my family. Thou robbest my head of reason. My cup of sorrow runneth over. Surely heroin addiction shall stalk me all the days of my life and I will dwell in the House of the Damned forever."

Also found in the car next to the young dead women was this note... "Jail didn't cure me. Nor did hospitalization help me for long. The doctor told my family it would have been better, and indeed kinder, if the person who got me hooked on dope had taken a gun and blown my brains out.

And I wish to God he had. My God, how I wish it."

I recently heard an ex-drug user/dealer, now a minister of the gospel, say..."Drugs will **take you farther** than you want to go, **keep you longer** than you want to stay, and **cost you more** than you want to pay."

I remember as a high school student leading the biggest drug dealer in school to the Lord. He was afraid that the pull of drugs would be so strong, that he would never be able to be a victorious overcomer. One of the things that shocked him was the fact that **Jesus** turned down drugs, when suffering the greatest pain anyone could suffer, while on the cross. And since Christ lives in you, you can overcome!!!!!!! (see 1 John 4:4)

He didn't even know drugs were found in the Bible. So I showed him in Matt.27:34, where Matthew tells us that before **Jesus** was crucified, He was offered "vinegar to drink mingled with gall", a form of a sedative to help deaden the pain of crucifixion. Upon tasting it, **Jesus** refused to drink it, because He wanted to suffer the full penalty for our sins. He could have taken that sedative to help numb his body, but by Him enduring that temptation, He won the victory for every addict that would ever live! Praise God! He is your hope if you're bound...He came to set the captives free. (Luke 4:18)

Jesus said in John 8:36 some good news for those of you who

are slaves to drugs,

> *"If the Son therefore shall make you free, ye*
> *shall be free indeed."*

<u>Some final words to parents</u>

As a parent, here are some warning signs to look for in your children to see if they may be taking drugs. Remember, it is a fact that most parents have no idea that their kids are on drugs. Don't lie to yourself, if your kid has these signs, beware!

•A change in appearance, neglecting personal grooming
•A dramatic drop in grades
•Unexplained periods of moodiness, depression, anxiety, irritability
•Refusing to look you in the eyes, becoming secretive
•A change in eating or sleeping patterns
•Acting intoxicated without the smell of alcohol
•Wearing sun glasses at inappropriate times
•Bloodshot or red eyes, droopy eyelids
•Ignoring curfews, staying out late, or not coming home at all
•Disappearance of money or valuables
•A major change in friends
•Laughing or crying for no apparent reason
•Phone calls at odd hours

•Scorched tinfoil, needles, powders, small bags, tablets, capsules
•Demanding alot of privacy
•Excessive talkativeness
•A unexplained large amount of money
•Being withdrawn, refusing to join family and friends
•Loss of interest in previously important things, (sports, etc.)
•Unusual smells or odors on clothes or in bedroom
•Unexplained weight loss or loss of appetite
•Abnormally pale complexion
•Changes in values, ideals, and beliefs

How to help your children say "NO" to drugs

*Develop a family altar, with prayer and reading the Word of God
*Show your love in a tangible way, hug and kiss your children
*Express your love verbally..."I really love you, son."
*Keep boredom out of your home...have family activities
*Become aware of various "pressures" on your kids
*Have a good listening ear...don't do all the talking
*Become informed of the facts concerning drugs and drug abuse
*Last, but most important...have a Christ-centered home!!

---

[1]NRD Journal, Oct. 1986, pg.9
[2]Circus Magazine, Apr. 17, 1979
[3]Circus Magazine, Apr.17, 1979
[4]Creem, Jan., 1984, pg.35

[5]Hit Parader, June, 1983
[6]Song Hits, May, 1984, pg.15
[7]Circus, Sept.30, 1983
[8]The Best of Metal, Vol. 1, No. 10, pg.5
[9]Newsweek, Aug.11, 1986, pg.15
[10]Better Homes and Gardens, Feb.1986, pg.26
[11]National Federation of Parents for Drug-free Youth
[12]The Toledo Blade, Oct.19, 1987, pg.19
[13]Penny Mann, "Marijuana Alert"
[14]U.S. Department of Health and Human Services
[15]Better Homes and Gardens, Feb.1986, pg.26
[16]Newsweek, Aug.11, 1986, pg.15
[17]National Federation of Parents, "The only thing wasted is you"
[18]National Federation of Parents, "The only thing wasted is you"
[19]USA Today, Sept.16, 1986, pg.4-D
[20]Delta-9-tetrahydrocannabinol, the main mind-altering (psychoactive) ingredient, a uniqe chemical found nowhere else in nature.
[21]Parents Drug Guide, pgs. 23-24
[22]National Federation of Parents
[23]Circus, Oct.12, 1981
[24]Creem, Dec.,1981
[25]Creem, Feb., 1984
[26]Creem, Aug., 1984
[27]Winston-Salem Journal, Jan. 17, 1988
[28]The Rock Yearbook, 1989, pg. 12
[29]Star Ledger, Apr. 26, 1988
[30]The Rock Yearbook, 1987, pg.130
[31]Life, June 16, 1967, pg.105
[32]Time, Sept.22, 1967, pg.62
[33]Rock and Roll Babylon, Gary Herman, pg.39
[34]Rock And Roll Babylon, pg.52
[35]Cavalier, June, 1968
[36]People, Apr.7, 1980, pg.61
[37]Rolling Stone, Nov. 5-Dec. 10, 1987, pg.32

[38]The Book of Rock Quotes, pg.64
[39]Time, Aug.9, 1969, pg.76
[40]Time, Jan.18, 1971, pg.34
[41]Life, June 28, 1968
[42]Rolling Stone, Feb.3, 1972, pg.30
[43]Rolling Stone, Jan.4, 1973, pg.16
[44]People, March 6, 1980, pg.30
[45]The Book of Rock Quotes, pg.95
[46]People, June 30, 1975, pg.60
[47]The Rock Yearbook, 1987, pg.134
[48]The Book of Rock Quotes, pg.97
[49]People, Sept.7, 1981
[50]Circus, Oct.31, 1984, pg.107
[51]The Rock Yearbook, 1984, pg. 208
[52]Middletown Journal, Oct. 25, 1983
[53]The Rock Yearbook, vol.5, pg.164
[54]People, July 21, 1986, pg. 35
[55]The Rock Yearbook, 1987, pg.174
[56]Rolling Stone, March, 1982
[57]The Rock Yearbook, vol.5, pg.166
[58]The Rock Yearbook, 1987, pg.133
[59]The Rock Yearbook, 1987, pg.133
[60]Creem, Dec. , 1983, pg.62
[61]OM, Oct., 1987, pg.33

────────────────────────────── 6

False Religions

"Christianity will go. It will go. It will vanish
and shrink. I needn't argue about it. I'm
right, and will be proved right. We are more
popular than **Jesus** now. I don't know which
will go first - rock 'n roll or Christianity."[1]
-John Lennon, (the first **Beatle** to die)

<u>DID YOU KNOW...</u>

*Representatives of 500 of the nation's largest Corporations,
including IBM, AT&T, and General Motors, meet regularly
to discuss how metaphysics, Hindu mysticism, and the occult
can help their executives to compete in the market place.

*Four thousand organizations are linked to this network in
U.S.A. alone.

*A 35,000 year old spirit named, "Ramtha", speaks through
its "psychic channel", J. Z. Knight. Ramtha has a mailing list

of 22,000 from all 50 states.

*In Lily Dale, N.Y., the world's largest "spiritualist summer colony," 20,000 visitors gather each July and August, hoping to get in touch with loved ones through mediums and to develop psychic powers.

*In cities like Phoenix, San Francisco, and Los Angeles, medium Kevin Ryerson, who played himself in *Out on a Limb*, the personal story of Shirley McLaine, consults with groups by channeling spirits. He has a yearlong waiting list for private sessions.

*New York City's Cosmic Contact Psychic Services, a small agency for "practitioners of the paranormal", has seen its business increase 400% since its start seven months ago, says director Michael Goodrich. Clients for the agency's astrologers, tarot readers, palmists and psychics include advertising execs, psychiatrists and stockbrokers whose chauffeured cars wait outside while they get market tips from mediums, he says.

*A recent gallop poll pointed out, over 30% (nearly 1 out of every 3) of Americans under 30 now believe in reincarnation.

*In public schools across America, where Christian prayer has been outlawed, yoga, eastern meditation, and visualization techniques, which are simply forms of Hindu prayer, are not only allowed but are actively promoted.

*At a Transcendental Meditation conference in India, a spokesman announced, "The entire mission of TM is to counter the ever-spreading demon of Christianity." They are well on their way to infiltrating every segment of our society.

*Leaders plan for the elimination of 25% of earth's inhabitants.

These are just a few of the startling facts about a worldwide organization called, "The New Age Movement". Its roots are in Hinduism, which is being deceptively packaged these days as "New Science".

The New Age Network is a worldwide movement composed of thousands upon thousands of organizations whose aim is to abolish all existing religions, create a New Age religion, and eventually establish a Department of Religion in the global government of the New World Order.[2]

Even *The Wall Street Journal* did a short article about this concept,

> "In Atlanta, clerical workers for Pacific Mutual
> Life Insurance Co. search their memories for a
> time when they felt 'victimized.' Trainers then
> ask them how they could have avoided that feel-
> ing by being more "accountable" for their actions.
> Later, with Dionne Warwick singing, 'What the
> Word Needs Now' in the background, the trainers

> pass out red carnations in an expression of corporate love." The article went on to say, "Abuzz with buzzwords, corporate America has launched one of the most concerted efforts ever to change the attitudes and values of workers. Dozens of major U.S. companies - including Ford Motor Co., Procter & Gamble Co., TRW Inc., Polaroid Corp. and Pacific Telesis Group Inc. - are spending millions of dollars on so-called New Age workshops."[3]

New Agers are encouraged through music, foods, books, and expensive seminars to get in touch with their "inner self". For most people, this means wearing crystals, sitting under a pryramid, or seeking advice from a spirit guide, which is simply glorified occult practice.

The New Age Movement is just another version of satan's very first package of lies..."you can become a god and have special knowledge". (see Gen.3:5) It has come packaged in all different ways, but it's universal "truth" is, Man doesn't need Jesus! Man can save himself.

What does all this have to do with Rock and Roll music? It has a great deal to do with it, because rock music has been a leading influence in changing the belief system of an entire generation. Such groups as the **Fifth Dimension**, with their song, "Age Of Aquarius", and more recently, the group **Yes**, from their *Big Generator* album, came the song "Holy Lamb

(Song for Harmonic Convergence)" are perfect examples of messages in songs that are strong themes of new age belief. Twenty years ago, what most Americans considered rather foolish, has today, become the very philosophies of millions.

For example, *reincarnation* was a dying concept of the Hindu religion, but now it has taken on a new appearance, and is believed by an ever-growing amount of people. Two basic concepts of God come from the eastern religions, *pantheism*, the belief that God is everything in the universe and that everything which exists constitutes God, and *polytheism*, the belief in and worship of more than one god. These teachings were generally rejected as eastern deception until the early '60's. Today, they are being taught at almost every major university. You are considered "close-minded" if you aren't open to the "universal consciousness".

Such terms as "mantra", "meditation", "reincarnation", "yantra", "enlightenment", "yoga", "psychic", "astral-projection", "karma", "chakra", "nirvana", etc. all began to find their way into American thinking through the introduction of rock music. And satan knew if he could cut the powerful Christian influence out of America, he could paralize much of the world from the gospel, due to the fact that America is the leading promoter of the "Good News"!!! What better way to change a generation's view of God, than through the power of music!!

In the previous chapter, we dealt with the influence of drugs in the rock culture. It was at this time that these "new concepts" began to take on "new meaning" to tens of thousands of young people. Drugs began to give that generation a more "open mind". (and I'm afraid it was so opened, most let their brains leak out!!!) Soon, some of the most popular groups in rock music openly practiced and encouraged eastern mysticism and Hindu teachings.

<u>Transcendental Meditation</u> (TM)

Transcendental Meditation has taken on many different titles. The **Guru Maharishi Mahesh Yogi** is the founder of the following organizations which bring TM to the masses...World Government of the Age of Enlightenment, Science of Creative Intelligence and the Technology of the Unified Field. Also, the World Plan Excecutive Council is the formal name for their U.S. non-profit educational organization.

Maharishi (meaning "great sage") Mahesh (his family name) Yogi (meaning "one who has achieved union with God") received his training from **Swami Brahmananda Saraswati** (Guru Dev) for 13 years in the Himalayas. There he was commissioned by Guru Dev to take meditation to the world. That was in 1957.

Not too many Americans had even heard of TM until 1967, when this virtually unknown Indian guru gained world-wide recognition overnight because of a visit from the **Beatles**. The Beatles were among the first to endorse Guru Maharishi

Mahesh Yogi.

It was in 1967, that all four **Beatles** along with **Jane Asher, Mia Farrow, Donovan, Mick Jagger** and his girlfriend, **Marianne Faithful** visited the guru in Bangor to receive "enlightenment" from TM. (This, by the way, was only one year after **John Lennon** told the London *Evening Standard* the "Christianity will go..." statement quoted eariler) While in Bangor, **Brian Epstein**, the Beatle's manager, committed suicide.

According to the teachings, one who desires to achieve "enlightenment" from TM is given a "mantra", a simple word or phrase that they are to repeat while meditating. This is believed to help relieve stress. Actually, there are only 16 mantras, which just so happen to be names, or close names of Hindu gods in Sanskrit, the classical language of India.

Shortly after the Beatle's "enlightenment", the **Beach Boys** joined in and became <u>devout</u> followers of the TM movement. Both **Mike Love** and **Al Jardine** became teachers of TM. In 1968, Maharishi toured with The Beach Boys, with the second half of the show given to the guru, who lectured the audience on "spiritual regeneration".

In 1976, the Beach Boys produced an album entitled *15 Big Ones* ending side one with the song "TM Song",written by **Brian Wilson**, which says,

"It's time for me to meditate...What time is this/How long has it been/Bubbles and ripples floating through my mind/I must have drifted away/Since I sat down, where have I been/ The mantra, my mantra must have took me away/It must have took me away/Maharishi gave it to me/And I wondered if it set me free/ And it did/And he'll tell you/Sometimes it goes real fast/And other times it goes real slow/Anyway you do it, well it's bound to work I know/Transcendental Meditation should be part of your time/It's simple, it's easy as making this rhyme/Transcendental Meditation, works for me good/More much more than I thought it would."

In 1978, the *M.I.U.* album was produced with its proceeds going to help build the M.I.U. (Maharishi International University) in Iowa. The record sleeve bears the M.I.U. emblem along with the slogan,

"Knowledge is structured in consciousness"

This was all the foundation satan was looking for. Because from the endorsement of these groups, satan was able to introduce America to a damnable doctrine that has swept this country. Over 6,000 U.S. doctors have learned TM and even the US Army has expressed interest in TM. Because of its "non-religious" system, it has had open doors in public schools from coast to coast. TM continues to grow among college campuses throughout the United States. *Students' International Meditation Society* chapters meet on 95% of all public universities, and more than 100 campuses and adult education programs offer the Maharishi's academically oriented Science of Creative Intelligence course for credit.[4] Today it is believed that over two and a half million people throughout the world practice TM, with 30,000 initiates joining each month!! The impact is obvious!

In 1970, the **Moody Blues** produced their album, *In Search Of The Lost Chord*, which has not only a song entitled, "OM", but the Hindu explanation inside the cover...

> "To anyone who has practiced meditation or Yoga; the word MANTRA is familiar as a word of power concentrated upon in meditation. The most important word of power in the Hindu scriptures is the word, OM, which pronounced, AUM, means, 'God', 'All', 'Being', 'The answer'. Thought or intentness on its meaning will cause the exclusion of all other thoughts, ultimately bringing about the state of mind to which the meditator aspires."

In other words, through the repetitions of the word, "OM", one will find total "peace of mind". This is exactly what **Jesus** taught against in Matt.6:7 when He said, *"But when ye pray,* *use not <u>vain repetitions, as the heathen do</u>...*"!

Also joining the TM movement were **Donovan, Paul Horn, Brian Jones** of the **Rolling Stones, Ray Manzarek** and **Robbie Krieger** of **The Doors, Mia Farrow, Skip Spence** of the group **Moby Grape,** and **Maurice** and **Verdine White** from **Earth, Wind and Fire, Larry Blackmon** from the group **Cameo.**

Another example of musician's influence on the message of TM being preached was **Stevie Wonder's** *Innervisions* album which shows a form of astral projection coming from his "third eye" with pyramids in the background. The song, "Jesus Children Of America" plainly says, "...transcendental meditation gives you peace of mind..."

Because of the fact that we are living in such a fast-paced "rat race", people are looking for a way out of tension and stress. TM does offer a measure of temporary relief simply because it helps a person get their minds off their temporal problems. But it does not solve man's problems. TM teaches that man's greatest need is happiness, which comes through relaxation and meditation. The Bible teaches that man's greatest need is salvation from sin, which comes through **Jesus Christ!** TM teaches man is good and is, in fact, one with God, therefore he is his own saviour. The Bible teaches that *"all have sinned and come short of the glory of God"* and all need the death and resurrection of Christ to pay for our plight.

"At that time Jesus answered and said, I thank thee, O Father, Lord of heaven and earth, because thou hast hid these things from the wise and prudent, and hast revealed them unto babes. Even so, Father: for so it seemed good in thy sight. All things are delivered unto me of my Father: and no man knoweth the Son, but the Father; neither knoweth any man the Father, save the Son, and he to whosoever the Son will reveal him." (Matt. 11:25-27)

Reincarnation, Karma

Many rock entertainers promote their belief in the teaching of reincarnation and the whole concept of "karma"...

Reincarnation is the teaching that after a person dies, his soul may return to life in a new body or form. It is also known as, "transmigration" or "metempsychosis" and is a major teaching in Hinduism and Buddhism. The law of **Karma** is the law of cause and effect; what one does in this life affects his next incarnation, so that wrongdoers are punished with suffering and the righteous are rewarded.

John Lennon wrote a song called, "Instant Karma", he also had a real belief in reincarnation.

The **BeeGees** album, *Spirits Having Flown*, from their own statements, was full of references to reincarnation.

Recently, **Gene Hoglan**, drummer for the heavy metal band, **Dark Angel**, told *RIP magazine*, "In 'Hunger of the Undead', I'm trying to point out other possibilities besides the usual heaven-and-hell stuff, such as karma, reincarnation, prolonged sleep or even complete nullification. I'm trying to stimulate people to think, not just accept God and the devil..."[5]

Culture Club had a hit entitled, "Karma Chameleon". Just as the chameleon changes, so in karma, you change.

The Brothers Johnson wish everybody "good karma" on the lyric sheet on their *Right On Time* album, saying,

> "Be peaceful to your brother/For Life wasn't meant to hate/Guide the hand of one who needs you/Good Karma breeds good fate."

For Everybody is the title of the album by the all-black group called, **Karma**.

Alexander O'Neal says about his spiritual awareness, "You know, the public has this strange notion that celebrities are excluded from ups and downs. No one is. I've learned about karma. What you put out is what you get back. I've learned my lessons."[6]

Robert Palmer claims in his next incarnation, "I want to become a dolphin...I think they're the creatures on earth at the moment."[7]

Chrissie Hynde from the **Pretenders** believes in reincarnation and regularly visits a Krishna temple near her home in London.[8]

Stevie Wonder, on his *In Square Circle* album, declares in the song, "It's Wrong (Apartheid)",

> "...the pain you cause in God's name, points
> only to yourself to blame, for the negative
> karma you will be receiving..."

The group **Journey** has an album entitled, *Next Journey* , which speaks of the next journey of a reincarnated life. The last song on the album is called, "Karma". Such albums as *Captured*, *Escape*, and *Departure* seem to give the order of death, reincarnation, death, reincarnation, etc. Journey has for a number of years used the Egyptian Scarab Beetle, which is a symbol of reincarnation.[9]

Blue Oyster Cult is another group who use the Scarab. On their album, *Fire Of Unknown Origin* , a coven (13) of witches are depicted with the leader bearing not only the pentagram on his chest, but also a scarab beetle on his forehead.

Journey also has a video game which you can play on your Atari that shows the group landing on a planet and getting out from the inside of a scarab. They adapted the infinity sign which also symbolizes an endless process of death and reincarnation. It looks like a number 8 laying on its side. (∞) The black magic tarot card #2, and the Magician also bear the infinity sign.

The Doors *Full Circle* album also depicts the sign of infinity along with the depiction of the various stages of adulthood ending in death, but coming back out the other side is an infant, showing the stages again into adulthood. "Break on through to the other side" was an important concept for the group.

Roger Daltrey, lead singer for the **Who**, has a solo album entitled, *One Of The Boys* which pictures a man looking in a mirror but seeing his back. This cover comes from the art work of Rene' Magritte, referring to the aberrant power of the mind to perceive past lives.

Linda Ronstadt is found sitting in a pig pen pleasantly smiling on the front cover of the *Silk Purse* album, which can be explained by reading the back of the album, "She believes in reincarnation..." People who believe in reincarnation also teach that some people will be reincarnated into pigs after this life! Watch out, Linda!

Jackson Browne says of his religious beliefs, "I kind of accept the idea of reincarnation. Only because it's inconceivable to me that we only get to be here once."[10]

Tom Araya, bass player for the group, **Slayer**, commenting on life after death says, "I believe in reincarnaton. Everybody's spirit comes back, and once you have reached your highest point, you move on to a higher plane."[11]

David Cloverdale, lead singer for **Whitesnake**, looking back over the way the band came together, claims, "...I believe more and more in destiny and karma, and there's a reason for these things."[12]

Even **Waylon Jennings, Willie Nelson, Johnny Cash**, and **Kris Kristofferson** dappled into reincarnation with their song, "Highway Man", which tells the story of their previous lives and further states that they will "be back again, again, again, and again..."

The Bible over and over again states otherwise:

Ecc.12:7, *"Then shall the dust return to earth as it was: and the spirit shall return unto God who gave it."* Your spirit goes back to God, not back to some animal, plant, or human.

Heb.9:27, *"...it is appointed unto man ONCE to die, but after that the judgement."* Not only will you die once, but you will stand before God in judgement following death.

In John 9:1-3, **Jesus** was asked if it were possible that this man who was born blind was suffering 'bad karma' because of his sins in the past? To that question **Jesus** gave a flat NO,

"Neither hath this man sinned, nor his parents: but that the works of God should be made manifest in him."

<u>2 Cor.5:8</u>, *"We are confident and willing rather to be absent from the body, and to be present with the Lord."* Plainly showing that Paul would leave this body on earth, and instantly go to be with the Lord, not returning as a plant, or cow, or even someone else.

<u>Luke 23:43</u>, **Jesus** speaking to the thief on the cross said, *"Verily I say unto thee, Today shalt thou be with me in paradise."* Notice **Jesus** did not tell him that he would come back again in the next life to suffer for his sin that brought him to a crucifixion.

Others try to use the verses that refer to John the Baptist having the spirit of Elijah, and claim this was through reincarnation. This is impossible because, first of all, Elijah never died! (2 Kings 2:11) He was merely translated! He appeared with Moses on the mountain. (Matt.17:3) And secondly, even John himself declared that he was not Elijah reincarnated (John 1:21) Luke 1:17 just refers to the characteristic and zeal of Elijah being upon John!

Reincarnation also denies resurrection, since, as reincarnation teaches, one spirit may easily live in a thousand different people, making resurrection impossible. And as 1 Cor.15:16-17 plainly says:

> *"And if the dead rise not, then is not Christ*
> *raised: And if Christ be not raised, your faith*
> *is vain; ye are yet in your sins."*

Those who believe in reincarnation are "yet in their sins"! There is no salvation for the reincarnationist. Only a series of life and death episodes, hoping to build one's 'karma', thereby working out one's sin and achieve perfection. But in Christ there is complete forgiveness and a brand new start in life as Paul said in 2 Cor.5:17:

> *"Therefore if any man be in Christ, he is a*
> *new creature: old things are passed away;*
> *behold, all things are become new."*

Yogi Paramahansa Yogananda

Elvis Presley was deeply influenced by **Yogi Paramahansa Yogananda**, the well-know guru and founder of the "self-realization fellowship". He wrote the book, *Autobiography of a Yogi*, one of Elvis' favorite books. According to *The Complete Elvis*, "Elvis became an avid reader during the 1960's and when he went back on the road he travelled with a portable bookcase that contained over 200 volumes of his favorite and newest books...the books most commonly associated with him over the years were: *The Prophet* by Kahlil Gibran; *The Impersonal Life* by Joseph Benner; *Autobiography of a Yogi* by Paramahansa Yogananda; *The Infinite Way*, by Joel Goldsmith; *The Mystical Christ*, by Manley Palmer

Hall; *The Life and Teachings of the Master of the Far East* by Baird Spalding; *The Inner Life* by Leadbetter; *The First and Last Freedom* by Krishnamurti; Cheiro's *Book of Numbers*. He was fascinated by the Dead Sea Scrolls, the Hebrew Cabala, the works of Albert Pike, Madame Blavatsky, May Heindel, mystics Corine Heline and Nicholas Roerich and Alice Bailey's book *Esoteric Healing*. The book he took to the bathroom on the day of his death was *The Force of Jesus* by Frank Adams."[13]

Anyone who doubts the mystic and occultic influence written in these books are either totally ignorant of the writings or are merely lying to themselves. **Elvis** was heavily involved in eastern philosophies and martial arts, based on occult practices!

Gary Wright was another follower of Yogananda. His album, *Dream Weaver,* was a very successful album for this former **Spooky Tooth** member. The title cut off the album refers to traveling on the "astral plane", a concept of astral projection. Wright told his manger, Dee Anthony, "Dee, you may be my business manger, but Paramahansa Yogananda is my spiritual manager."[14]

The group, **Yes**, have also studied and promoted Yogananda. On the back of the *Tales From Topographic Oceans* album, they go into great detail explaining how the "Autobiography of a Yogi" had inspired the material on that album. Claiming, after reading a lengthy footnote, they were inspired and "at once began holding sessions by candlelight" to help them come up with the material for the album, afterwards saying, "It was a magical experience which left both of us exhilarated for days". The album cover depicts a Persian pyramid being lit by the light of a full moon. Their album, *Big Generation*, ends with the song, "Holy Lamb (song for harmonic convergence)", a song dedicated to the celebration of the New Ager's dawning of a new age of world harmony and peace, also known as the Age of Aquarius.

Santana's album, *Caravanserai*, has a quote from Yogananda's *"Metaphysical Meditations"*,

> "The body melts into the universe. The universe melts into the soundless voice. The sound melts into the all-shiny light. And the light enters the bosom of infinite joy."

This, of course, is the teaching of pantheism, that we all will become part of the universal God. But God says:

> *"Ye are my witnesses, saith the Lord, and my servant whom I have chosen; that ye may know and believe me, and understand that I am he: before me there was no God formed, neither shall there be after me."* (Isa. 43:10)

<u>Yoga</u>

Yoga is considered both a form of meditation and a practical discipline. In yoga (meaning "union"), one attempts a mystical union with the Universal Soul through the physical body in a long series of physical and mental exercises.

Kundalini is a form of yoga that claims one attains a psychic energy by meditation, when energies are released through the major 'chakras' in the spinal cord by the passing up of a serpent in the spine to the brain. Instructors warn that unless this ascent is carefully guided, insanity may result. I believe this insanity is the result of demon take-over, due to the fact one has opened himself to the spirit realm by this practice.

Earth, Wind, and Fire have an album entitled, *Powerlight*, that shows the 7 major chakras being encircled with light. Also very obvious is the infinity sign with a burst of an energy passing through the head, also known as astral projection.

Styx also extols this concept in their song, "The Serpent Is Rising",

> "The serpent is rising, uncoiling in your
> spine, bringing you light from the depths of
> your mind."

Yoga claims to be the path to liberation from the bondage of reincarnation and teaches that man attains samadhi, "final bliss", through postures. And since the body is believed to be the physical instrument through which these goals are achieved, man becomes his own form of liberation through self-discipline and self-control. This, of course, nullifies the need of the atoning death of Christ on the cross. Man's hope comes not through looking inward, but looking to **Christ Jesus!** Paul said:

> *"For I know that in me (that is, in my flesh,) dwelleth no good thing...O wretched man that I am! who shall deliver me from the body of this death? I thank God through Jesus Christ our Lord."* (Rom. 7:18, 24-25)

Krishna Consciousness

Probably one of the most popular artists to promote the Krishna Consciousness group would be **George Harrison.** His song, "My Sweet Lord", goes through the entire 16-word "mahamantra", "Hare Krishna, Hare Krishna, Krishna, Krishna, Hare, Hare, Hare Rama, Hare Rama, Rama, Rama, Hare, Hare" This chant is part of the Krishna Consciousness group's strict discipline. Normally, the chant is quoted over and over about 3 hours a day.

Looking back at **Harrison's** devotion to Eastern religions in the '60's and '70's, some have asked if it still holds an important place in his life. "It's gone deeper and more personal," he says. "There's no point in talking about it. I still believe the purpose of our life is to get God-realization. There's a science that goes with that, the science of **self-realization**. It's still very much a part of my life, but it's sort of very personal, very private."[15]

Harrison was the one who financed Monty Python's *Life Of Brian*, a film that blasphemed the life of our **Lord Jesus**. One popular magazine described the movie as "one of the most irreverent"[16] I find it very interesting that Harrison and others must work so hard to try and put down **Jesus**! If He isn't anything to worry about, why all the constant attack on the person of **Jesus** Christ?! Of course, those who agree with the Krishna group believe that **Jesus** was a pure devotee of Krishna, only visiting here from another planet. And the Bible? Well, it got distorted in translation and interpretation over the centuries, therefore, only the Hindu Scriptures are valid!

What got Harrison into all of this? Drugs! *Rolling Stone Magazine* interviewed Harrison concerning the Beatle's popularity, (R.S.) "Did your interest in Transcendental Meditation and other spiritual disciplines help you get a handle on some of this?" (G.H.) "All the panic and the pressure? Yeah! Absolutely, I think. Although up until LSD, I never realized that there was anything beyond this state of consciousness. But all the pressure was such that, like the man said, 'There must be some way out of here.' I think for me it was definitely LSD. The first time I took it, it just blew everything away. I had such an overwhelming feeling of well-being, that there was a God, and I could see him in every blade of grass."[17]

Neil Diamond's album, *Jonathan Livingston Seagull*, opens up to reveal some rather interesting things. The inside record sleeve shows such books as *Bhagavad-gita, As It Is*; *The Sermon on the Mount according to Vedanta*, by Swami Prabhavananda; *KRSNA Supreme Personality of Godhead*; *The Aquarian Gospel of Jesus the Christ*; and *Religions Of The World*.

Annie Lennox, lead singer for **Eurythmics** started exploring the realm of Krishna Consciousness after marrying her husband, a West German Hare Krishna devotee.[18]

Cro-Mags, a hard-core band from New York, promote the Hare Krishna philosophy. Unlike many punk-type groups, politics isn't their theme, "We've seen that it doesn't work politically. You can't solve politics by more politics. So the only way to solve these all is if we become concerned with self-realization. Then there'll be peace on the planet."[19]

Again, man's hope does not come through looking inward. The only real self-realization you will get is what Jeremiah says:

> *"The heart is deceitful above all things, and*
> *desperately wicked: who can know it? I the*
> *Lord search the heart..."* (Jer. 17:9-10)

Buddhism

George Michael, formerly with **Wham**, claims that even though he's not a Buddhist, "I think the Buddhist religion is the most constructive religion that I've ever come across...I've never seen Buddhism do anything but good."[20]

Lisa Bonet, the delightful daughter on *Cosby*, played the role of a voodoo sex goddess in her first movie, *Angel Heart*. She appeared nude in a love scene, practices voodoo, and has an illegitimate baby. Where does she get her inspiration..."There's a sign on my dressing room which says, 'Om Namah Shivaya', It's a mantra which means, "I honor my self within." I guess that's where I am right now."[21]

Tina Turner is another devout Buddhist. In an interview with *Life* magazine, Tina, who chants regularly at her own Buddhist altar says, "In this faith you decide what is right and wrong."[22] She is a firm believer in reincarnation, acupuncture, crystal healings, and believes that she once lived in Egypt many lives ago. "Psychics are my drugs. My real goal in life is opening that third eye."[23]

Suzanne Vega, with the very successful *Solitude Standing* album, brings her concepts from her Buddhist faith, which she has been a part of since she was 17. She likes to spend her few free hours chanting at a small, wooden altar.[24]

TV Guide published the feelings of **Patrick Duffy**, who plays the role of "Bobby Ewing" on *Dallas*. He claimed he chanted with his wife before their Buddhist altar for several weeks, and sought advice from a spiritual mentor, which happens to be a greengrocer, to obtain guidance before agreeing to return to the TV show. (Now we know who's behind Dallas! Ha!)

Herbie Hancock also is a devout Buddhist. Twice a day **Hancock** kneels before his own rosewood altar, when he is home and rings a bronze bell and chants the words 'nam-myohorenge-kyo' for up to an hour.[25] His album, *Sextant*, shows his confidence in the Buddhist religion with Buddhist prayer beads shown right on the album cover, which he has been practicing for over 15 years.[26]

Buddha Records, Inc. is the name of the record company that has distributed many popular artists for years. Their logo is simply a oversized, smiling Buddha. They now use the Sutra, Beckett, Sunnyview, and Streetwise labels.

Bob Dylan, a man who can't seem to find what he's looking for, had an album entitled, *Desire*. The back side of the album shows him smoking pot in one corner, a black magic tarot card in another corner, and a huge Buddha in the bottom corner. Next to the Buddha are these words, "I have a brother or two and a whole lot of karma to burn...Isis and the moon shine on me."

Cat Stevens, who is now known as, **Yusuf Islam**, claimed that **Jesus** was merely a reincarnation of Buddha on the *Buddha And The Chocolate Box* album. *Footsteps In The Dark* was the latest from Stevens and is a "greatest hits" type album with his comments on the back as follows:

"A long time ago I started my quest for peace and enlightenment. I took a strong interest in Eastern religions and philosophies and was just beginning to discover the conscious self within me...I was almost at the point of giving up when one day it happened — my brother, who had just come back from a visit to Jerusalem, handed me a copy of the Holy Qur'an. After I had read *The Opening*, it was as if suddenly, someone, somewhere, had switched on the lights and I was able to perceive the wonderful order of things which, before, I could barely feel in the dark. The Qur'an was like no other book I had come across. The words all seemed strangely familiar and yet so unlike anything I had ever read before, but what moved me most was its message — the absolute and uncompromising belief in one universal God (Allah), the sole Creator and Sustainer of the heavens and the earth. This belief somehow had a direct effect on my inner psyche and on my view of life. I realized that this "oneness" was the purpose behind the universe...The Word, *Islam,* itself means "submission" or "entering into peace". Therefore, it was not a new religion, but the original faith which God inspired to messengers throughout human history: Abraham, Moses, **Jesus** and lastly, Mohammed. Peace be upon them, <u>they were all prophets and messengers</u> of the one God..."

One problem with all this....**Jesus never claimed to be a prophet!** He claimed to be equal with God!! I've studied many different religions and found it interesting that they all claim **Jesus** was a very good "teacher", but how could they believe that if they won't believe His teaching?!?! To put **Jesus** on the same level with Abraham, Moses and Mohammed is calling Jesus a Liar!! Jesus said, *"Before Abraham was, I AM!"*...When Jesus was on the mount of transfiguration, Moses and Elijah appeared and spoke with Him. Then the voice of God spoke from heaven and said, *"This is my beloved Son, hear ye HIM!"* Not Moses, not Elijah!! Before Buddha died he said, "I'm still searching for truth.", but Jesus said:

> *"I am the Way, the Truth, and the Life: no*
> *man cometh unto the Father but by me."*
> (John 14:6)

Taoism

Rick Springfield's album, *Tao,* is dedicated to the concept of the ancient Chinese philosophy known as Taoism.

The word, **Tao,** means "a path, a way". Lao Tzu, the author of *Tao Te Ching* (meaning "the way of virtue") taught that Tao existed before God was. It is therefore, the Ultimate Reality; the Principle controlling the universe; and the way of living in harmony with universe. It is actually a form of Pantheism (God is everything in the universe and everything which exists constitutes God.).

Peter Tork, bassist for **The Monkees** claims his religion is also based on the "Eastern Taoist thinking".[27]

The concept of **Yin and Yang** is a major belief behind Taoism. Yin and Yang is the belief that two great opposite principles interplay. Therefore, everything in the universe depends upon this unity. Yin represents the female, and is dark and negative, while Yang is male, light and positive. The same concept is that of the "Force" in *Star Wars*, having a "dark" or "light" side. Martial arts, acupuncture, yoga, and I Ching all stem from this "doctrine of devils"!

I Ching, a form of Chinese divination, is where "guitar wizard", **Pat Martino,** gets his creation of a sonic language. He told *Guitar World* that his guitar is "...an ancient instrument. Ancient. It goes back to 5000 B.C. in China, the system of hexagrams from the "I Ching" in which they have are six line figures. If I asked you how many lines, how many strings do you have on your guitar? Six. Then your guitar is a hexagram."[28] (a hexagram is an occultic term from which a "hex" or "a curse" comes)

Robert Fripp, from the group, **King Crimson,** also speaks of the more mystical side of guitar playing, "In Eastern and Asian cultures the musician spends a lot of time not learning to play the instrument, but finding a relationship with himself so that if one changes state, one is in a position where music can occur...And if one has the shift in state, then one is at a place where music can present itself. It's not really possible to make a change of state unless you relax. So there will be yoga..." He went on to say, "That certain feeling happened to me in a big way quite often with the first King Crimson. Amazing things would happen — I mean, telepathy, qualities of energy, things that I had never experienced before with music...you can't tell whether the music is playing the musician or the musician is playing the music."[29] He is a follower of **Gurdjieff**. Gurdjieff taught a "Golden Ladder" concept of truth. Man exists on one of seven rungs of an evolutionary ladder. The ladder can be ascended not by logical knowledge, but by psychological wisdom — self-study, self-awareness, self-remembering and the discovery of the essential unchanging, "I".[30] **Roger McGuinn**, of **The Byrds** and **Keith Jarrett** were also followers of Gurdjieff's teachings. This is what Paul meant when he said:

"Ever learning, and never able to come to the knowledge of the truth." (2 Tim. 3:7)

Baha'i Faith

Seals and Crofts are probably the best-known rock and roll converts to Baha'i. Most of their albums are given to the promotion of the Baha'i faith, with the American Headquarters address found next to the "Seals & Crofts Fan Club" address.

Many of their songs, such as, "Hummingbird", are footnoted with "From the Baha'i Scriptures". One of their songs entitled, "East If Ginger Trees", says, "...Pepare to meet Baha'u'llah in the Garden of Clove.", (Baha'u 'llah was the founder of Baha'i). In their *Takin' It Easy* album, the group ends the album with the song, "A Tribute To 'Abdu'l Baha'"

Baha'i is a religion which teaches that Divine Revelation is continuous and progressive, that religious truth is not absolute, but relative. Their central teaching is that all religions are one. To be a Baha'i, one must accept the divinity and truth of all revealed religions and to accept all people as children of the One God. Baha'u'llah, the Prophet Founder of the Baha'i Faith fulfills the promises of **Jesus**, Mohammed, Moses, Krishna, Buddha, and Zoroaster that at a given time, God would send One who would unite all the peoples of the world into one common faith. **Jesus**, of course, never said He was one of the many ways to God or truths, He said *"I am THE WAY, THE TRUTH, AND THE LIFE, NO man cometh unto the Father, but BY ME."* (Jn.14:6)

Rastafarianism

The **Rastafarians** believe themselves to be "the true Israel of God". They believe that God, **Jesus**, the Israelites and the early Christians were all black and that all white men are devils. They believe that **Haile Selassie** was God in the flesh and that, although he died, he is still alive in "another dimension". And since the Bible was written by and for black people, no one else can properly interpret it. They also believe that smoking pot, (what they call, "ganja" or "wisdom weed"), helps one have communion with Jah and gives them health.

Bob Marley, called the "King of Jamaican Reggae" died in 1981 being treated for lung, liver and brain cancer, no doubt brought about by his devotion to marijuana, "the sacred weed". It was believed that Marley smoked an average of a pound of prime Jamaican Ganja a week for many years. Marley was considered the most important figure in spreading this Jamaican religion. His concerts were widely attended and his album sales were considered above normal in England and America. Reggae has had a real impact from him and his band, **The Wallers**. Many other groups such as **UB40's, Third World, Jah Warriors, Black Roots, Gregory Isaac, Aswad, Ini Kamoze, Maxi Priest, Yellowman, Black Uhuru, and Wailing Souls** all are devoted to their "preaching" through Reggae.

Sri Chinmoy

Sri Chinmoy teaches basic Hinduism including the way of yoga and meditation towards enlightenment. He, like all gurus, teaches one must go through him to reach God. Even though his following is quite small, he leads the United Nation's meditation program and has some very popular rock stars as disciples.

In 1973, Carlos Santana, a disciple of Sri Chinmoy, changed

173

his name to **Devadip**, which means, "The Lamp of the Light of the Supreme". On his *Oneness* album, **Santana** fills the album with quotes from Chinmoy and even gives his address, encouraging his fans to write and find out more about Sri Chinmoy.

Another disciple of Sri Chinmoy is **Clarence Clemons**, the saxophonist for **Bruce Springsteen**. Offstage, Clemons has adopted the spiritual name Mokshagun (Sanskrit for Lord's All-Illuminating Liberation Fire) and rarely goes 24 hours without meditation.[31] His solo album, *Hero,* has a quote from Sri Chinmoy on the record sleeve along with this statement on the credit lines,

> "Special thanks to the Supreme Being for
> blessing us with Strength & Love—To Guru
> Sri Chinmoy for Soulful Inspiration & Joy."

A "Sri Chinmoy Oneness-Home Peace Run", in 1987 was billed as the world's longest relay, covering 27,000 miles in 55 countries and was supported by Clemons who claimed, "The earth is our home. We are one people, and we're striving for this oneness."[32] Also joining him was **Jon Anderson**, singer for the group, **Yes**.

Others such as **John McLaughlin**, leader of **Mahavishnu Orchestra** also follow **Sri Chinmoy**. His album, *Apocalypse,* bears a poem written by Chinmoy on the back. **Mahavishnu** is the combination of two Hindu deities, "Hahadeva", the god of creative power, as well as destruction, (also known as Shiva). "Vishnu" is the second of three Hindu supreme deities. He is considered to have been the incarnated Rama, Krishna, Buddha, and others and is the "preserver of the universe".

Meher Baba

"When I break my silence, the impact of my love will be universal and all life in creation will know, feel and receive of it. It will help every individual to break himself free from his own bondage in his own way. I am the Divine Beloved who loves you more than you can ever love yourself. The breaking of my silence will help you to help yourself in knowing your real Self."[33] Those were the writings of **Meher Baba**, an Indian mystic. He died in 1969 at the age of 74, but he never broke his 43 years of silence, he died before he could!

Meher Baba is the spiritual avatar to **Pete Townshend** of **The Who,** and **Ronnie Lane,** from **Faces.** He believed himself to be the final incarnation of God for this age, following and fulfilling the steps of Zoroaster, Krishna, Rama, Buddha, **Jesus** and Mohammed. He taught that he was the One and Only and total devotion to him was necessary for one to attain oneness with God. "There is no doubt of my being God personified...I am the Christ...I am everything and I am beyond everything."[34]

Pete Townshend's album, *Empty Glass,* shows Townshend

with an aura, or force field around his head. On the record sleeve is found this quote from Meher Baba,

> "Desire for nothing except desirelessness, hope for nothing except to rise above all hopes, want nothing and you will have everything."

On his *Who Came First* album, Townshend is shown standing with his full weight on a row of uncracked eggs while wearing a button of his "god". The album, which depicts Baba a number of times, ends with a 6 minute and 43 second song adapted from Meher Baba's "Universal Prayer".

1. Meher Baba offers no hope to the sinner, **Jesus** came to pay the penalty of every sinner...
2. Meher Baba died...**Jesus** died, AND ROSE AGAIN...
3. Meher Baba died before breaking his oath of silence which he claimed he would do, which would free mankind...**Jesus** completed his work on the cross when he <u>spoke</u>, *"It is finished!"*...

Which will you follow?

<u>est. or Erhard Seminar Training</u>

John Denver shows his faith in **Werner Erhard** on the inside of the *Back Home Again* album, in which he states,

> "My purpose in performing is to communi-
> cate the joy I experience in living. It is the al-
> iveness already within you that my music is
> intended to reach. Participating in *est* has
> created an amazing amount of space for joy
> and aliveness in my life. It pleases me to
> share *est* with you."

And again on the *Wingsong* album, Denver dedicates "Looking For Space" "...to Werner Erhard and everyone in est".

Werner Erhard basically has a pantheist view on life. We are
all just little "gods". There is neither wrong nor right. This
movement is subtly based on Zen Buddhism and teaches the
disciple never to use the rational mind, but to open up to the
so-called, "ever present now."

Carl Jung

Synchronicity was one of the last albums from the group,
Police. The album cover shows **Sting** holding a book called,
"Synchronicity", written by Carl Jung. Jung was a psychiatrist who began studying alchemy, astrology, spiritualism and
esoteric teachings and mixed the occult with psychiatry. The
album not only depicts a goat's head (a symbol of satanism),
but also acupuncture (an occultic form of Taoism). Sting, the
lead singer for the group who now has a solo career, says,
"There are demons inside of me, but I manage to use them for
my furtherance."[35]

Dr. Arthur Janov

The group, **Tears For Fears**, got their name from the concept taught by Janov in his book, *Primal Revolution*. **Curt Smith** of the group says, concerning the title of the group, "It means tears as a replacement for fears...It's based on Janov's theory...And basically all our songs are about this particular subject..."[36] The primal scream theory teaches man must scream all his problems away! By yelling, one can "cleanse himself". This concept is a perfect example of what Paul meant when he said in Col.2:8-10:

> *"Beware lest any man spoil you through philosophy and vain deceit, after the tradi-tion of men, after the rudiments* (principles) *of the world, and not after Christ. For in him dwelleth all the fulness of the Godhead bodily. And ye are complete in him, which is the head of all principality and power."*

Mormonism

No doubt one of the most popular Mormon families would have to be the **Osmonds**. Their squeaky clean image has opened many people to the teachings of **Joseph Smith** and the **Latter Day Saints**. Their album, *The Plan,* gives a quick run down of the basic teachings of the Mormon church. The album opens to reveal nine stages of life from a L.D.S. viewpoint...

1. The pre-existent spirit coming to be born
2. Childhood
3. Wisdom and training
4. Marriage
5. Career
6. Having children
7. Grief
8. Old age
9. Death and back into spirit form

And then, up in the upper-right hand corner, you'll find the words...

"As man is, God once was-As God is, man may become"

When the record sleeve is pulled out, one will find the phrase..."KOLOB—The First Creation", along with the scripture reference from the *Pearl of Great Price*, considered to be a sacred Mormon book. Kolob is taught to be a star/planet that Mormon men go to so they may have sex with as many women as possible, so they might produce "spirit children" in hopes of one day being a god over some other planet! (So much for a squeaky clean image!)

Jehovah's Witnesses

Lester Bangs, the famous rock critic, **George Benson, Ornette Coleman,** jazz musician, **Larry Graham of Graham Central Station, Michael Jackson, Hank Marvin of**

the **Shadows, The Modern Jazz Quartet, Van Morrison, Huey "Piano" Smith,** famous New Orleans pianist, **David Thomas** of **Pere Ubu** are all listed among J.W.'s.

The **Jehovah Witnesses** are considered one of the fastest growing cults in our land. They deny the deity of Christ, the atonement on the cross, the physical resurrection of Christ, the trinity, the existance of hell, immortality, and many other basic Biblical teachings. They have repeatedly sets dates for the return of Christ and the end of the world... 1914, 1918, 1925, 1926, 1935, 1947, 1975.

Others like **Peter Green** from **Fleetwood Mac** and **Jeremy Spencer,** have joined **The Children Of God.**

Down through the many millenniums that mankind has lived, Satan has offered us all forms of "religion", which has placed mankind under satanic deception. **Religion is merely man's search for God...Christianity, in the true sense of the word, is not a religion, but a relationship!** It is a relationship with God brought about through the death and resurrection of **Jesus Christ our Lord!!** For in every "religion", man must <u>do something</u> to become right with their "god" or to attain into some form of "godhood"; but only in Christianity does God come down to mankind in love and forgiveness! Religion turns people into slaves that are never quite able to please their god, but Christianity shows God's true nature...LOVE!!! And the resurrection sets Christianity apart from all other religions.

Eastern religion and cults all say man must earn his way through his good deeds and works, the Gospel says, "Jesus **paid it all, all to Him I owe**"!

---

[1]The Book of Rock Quotes, Jonathon Green, pg.61
[2]From Jack Van Impe Ministries International Newsletter and USA Weekend, Jan.9, 1987, pg.4
[3]The Wall Street Journal, July 24, 1987
[4]The Mystical Maze, Pat Means, pg.133
[5]RIP October, 1987, pg.10
[6]Black Beat, Nov., 1987, pg.15
[7]Rock 'n Roll Handbook, pg.27
[8]People, Mar. 23, 1987, pg.68
[9]The Egyptians believed the scarab represented the force that made the sun come to life again each day and cross the heavens. They would place scarab charms inside the Egyptian tombs to help the soul of the dead person be reborn-reincarnated, just as the sun is reborn when it rises.
[10]Rolling Stone, Nov. 5- Dec. 10, 1987, pg.161
[11]Metal Mania, Dec., 1987, pg.34
[12]Metal Creem Close-up, Sept., 1987, pg.15
[13]The Complete Elvis, Delilah, pg.141
[14]Rock and Roll Babylon, Gary Herman, pg.159
[15]People, Oct.19,1987, pg.64
[16]People, Feb.23, 1981, pg.40
[17]Rolling Stone, Nov. 5-Dec. 10, 1987, pg.48
[18]USA Today, Aug.9, 1984, D-1
[19]Metal Mania, Dec., 1987, pg.56
[20]No. 1, June 6, 1987, pg.10

[21]USA Weekend, Mar.6, 1987, pg.8
[22]Life, Aug., 1985
[23]People, July 15, 1985, pg.46
[24]People, June, 8, 1987, pg.72
[25]People, Jan. 9, 1987, pg.69
[26]Ebony, Mar., 1987, pg.136
[27]Movie Stars, June 28, 1968, pg.37
[28]Guitar World, July, 1985, pg.22
[29]Down Beat, June, 1985, pg.61
[30]A Book Of Beliefs, John Butterworth, pg.80
[31]People, Nov.4, 1985, pg.58
[32]New York Daily News
[33]"Universal Message" by Meher Baba
[34]A Book Of Beliefs, John Butterworth
[35]Hit Parader, July, 1983
[36]"Tears For Fears" Will Hall, Zomba Books, pg.12-13

7

Violence

> "I think rock 'n roll in its highest form is a
> *death* cult. The gods of rock 'n roll are all
> dead...Sid Vicious, Janis Joplin, Jimi Hen-
> drix, Jim Morrison. The best thing you can
> do in rock 'n roll is die."[1]
> -Sting, the lead singer for the group **Police**

•In Georgia, 15-year old Janet Weaver wanted to kill her
sister. So she, and her friend, 22-year old Renee Thomas,
cornered 17-year old Yuette Weaver in her bedroom and
stabbed her 51 times, later dumping her body on a neighbor's
property. For three days Janet remained silent, watching cartoons while the police searched for clues in the blood-
spattered bedroom. Finally, after questionings, both Janet
and Renee broke down and told the gory details of the murder.

•In Texas,14-year old Arthur Baters broke into 60-year old
Lillian Piper's home. He strangled her to death and then raped

her. As if nothing happened, he proceeded to the freezer and helped himself to some butter-pecan ice cream. He then drove off in Mrs. Piper's Cadillac. After the police caught him, he immediately confessed and added, "You can't do anything to me. I'm just 14."

•In Illinois, 16-year old David Joseph, a product of a broken home, had high hopes of going to law school. He made good grades. Going through a rebellious stage, David got a modified punk haircut, started dressing punk with a jacket bearing the message, "HELP", on the back, written out by safety pins. One Friday morning, David woke up from his 6:30 alarm, pulled on a pair of rubber gloves, took a pistol from his father's gun collection and shot his dad through the head, killing him instantly. To give the appearance of a robbery, David and a friend took some of the video and audio equipment and put it in the Corvette. David then went back into the bedroom, shot his father again, this time in the chest. He took his father's credit cards and Corvette, and that evening took a date to the homecoming dance and treated his friends to dinner totaling $147.00. Over the weekend, he charged another $6,000 at the local malls. Finally, on Monday evening, he called his mother and told her that he found his father dead in bed. Police were able to uncover the murder easily under questioning.[2]

•In Mass., 15-year old Rod Matthews showed no reaction when the verdict of second-degree murder and his sentence of life in prison was announced. Matthews said he had plotted the killing for a month to experience what killing someone was like, according to testimony from two classmates who were shown the body by Matthews before a pre-Thanksgiving pep rally.[3]

Violent crimes among adolescents...a very scary problem in our nation. But how to deal with it is even more frightening! *Newsweek* magazine brought this out so vividly in their article, "Children Who Kill"..."Kathleen M. Heide, a criminologist at the University of South Florida, interviewed 59 male adolescents convicted of homicide and attempted murder in Florida during a 25-month period. She found they could be divided into seven categories, ranging from the fearsome nihilist who killed because he wanted to hurt people, to the action seeker who regards crime as good sport and homicide as a random event in an otherwise businesslike robbery. Her group also divided along one basic question: did the killer feel remorse? About 40% *did not*, she reports, preferring to blame the victim for not responding appropriately to a demand, or, incredibly, for failing to duck."[4]

Violence, including car accidents, has become the leading killer of the nation's young people, according to a study by Dr. Robert Blum published in the *Journal of the American Medical Association*. Blum is the director of the Adolescent Health Program at the University of Minnesota. Seventy-five percent of 15-to 24-year olds who die are victims of *violence*. Accidents, primarily auto accidents, account for over 53% of the fatalities and remain by far the leading cause of death in this age group. *Homicide* deaths have climbed 300% among young people in the past three decades to become the *number two killer*. *Suicide* has surpassed disease to become the *third-leading cause of death.*[5]

Violence has become so interwoven into the fabric of our society that we have become used to it. And the only way to see just how far we have come is to look back over our past. Do we have less violence or more violence today? Ezekiel speaks about a chain that binds cities:

> *"Make a chain: for the land is full of bloody crimes, and the city is full of violence."*
> (Ezek.7:23)

• In Newark, New Jersey, a young 14-year old Thomas Sullivan, Jr. took a knife and attacked his own mother, stabbing her over two dozen times in the neck and chest area, then attempted to set the house on fire to kill his father and brother. He then ran into a neighbor's backyard, slit his own thoat and wrist, leaving a suicide note. Later, the father reported that his son had changed drastically over the previous two weeks after doing a study on the occult. Mr. Sullivan also told the New York Daily News that in the week before the violence, his son had sung a song "about blood and killing your mother". The boy claimed that satan appeared to him in a dream and told him to kill his parents, and preach satanism to the world.

• In Rochester, Minn., a 16-year-old teenager took an ax and murdered his mother, father, sister, and brother. The bloody, 28-inch ax was found in the basement. David Brom, who faces four charges of first-degree murder had expressed frustration and anger about his parents and was drawn to hard-core, punk-rock bands with songs of pain, insanity, and death. A favorite of David's, according to one friend, is the group "Suicidal Tendencies." A song on its latest album describes "the maniac I'll meet. His love for me is like a father to a son. And now the maniac and I are one."[6]

An interesting survey showed the major offenses in public schools, which have changed quite a bit in four decades...

<u>In the 1940's, teachers listed these seven major offenses:</u>
1. Talking
2. Chewing Gum
3. Making Noise
4. Running in the Halls
5. Getting Out of Turn in Line
6. Wearing Improper Clothing
7. Not Putting Paper in Wastebaskets

<u>Now, in the 1980's, teachers list these as the top offenses:</u>
1. Rape
2. Robbery
3. Assault
4. Burglary
5. Arson

6. Bombings
7. Murder
8. Suicide
9. Absenteeism
10. Vandalism
11. Extortion
12. Drug Abuse
13. Alcohol Abuse
14. Gang Warfare
15. Pregnancies
16. Abortions
17. Venereal Disease[7]

What is the cause of this onslaught of violence in our society today? I believe we can find much coming through the media. Movies, television, and music are leading the way. According to a new survey sponsored by the *Motion Picture Association of America*, 123.6 million people go to the movies at least once a year.[8] The most popular movies among teenagers today are the ones that seem to major in violence and horror! But one no longer has to go to a movie theater or cinema to view such "slice and dice" films, now we have VCR's and cable movies!! It is a sad fact that the average teenager will see 150,000 violent acts and 25,000 violent deaths on just regular television programs by the time he turns eighteen.[9]

A study by the *U.S. National Institute of Mental Health* concluded there was "a clear link between watching violence on TV and aggressive behavior in children." Says Dr. David

188

Pearl, who headed the study, "We found children act more violently when TV teaches them violence is normal. From all we've learned, I'm sure these new rock concerts and videos have the same effect. You can't say viewing violence is the only cause of any particular act, but when the conditions are right, we know it's a *strong contributing factor*."[10]

MTV, (Music TeleVison, which could just as easily stand for "Masochistic Type Violence") has certainly added it's influence to violence. It is being piped into the ears and eyes of nearly 30 million cable owners. Mixed in with the normal sounds of rock and roll, comes the fast-paced video production of many various tastes.

"The intense sadistic and sexual violence of a large number of rock music videos is overwhelming," says Dr. Thomas Radecki, the psychiatrist who leads the *National Coalition on Television Violence*. "It's shocking to see this subculture of hatred and violence becoming a fast-growing part of rock music." In its latest report on music videos, the *NCTV* charges that video clips shown on *MTV* and *WTBS's Night Tracks* average 17.9 violent acts per hour. The study, which surveyed more than 900 rock videos, finds that 46% of the clips contained violent action or suggestions of violence.[11]

Of all styles of music, Punk and Heavy Metal bands are probably best-known for their violence-oriented music. Just a casual look at the titles of some of the bands reveals alot. Here are just some titles of various punk, speed metal, and

189

hard-core heavy metal bands...

- Cryptic Slaughter
- Blood Death
- Axewitch
- Original Sin
- Metal Massacre
- Hellion
- Slayer
- Megadeth
- Dead Kennedys
- Laughing Dogs
- The Damned
- Fear
- Blasters
- Blood Feast
- At War
- Savage Steel
- Necrophagia
- Indestroy
- Executioner
- Rosemary's Baby
- Agnostic Front
- Undead
- Manson Youth
- Evil
- Dead Milkmen
- Onslaught
- Blessed Death
- Abuse
- Slaughterhouse
- Doom
- Sluts
- Corruption
- Death
- Discharge
- Overkill
- Sword
- Primal Scream
- Poison
- Iron Maiden
- Dictators
- Kamikaze Klones
- Weirdo
- Flesh Eaters
- Death Squad
- Crucifix
- Skulls
- Icons Of Filth
- Voodoo Church
- Septic Death
- Crown Of Thorns
- Stillborn Christians
- Ultra Violence
- Criminal Youth
- Dayglow Abortions
- Destruction
- Impaler
- Thrasher
- Sacrifice
- Deathcorp
- Trashbrats
- Snakepit
- Necros
- Intense Mutilation
- Sodom
- Gravestone
- Pain
- Deathrow
- Venom
- Lizzy Borden
- Mercyful Fate
- Stranglers
- Monster
- Castration Squad
- Dead Boys
- Homicide
- Corpse Grinders
- Child Molesters
- Legal Weapon
- Suicidal Tendencies
- Millions Of Dead Cops
- Graven Image
- Sick Pleasure
- Condemned To Death
- Violent Children
- Bloodlust
- Aggression
- Grave Digger
- Possessed
- Black Death
- Pestilence
- Post Mortem
- Slow Death
- Germs

•Warlord	•Bitch	•Pandemonium
•Civil Death	•Urinals	•Corporate Whores

Again, let me say, those are names of actual bands playing in various cities I've been to. But it doesn't stop at just the names, these groups actually promote the concept of destruction. Keep in mind before reading the following examples that Jesus said in Matt. 18:7:

> *"Woe unto the world because of offences! for it must needs be that offences come; but woe to that man by whom the offence cometh!"*

Iron Maiden, who got their name from a torture devise used to kill their victims slowly, doesn't try to hide its violence. Their zombie mascot, 'Eddie', keeps coming back album after album. The *Killers* album shows smiling Eddie with an axe dripping blood as he just killed another victim. With one of their albums, Maiden has Eddie killing Margaret Thatcher with a knife. When flipped over on the back, the album depicts the group standing in front of a disemboweled victim hanging by his neck.

I remember one night after one of our crusades, a young man came over to me and said, "Mister Muncy, it's obvious that you don't know what you're talking about." I asked him why he said that. "Well, for one, **Iron Maiden**. Man, those guys are all Christians." I almost laughed, but I could tell he was serious. I said, "What makes you think those guys are Christians?" "Well," he said, "they have scripture verses on the back of alot of their albums." I said "Well, it's obvious you don't know what you're talking about." I went ahead and showed him a perfect example...

On the back of their *Piece of Mind* album is a reference to a verse found in the book Revelation. Although most Iron Maiden fans claim this is a verse in the Bible, they fail to realize that *one word* was changed. The verse quoted on the album speaks about going to heaven where there "will be no more brain". They claim that Christians are going to be a bunch of brainless idiots if they go to heaven. Actually the scripture really says in that verse that in heaven there *"will be no more pain"*!!! But they take upon themselves to change the Word of God, which is forbidden according to Rev. 22:18. It's interesting to note that the album shows Eddie with his skull cut open and then screwed back together. His brain was removed and by pulling out the record sleeve, you will see that his brain is being served at the supper table of the band.

> *"The God of my rock; in him will I trust: he is my shield, and the horn of my salvation, my high tower, and my refuge, my saviour; **thou savest me from violence**."*
> 2 Samuel 22:3

Damaged is the title of one of **Black Flag's** albums showing a young man smashing his fist into a mirror with his own face as the target. A form of self-hatred that is causing many kids to dress and act the way they do. Another one of their albums entitled *Family Man* depicts on the cover a man who has just shot his wife, son and daughter is getting ready to commit suicide with the gun to his head.

Sodom has an album entitled, *Obsessed by Cruelty*, showing a human skull dripping in blood while being scratched with long fingernails. Everytime I see that album, it reminds me of a young man whom I met at one of our crusades. He brought me a collection of his artwork, which was made entirely of violent and gorey drawings. One poster he drew was full of nothing but guns, knives, axes, swords, machine guns, bombs and other such things used to torture and maim others. In talking to him I found he didn't even think about what he was drawing, it just came from him "naturally". He was *obsessed by cruelty.*

Wendy O. Williams, a former porno-queen, is now known for stage shows including blowing up cars, TV's, and simulating masturbation with a sledgehammer says, "I like being the roughest, toughest woman in rock 'n roll. I'm a specialist."[12] She has certainly lived up to it!

Dayglow Abortions have an album picturing former President and Mrs. Reagan sitting at the supper table with an aborted baby laying on a bloody plate.

> *"If thou seest the oppression of the poor, and*
> *violent perverting of judgement and justice*
> *in a province, marvel not at the matter: for he*
> *that is higher than the highest regardeth;*

and there be higher than they." (Ecc.5:8)

Van Halen's earlier album, *Fair Warning,* not only depicts a man beating another man, but also shows a man ramming his head against a wall. This is where we get the term 'head banging music'; some young people will literally bang their heads against the stage while listening to the music.

While in a crusade in California, a gentleman asked me to help him with his son. He had decided not to let his 15 year old son listen to rock music in the house anymore, according to Deut.7:25-26. His son soon began to literally slam his head into walls and doors of the house. While speaking at a school in North Carolina, one teacher told me about a young man in her class who would suddenly go into a rage and would begin to beat himself against the brick wall until the blood would flow. In Ohio, I received a call from a Pastor who asked for some advice concerning a teenager in his youth group. His parents refused to allow him to go to a Ozzy concert, and he threw himself down and began to scream. Many would just excuse these things as bad temper problems. But I find a certain similarity with many of these kind of things with the accounts in the Bible, Luke 4:33-35:

> *"And in the synagogue there was a man, which had a spirit of an unclean devil, and cried out with a loud voice, saying, Let us alone; what have we to do with thee, thou Jesus of Nazareth? Art thou come to destroy*

us? I know thee who thou art; the Holy One of God. And Jesus rebuked him, saying, Hold thy peace, and come out of him. And when the devil had thrown him in the midst, he came out of him, and hurt him not."

Mark 9:17-18, 21-22,

"And one of the multitude answered and said, Master, I have brought unto thee my son, which hath a dumb spirit; and whereso-ever he taketh him, he teareth him: and he foameth, and gnasheth with his teeth, and pineth away...And ofttimes it hath cast him into the fire, and into the waters, to destroy him..."

Metallica has an album entitled, *Creeping Death,* with a huge human skull hidden in the drawing on the cover. Their album, *Kill 'Em All,* shows a bloody hammer on the front cover while the back cover says, "Bang that head that doesn't bang"!

"The mouth of a righteous man is a well of life: but violence covereth the mouth of the wicked." (Prov.10:11)

Omen's album, *Battle Cry,* depicts a number of huge skeleton-type warriors decapitating and maiming people with huge axes and swords with blood splattered everywhere.

Exciter shows a double-fisted grip on a knife ready to be used on their album, *Feel The Knife*. Another title of their album is simply called,*Violence and Force*.

Venom's album, *Nightmare,* shows a nude girl laying dead on her bed with her head hanging over the side while a demon sits on her, eating part of her stomach.

Kreator has an album entitled, *Pleasure to Kill,* showing a man surrounded by sword and axe bearing skeletons.

"...violence covereth them as a garment." (Psa.73:6)

Slayer, which isn't a very subtle name for a group, has one album entitled, *Show No Mercy,* complete with a sword-bearing, ritualistic Satanist, wearing a goat's head, standing next to an inverted pentagram with another one carved on the goat's forehead. Another album entitled, *Reign In Blood* shows Satan's slaves carrying him through knee-deep blood, as decapitated heads float around in it, while other victims hang on the walls.

Malice has an album entitled, *License To Kill,* which shows a masked man taking an axe and spattering the blood of his victim on the album cover.

"Let not an evil speaker be established in the earth: evil shall hunt the violent man to overthrow him." (Psa.140:11)

Thin Lizzy has an album titled to appear as if written in blood, *Lizzy Killers*.

The **Death Metal** collector's album depicts a man ripping open the stomach of a victim he just killed and taking both hands to stuff his mouth full of the intestines of the dead rocker laying before him. In the background, three others are hanging.

> *"A violent man enticeth his neighbour, and leadeth him into the way that is not good."*
> (Prov.16:29)

Grim Reaper shows the death reaper with blood dripping from his blade on the *See You In Hell* album. Many bands brag about going to hell.

Megadeth brags on one of their albums, "Killing is my business...and business is good." The album shows a human skull which was used in some form of torture with chains and hooks. Behind the skull is a knife, and a candle burning in a human bone.

AC/DC tells their fans, *If You Want Blood You Got It*, while one member of the band is impaled by another member with his guitar.

The **Live Undead** album shows partially decomposed bodies of dead men playing in a fog-filled graveyard.

Poison Idea's album, *Kings Of Punk,* shows the abdomen area of a member of the band after he took a pen knife and cut into his flesh the name of the band.

The Bible many times refers to this practice...

In 1 Kings 18, we read the story of Elijah challenging the prophets of Baal to call on their gods to send down fire from the sky. In doing so, verse 28 says:

> *"And they cried aloud, and **cut themselves**
> after their manner with knives and lancets,
> till the blood gushed out upon them."*

The Bible tells us in Mark 5 about a man who was possessed with an unclean spirit and how he would, as verse 5 says:

> *"And always, night and day, he was in the
> mountains, and in the tombs, crying, and
> **cutting himself** with stones."*

(It is worth notice that when the spirits were cast out of this man, they entered into a herd of swine which in turn *"...ran violently down a steep place, (they were about two thousand;) and were choked in the sea."*

Again the Bible tells us not to carve into our bodies. Lev. 19:28 says:

> *"Ye shall not make any cuttings in your flesh for the dead, nor print any marks upon you: I am the Lord."*

Again in Deut.14:1, God says:

> *"Ye are the children of the Lord your God: ye shall not cut yourselves..."*

Abattoir has an album, *Vicious Attack*, which shows a man holding a woman with a twelve-inch blade to her waist and a huge hook to her half-exposed breast. Tattooed on his arm is the word, Maniac, with two skeletons carrying axes.

Impaler's album, *Rise Of The Mutants*, shows a member of the band laying on the stage with pieces of a woman's bloody body in his mouth and hands. The back side of the album shows the drummer beating a woman unconscious with a cross shaped board.

> *"His mischief shall return upon his own head, and his violent dealing shall come down upon his own pate."* (Psa.7:16)

Cheap Trick's album, *Dream Police*, shows one member of the band holding a chain saw while a manikin lays cut-up on the ground.

An early **Beatles** album entitled, *Yesterday and Today*, depicted the band sitting around in smocks, smiling as they hold pieces of meat alongside decapitated baby dolls. The album cover was so offensive at that time that they were forced to re-release it with another cover. I'm sure if it were released in our day, it would have made it with no trouble.

Mick Jagger of the **Rolling Stones** says, "The best rock & roll music encapsulates a certain high energy — an angriness — whether on record or onstage. That is, rock & roll is only rock & roll if it's not safe…Violence and energy — and that's really what rock & roll's all about."[13] This throws some light on the infamous 1969 free concert at California's Altamont speedway which resulted in four deaths, one at the hands of a knife-bearing member of the Hell's Angels, hired by the Stones as security.

Rod Stewart sings the title cut off the album, *Foolish Behavior*:

> "I'm gonna kill my wife, I'm really gonna
> take her life…maybe blow out her brains
> with a bullet, they'll think it's suicide, they
> won't know who done it…I've got my hand
> locked around her thoat."

Alice Cooper, who claims he watches two or three "blood-and-guts splatter movies" a night for "relaxation"[14], was one of the first "shock rockers". As a matter-of-fact, his song, "He's Back", was the theme for *Friday the 13th-Part VI*. He was able to sing about everything from "Dead Babies" while chopping up life-like baby dolls filled with blood capsules to "Cold Ethel" and "I Love The Dead", both songs about having sex with a dead corpse. His 1986 come-back concert in Detroit on Halloween night included all his "normal acts" including snakes, chopped-up baby dolls, hanging, all complete with his own execution by a guillotine. The concert, seating 15,000 people, sold out in two hours.

Ohio Players album, *Climax,* shows a man and a woman having sex with the women stabbing the man in the back with a large knife.

Lizzy Borden has an album entitled, *Love You To Pieces,* which shows a beautiful woman laying on a bed while the mirror reflects a man with an axe in his hand ready to strike. The back cover shows the axe dripping with blood lying next to the woman's shoe. One rock magazine writer tells of her experience at one of their live concerts, "One of the many high points of the performance was watching Lizzy chase a man carrying a PMRC briefcase around the stage with his baseball bat and, to the crowd's delight, pulling a pistol and shooting him dead in his tracks. Lizzy showed the crowd how 'Love Kills' by first physically assaulting (for want of a better term) a woman and then dragging her screaming into his box, where he abruptly ended the affair with the almighty axe. With his victim's remains splattered all over his costume, he finished the song, then left the stage only to return draped in the stars and stripes for a dose of 'American Metal'."[15] Sounds like the kind of entertainment every teenager should see!

Molly Hatchet, which has a great many bloody album covers claim on the back of one of their albums that their name came "from 17th Century Salem where one legendary lady (if one could call her that) named Hatchet Molly would behead her lovers with that hand tool Lizzie Borden made famous."

> *"Keep me, O Lord, from the hands of the wicked; preserve me from the violent man; who have purposed to overthrow my goings."*
> (Psa.140:4)

Motley Crue have a number of songs given to violence. A record sleeve from their first album shows the band standing under an inverted pentagram in the middle of black candles, while holding human skulls.

Their song, "Knock 'em Dead, Kid" speaks of a person who is "...primed for hate..." with the chorus saying, "Knock 'em dead, kid, the blade is red, kid...knock 'em dead!"

Another song entitled, "Too Young to Fall in Love" says, "...I can just taste the hate/Well, now I'm killing you/Watch your face turning blue..."

Still another song after the *Shout At The Devil* album called, "Bastard" says, "Out go the lights/In goes my knife/Pull out his life/ Consider that bastard dead...make it quick, blow off his head."

> *"Then he said unto me, Hast thou seen this,*
> *O son of man? Is it a light thing to the house*
> *of Judah that they commit the abominations*
> *which they commit here? For they have*
> *filled the land with violence..."* (Ezek.8:17)

From **Motley Crue's** *Girls, Girls, Girls* album comes the song, "You're All I Need", a song about a young man who kills his girlfriend. "You're all I need, make you only mine/ I loved you so I set you free/I had to take your life...Laid out cold/Now we're both alone/But killing you helped me keep you home..."

Much of the violence is pointed toward women, as in the example from **Guns N' Roses** album, *Appetite For Destruction.* Their choice of a title for the album says a lot in itself! Jesus said in John 10:10:

> *"The thief [Satan] cometh not, but for to*
> *steal, and to kill, and to destroy: I am come*
> *that they might have life, and that they might*
> *have it more abundantly."*

That "appetite for destruction" comes from Satan himself! The song, "Anything Goes" describes the same thing the record sleeve shows...a rape...

> "I been thinkin' 'bout/Thinkin' 'bout sex/
> Always hungry for somethin'/That I haven't
> had yet/Maybe baby you got somethin' to
> lose/Well I got somethin', I got somethin'
> for you/My way-your way/Anything goes
> tonight/My way-your way/Anything goes/
> Panties 'round your knees/With your a— in
> the debris/Doin' dat grind with a push and
> squeeze/Tied up, tied down, up against the
> wall/Be my rubbermade baby/An' we can do
> it all"

As I just mentioned, the record sleeve shows a young girl, just raped, leaning unconscious against a wall, her dress ripped open, exposing one of her breasts, her panties are pulled down below her knees. **Guns 'N Roses** had to deal first hand with disaster when, during their set at the Castle Donington festival, two fans who were only feet from the stage were crushed to death.[16]

But the question is, "Can we say that this really causes people to become violent?" Are you willing to take a chance? I think the problem is very obvious, and I believe it could 'tip the scale' for many people. For example, read the following and ask yourself if there could be a same percent chance this could effect somebody's decision who might be considering murder...

Police have an extra song on the cassette version of their

Synchronicity album entitled, "Murder By Numbers" which says,

> "Once that you've decided on a killing/First you make a stone of your heart/And if you find that your hands are still willing/Then you can turn a murder into art/There really isn't any need for bloodshed/You just do it with a little more finesse/If you can slip a tablet into someone's coffee/Then it avoids an awful lot of mess/Now if you have a taste for this experience/And you're flushed with your very first success/Then you must try a twosome or a threesome/And you'll find your conscience bothers you much less/ Because murder is like anything you take to/ It's a habit-forming need for more and more/ **You can bump off every member of your family**/And anybody else you find a bore..."

The Wall Street Journal had an interesting statement about the young man who attempted to assassinate President Reagan back in 1981..."While not much is known about his (John W. Hinckley, Jr.) personal likes, he did have a reputation in Denver for liking rock 'n roll music, and had recently been a fan of and attended a concert by his current favorite, a punk rock group called the **Kamikaze Klones**, who played such songs as, "Death Can Be Fun" and "Psycho Killer"."[17]

Listen to what the promoters of many of these groups say...Heavy metal "has all the extreme qualities that make rock 'n roll something for kids and not adults, it belongs to kids exclusively." says Bill Kaiser, MTV vice president of programming. "We call it **music to kill your parents by.**" says MJI Broadcasting president Joshua Feigenbaum.[18] Think about it!!!

> *"O God, the proud are risen against me, and*
> *the assemblies of violent men have have*
> *sought after my soul; and have not set thee*
> *before them."* (Psa.86:14)

Fans, starting as young as eight and nine years-old, are attending concerts in increasing numbers. And they certainly are not known for their safety. Riots, beatings, stabbings, assaults and murders are occurring in increasing numbers in many rock concerts! In 1986 alone, three deaths, 124 injuries, and 91 arrests resulted from episodes of concert violence.[19]

But it doesn't stop at Heavy Metal...Rapping groups such as **Run-D.M.C.** have had their dealings in violence. Their tour, "Raising Hell", seemed to do just that! Arrests were made after outbreaks of violence during their concerts in Cleveland, New York, Atlanta, and Pittsburgh. **Garfield Brown, a** bodyguard for the group has been charged with murder in a fatal beating backstage at a concert in California. Alex Baldwin was taken backstage, thrown to a concrete floor and kicked. He died the next day from head injuries. A rap concert featuring **Run-DMC, L.L. Cool J** and **Whodini** at the 14,500 seat Long Beach Arena had to be stopped by police after a riot broke out. Forty-two people were beaten or stabbed and one person suffered a gunshot wound. Police reported that the seats, the glass and other furniture inside the arena were smashed.[20] A rap concert in Brooklyn called, "Monster Jam '86", was halted when gun fire erupted from the crowd. A 14-year-old boy was killed and three others wounded. A rap concert by **Public Enemy No. 1** attended by nearly 6,000, held in Nashville, had at least 26 people injured and sent to hospitals while two teen-age girls were crushed to death.[21]

I believe that the scriptures show us that there is a spiritual influence behind all this violent mentality. The Bible speaks of those who had a spirit working in them,

> *"Wherein in time past ye walked according to the course of this world, according to the course of this world, according to the prince of the power of the air, the spirit that now worketh in the children of disobedience: among who also we all had our conversation in times past in the lusts of our flesh, fulfilling the desires of the flesh and of the mind; and were by nature the children of wrath, even as others."* (Eph.2:2-3)

It's sad to see many who claim to want peace, but they can't even live at peace in their own home. I remember the '60's "peace demonstrations", when people would "fight for peace"! What a foolish thing! But we know that people without Christ are "*by nature the children of wrath*". They have a spirit that works in them, causing them to disobey the law of the Lord, "to love". This spirit is from the "*prince of the power of the air*", a phrase use to describe Satan. And again, we know that during the fall of Satan, he was filled with violence...Ezek.28:13-16:

> *"Thou hast been in Eden the garden of God; every precious stone was thy covering, the sardius, topaz, and the diamond, the beryl, the onyx, and the jasper, the sapphire, the emerald, and the carbuncle, and gold: the workmanship of thy tabrets and of thy pipes was prepared in thee in the day that thou wast created. Thou art the anointed cherub that covereth; and I have set thee so: thou wast upon the holy mountain of God; thou hast walked up and down in the midst of the stones of fire. Thou wast perfect in thy ways from the day that thou wast created, till iniquity was found in thee. By the multitude of thy merchandise they have filled the midst of thee with violence, and thou hast sinned: therefore I will cast thee as profane out of the mountain of God: and I will destroy thee, O covering cherub, from the midst of the stones of fire."*

It would only seem normal for Satan to continue that spirit of violence through his music today. He is the author of destruction! He has no concept of love and peace! He is a father of hate and greed!

Actually, the violence we are seeing and hearing of today is a mark of the last days. Jesus said that right before He returns, people would begin to be as they were in Noah's day. (see Matt.24:37-39) In Genesis we are told about the wicked condition of that generation of people...Gen.6:11-13:

> *"The earth also was corrupt before God, and the earth was filled with violence. And God looked upon the earth, and, behold, it was corrupt; for all flesh had corrupted his way upon the earth. And God said unto Noah, The end of all flesh is come before me; for the earth is filled with violence through them; and, behold, I will destroy them with the earth."*

The Bible also tells us in 2 Tim. 3:1-4 what the personality traits of the last-day generation would be like...

> *"This know also, that in the last days perilous times shall come. For men shall be lovers of their own selves, covetous, boaster, proud, blasphemers, disobedient to parents, unthankful, unholy, without natural affec-*

> *tion, trucebreakers, false accusers,*
> *incontinent, fierce, despisers of those that*
> *are good, traitors, heady, highminded, lov-*
> *ers of pleasures more than lovers of God;"*

We need to realize violence is just one of the many qualities of a fallen nature in man, and only the love of God can set a man free from hatred! And that can only come as one yields himself to the Lord Jesus in sincere repentance!

Jonah's message to sinful Nineveh was...

> *"...let them turn every one from his evil way,*
> *and from the violence that is in their hands."*
> (Jon.3:8)

"...Do violence to no man..." (Lk.3:14) was the reply John the Baptist gave to those who enquired of him concerning following God.

And if you are to ever find peace, and if you want to follow the Lord, you too must turn from your evil ways and violence. Turn to the Prince of Peace and He will speak peace to the storm that rages in your heart!

Oh, for the days that Isaiah spoke of in Isa. 60:18,

> *"Violence shall no more be heard in thy*
> *land, wasting nor destruction within thy*

borders; but thou shalt call thy walls Salvation, and thy gates Praise."

[1]The Rock Yearbook 1984, pg.203
[2]Newsweek, Nov.24, 1986, pg.93-94
[3]Lake County Record-Bee, Mar. 11, 1988, Pg.A-5
[4]Newsweek, Nov.24, 1986, pg.94
[5]NFD JOURNAL, August, 1987, pg.15
[6]The Record, Feb. 21, 1988, pg.A-13
[7]The Cause, July, 1986, pg.17
[8]USA Today, Nov., 1987
[9]Reader Digest, Jan. 1983
[10]Woman's World, Apr.2, 1985
[11]Video Magazine, May, 1985, pg.122
[12]The Rock Yearbook, Vol.8, pg.57
[13]Rolling Stone, Nov. 5-Dec. 10, 1987, pg.34
[14]Blast, Aug.8, 1987, pg.14
[15]Concert Shots, Nov., 1987, pg.29
[16]Music Express #132, 1989, pg. 29
[17]Wall Street Journal, Apr.1, 1981, pg.14
[18]USA Today, June 10, 1987, pg.D-1
[19]The Record, Winter, 1987
[20]Rolling Stone Magazine, Sept.25, 1986
[21]Middletown Journal, Dec.21, 1987

8
Sexual Perversions

"Gay politics is obviously one of the most important things in our lives." - **Jimi Somerville, Bronski Beat**

I flipped on the TV to catch the news one evening, while holding a crusade in Toledo. The leading story was about a little 8 year-old girl who was reported missing. The little girl's parents and neighbors were terrified because she had never been the type to leave the neighborhood. The report ended with a picture of the cute little girl and said if you see her to report it to the police. Carolyn and I both were deeply moved and prayed for her. What we didn't know was that the little girl was already dead by that time. Two days later the papers revealed the tragic findings...little 8 year-old Constance was found dead, buried under a crawl space of a neighbor's house.

As the story unfolded, a cold chill went down my spine. A 25 year-old unmarried man had talked young Constance into his house, afterwards grabbing her and pulling her into his bathroom and attempted to drown her in the bathtub. Finally, he took a brick and beat her over the head till she died. Then space. At his own testimony he revealed, "The following day, I had anal intercourse with the corpse, and I used my finger in her vagina."[1] All kinds of mixed feelings went through my mind as I read those words, but most of all I thought, '*How could anyone do such a wicked thing?*'. The truth is, things like that happen nearly everyday somewhere in the United States! Some of the most perverted acts imaginable have almost become common news today. People aren't quite as shocked to hear it anymore.

The next night on the evening news, neighbors said of Pons, the murderer, that he was a likeable guy, *a son of a doctor* and was very quiet, but that, 'he listened to weird music all the time'! It was easy for me to preach that week on the sexual perversion in some rock music! We had a case to back it up.

Now, let me be quick to say that I'm not saying that rock music alone caused this man to commit perverted acts on this young girl, but I will say that it probably fueled the flame!

Again, I entitled this chapter, "Sexual Perversions", and by that I am refering to the perversion, the corruption, the pollution, and the contamination of something very beautiful and pure...SEX. Satan is the ultimate pervert, and he has perverted that which is wholesome into pure rot. Such is the case with some music today. It is easy to call some rock music, "Porn Rock". Its themes seem to dwell on the indecent, immoral, immodest, filthy, lewd, vulgar, uncouth, dirty, impure, unclean, foul, nasty, vile, depraved, decadent, debased, degraded, debauched, and whatever words might be used to describe the depths to which some will sink. But sex doesn't have to be that way.

God created sex for a two-fold purpose...First, to procreate the human race through man and his wife...Second, to enhance the love and affection of man and his wife. Marital love is considered by God as something sacred and private, something that two commited people share together with the blessings of Almighty! But what happens to a teenager who has "done it all" before marriage? Marriage has nothing to offer to these but commitment, and most who have gone this far are not really into commitment too often. Marriage has lost its mystery! It has lost its appeal! When sex loses its God-given purpose, it becomes a source of destruction and disaster, rather than blessing and benefits.

Such rock groups as **Poison** brag about their sexual lifestyles saying, "We're not the guys to speak to if you're doing one of those 'safe sex' campaigns."[2] *Creem Magazine*, a rock magazine for young people, went to one of **Poison's** concerts in Charleston, W.V. and described some of the things that happened that night, on the stage made up to look like a woman's torso, with spread legs; complete with fishnet hose and garter...

> "A dozen girls came on stage totally "topless", got down on their knees and simulated sex while massaging a two-foot dildo. Dur-

sex while massaging a two-foot dildo. During the last song, a "slew of girls" from the audience also joined the others on stage by taking off their tops."[3]

So much of today's music is sexist! Degrading women is one of the first stages of perversion. Most rock videos portray women as little more than "sex objects". This not only gives young men a misconception of true sexuality, but also gives unrealistic roles (almost as prostitutes) for young girls to try and fulfill. **Whitesnake**, who have such album titles as, *Slide It In*, are known for their sexist-type messages. **David Coverdale**, lead singer for the group says concerning the sexist messages in their songs, "There's an area in the press that call it sexist, but I say it's sexy. I write a lot of sex songs, and if I write a negative song about a woman, it's because it was a negative experience."[4]

Paul wrote about the slow decline of sexuality in mankind when he said in Romans 1:18-32:

> *"For the wrath of God is revealed from heaven against all ungodliness and unrighteousness of men, who hold the truth in unrighteousness...Because that, when they knew God, they glorified Him not as God, neither were thankful: but became vain in their imaginations, and their foolish heart was darkened. Professing themselves to be*

> *wise, they became fools...Wherefore God also gave them up to uncleanness through the lusts of their own hearts, to dishonour their own bodies between themselves: Who changed the truth of God into a lie, and worshipped and served the creature more than the Creator, who is blessed for ever. Amen. For this cause God gave them up unto vile affections: for even their women did change the natural use into that which is against nature: And likewise also the men, leaving the natural use of woman, burned in their lust one toward another; men with men working that which is unseemly, and receiving in themselves that recompence of their error which was meet. And even as they did not like to retain God in their knowledge, God gave them over to a reprobate mind, to do those things what are not convenient...Who knowing the judgment of God, that they which commit such things are worthy of death, not only do the same, but have pleasure in them that do them."*

This puts an entirely different view on sexual perversion than our modern-day psychologists see it. Instead of blaming our environment, Paul claims that man's problem is a **heart** problem that starts in the **head**. Man stops honouring God who made him and becomes vain and proud in his "wisdom" talk like a fool, or an animal, as we are taught by Darwinism. When this happens, God releases man to his own corruption, allowing him to dishonour himself into all kinds of "vile affections" and "lusts", which, in turn, destroy man, who by this time has a reprobate mind! With the mind in a reprobate (depraved, unprincipled) condition, all that follows is sexual suicide!

Let's deal with some of the direction sexuality is going under the modern day "new morality" concepts, and see if it really is as great as some would have us believe...

<u>Masturbation</u>

Someone once said, "Perhaps no other form of sexual activity has been so soundly condemned and yet more universally practiced as masturbation." Masturbation comes from two Latin words: *manu* (meaning "hand") and *turbation* (meaning "to disturb or agitate"). Masturbation is the practice of self-stimulation of the sex organs, usually with the hand, resulting in orgasm.

Regardless of its controversy, masturbation is given such a prominent position by the average "sex education" classes in our local schools, that if one does not masturbate, he or she is supposedly missing out on a real form of sexual fullfillment. **Marc Almond**, formerly with **Soft Cell** and **Bronski Beat** says, "I'm one of those people who think that masturbation should be taught in schools. It's especially important in should be taught in schools. It's especially important in today's climate of safe sex."[5] Sad to say, the issue of self-control is hardly (if ever) even considered in today's "safe sex" society. It seems so clear to me that self-control is the real issue and that the answer to much of our problems concerning "safe sex" is taming the drive, not pacifying it! Instead of man controlling sex, sex is controlling man, and this *never* leads to true fullfillment, but only to perversion.

Mixed in with heavy breathing, **Cyndi Lauper** introduces her fans to "the danger zone" that she "can't stop messin' with". Her hit single, "She Bop" stayed at the top of the charts for 14 weeks, telling fans about masturbation with pornography...". Cyndi explains that the song came about one day when she and some of her collaborators happened to be looking over a copy of *Blueboy* magazine (A homosexual magazine). They got to talking about how no one's ever written a song about *that* subject, and before they knew it, they were working on what might be the first-ever rock paean to masturbation."[6]

John Crawford, from the group, **Berlin**, says concerning their song "When We Make Love", "...'a song about a woman who brings men home, makes love to them, videotapes the proceedings, then plays back the tapes when she's alone'...That song is purely about masturbation. I think everyone should masturbate."[7]

Prince uses a special-made guitar which he sticks between his legs and begins to stroke the neck as if masturbating, complete with white fluid shooting out the end, as seen at the end of his movie, *Purple Rain.* On live stage, he proceeds to lick the neck of the guitar after its "ejaculation". He sings in his song, "Darling Nikki",

> "I once knew a girl named, Nikki, you could say she was a sex fiend, I met her in a hotel lobby, masturbating with a magazine."

The Book Of Rock Lists, published by *Dell/Rolling Stone Press* include the following songs as "Songs about Masturbation"...

"Cool Jerk", **The Capitols**
"Dancing with Myself", **Gen. X**
"Fiddle About", **The Who**
"Going Home", **The Rolling Stones**
"Imaginary Lover", **The Atlanta Rhythm Section**
"In My Room", **The Beach Boys**
"Jamaica Jerk-Off", **Elton John**
"Love or Confusion", **Jimi Hendrix**
"Pump It Up", **Elvis Costello**
"Rattlesnake Shake", **Fleetwood Mac**
"Rocks Off", **The Rolling Stones**
"Shake a Hand", **Faye Adams**
"Slippery Fingers", **Grin**
"Whip It", **Devo**[8]

Such titles of groups as **The Buzzcocks, The Sex Pistols, Steely Dan, The Vibrators, Cream, The Lovin' Spoonful** and even **10cc** are all reported to be titles dedicated to female or male masturbation.

I believe that masturbation is a rip-off to true sexual fulfillment and a step towards perversion because of the following five reasons...

1. It is a solo act, and God never intended sex to be solo. We find in Gen. 2:24-25 God's purpose in sex...

> *"Therefore shall a man leave his father and his mother, and shall cleave unto his wife: and they shall be one flesh. And they were both naked, the man and his wife, and were not ashamed."*

This is how God intended sex to be; an intimate sharing and communication of two people knitted together by a permanent commitment to one another. He created our bodies so that *man* and *his wife*, unashamedly can be naked and unite their bodies in one flesh. Masturbation robs that precious fulfillment of physical union between two people in married love, and makes sexual fullfillment a second-rate experience.

Many use masturbation as a way to escape loneliness as **Billy Joel** sings in his song, "Captain Jack", a song that tells of a lonely boy who, while his parents are gone, and his sister is on a date, will "sit at home and masturbate". This is too true for literally thousands of teens, who instead of trying to develop relationships, lean on masturbation as a crutch that they can always turn to and lean on. The concept of love or commitment is absent, fulfillment is based only on the pleasure of self, which leads to the second reason...

2. It is a form of selfishness, the ultimate act which destroys true love. It is sad to say, but we have become the generation Paul spoke about when he said in 2 Tim. 3:2:

"For men shall be lovers of their own selves..."

When a person gets into the mode of pleasing themselves, it gets very easy to "love" for what you can *get out of it*, rather than how *you might give*. Love, by definition from 1 Cor. 13:5, is something that *"seeketh not [its] own"*, which simply means it is not self-centered. Masturbation, in simple terms is "fruitless", it produces no love for another person, but is bent only towards self-love. This brings the act of sex down to *lust* rather than *love*, which brings us to the third problem...

3. It fuels the fire of lust, living off of fantasy. Studies have shown that up to 95% of males have masturbated, while as many as 79% of men continue to masturbate even after marriage! The reason is simple, fantasy is better than reality to most people! Sex researcher A.C. Kinsey and his colleagues discovered that some 90% of all males who masturbated had used fantasies as a source of stimulation during masturbation.[9] The problem with this is that the person who has become an habitual masturbator actually can become a victim of his own little world, finding "real sex" less erotic than his "fantasy sex" and therefore enjoying solo sex better, since the mind is able to produce the "perfect" act, which leads to my next point...

4. In most cases, masturbation and pornography go hand in hand. "Voyerism" and masturbation are twins to millions of men and women across this nation. Since the mind is the most important sex organ, pornography helps to produce strong images of sensuality which further enhance lust. Clearly this is what the Lord was saying when He addressed lust in the mind in Matt. 5:27-28:

> *"Ye have heard that it was said by them of old time, Thou shalt not commit adultery: But I say unto you, That whosoever **looketh** on a woman **to lust after her** hath committed adultery with her already **in his heart.**"*

What started out as maybe a curious peek can become a vicious circle which leads to deeper and deeper perversion, and has destroyed many lives, including ministers. After all, the Bible says in Prov.27:20 "*...the eyes of man are never satisfied*", which leads to my last point...

5. It can become habit forming. For many, masturbation has become "master-bation" because it masters their lives. I've lost track of how many young men have come to me in confidence desiring prayer for freedom from the grip of masturbation. Many people have confessed that masturbation not only became compulsive and addictive in their lives, but came to the point of actual obsession.

Many young men have been taught that masturbation helps release the tension or pressure of lust, but just the opposite is true...rather than curbing the sex drive, masturbation tends to stimulate it and then becomes a further form of bondage and enslaves more and more. Paul said in 1 Cor. 6:12:

> *"All things are lawful unto me, but all things are not expedient: all things are lawful for me, but I will not be brought under the power of any."*

Paul was saying he considered anything that would bring you into bondage or that would overpower you to be wrong. We are to be slaves to nothing but **Jesus**, and He would never mistreat any!

There are, no doubt, many of you who are reading this now, finding a real stuggle in this area of your life. It's not so much a problem because you do it as much as *"why"* you are doing it. Insecurity, lonliness, lack of proper self-esteem, wrong concepts concerning sex, and others reasons all can be causes that make masturbation such a part of your life. Regardless of the reasons, every time you come to God for help, He is more than able to give you victory if you will work with Him in your life. Here are some pointers to obtaining victory over masturbation:

1. Realize that you are not alone in your temptation to masturbate. As mentioned earlier, a large percentage of people have masturbated. The Bible makes it clear that our temptations are *"common to man"* (1 Cor. 10:13) and that even **Jesus** was *"in all points tempted like as we are, yet without sin."* (Heb. 4:15) Temptation is merely Satan's attempt for you to ruin your relationship with God! Satan wants to tempt you to obey the flesh rather than the Lord. Being tempted is not the sin, it's just the open door that invites you in; you can go in or walk on by.

2. Read some good Christian books on sex, and get a healthy outlook on this gift from God. We have all seen and heard enough false information on sex presented to us by the world, now it's time to get God's perspective on it! Go to a local Christian bookstore and pick up a couple of books written by men and women of God who give Biblical teachings on this wonderful gift from God to you. Of course, no book could be better on the subject than the Bible! *Read the book of Ruth instead of Dr. Ruth!!!!*

3. Spend your free time in constructive things. Some teach that exercise can lower the sex drive. That simply is not true; if it were true, athletes would have the lowest sex drive and those who have little or no exercise would have the strongest sex drives. Sexual desire is not determined by how active one is physically, but how much control one has over their mind, the main sex organ! Too often, temptation will overcome you if you have never learned to "*gird up the loins of your mind*" (1 Pet. 1:13) Even though the following statement is not in the Bible, it's still a true saying: "The idle mind is the devil's playground"! Fill your time with godly friends and wholesome activities. Develop a hobby, play games, sports, get involved in some church activities, but most important of all, READ THE WORD OF GOD! Memorize scriptures. (1 Cor. 10:13 would be an excellent one to start with!) Instead of allowing your mind to be filled with junk, fill it with "*whatsoever things are true, honest, just, pure, lovely, and of good report*" (Phil.4:8)!

4. Get rid of anything that tempts you. It might be a pile of magazines, romance novels, pictures, posters, books, records, tapes, and other such things that seem to fuel the flame of passion. It might be necessary for you to stop watching certain programs on T.V. and going to movies. It might be necessary to stop heavy kissing on dates, or being alone to break the pattern of temptation, but you must be determined to stop whatever is leading you into temptation. This is how you will show God just how serious you really are! You'll never get victory over a sin that you keep feeding!

<u>Pornography/Exhibitionism/Voyeurism</u>

The former all-girl group, **Go-Go's**, decided to appear on the front cover of *Rolling Stone Magazine* only in their underwear. Their album, *Beauty And The Beat* showed them sitting together on the front cover wearing only towels, with one of the girls on the back cover in the bath tub reading a pornographic book entitled, "H is for Harlot". This would have been totally unheard of when rock music first came out, but now nobody even blinks an eye at it! It is all because we have become so desensitized! But, to be honest with you, this is a perfect example of pornography...

The word *pornography* comes from two Greek words, *porne*, meaning "whore" and *graphein*, meaning "to write or draw". The word, *fornication*, found a number of times in the New Testament also comes from the same root wording. Pornography is obviously a forbidden thing from scriptural standpoint, but is a major part of American "culture". It can be bought in almost any magazine shop, and watched on almost every cable movie channel, and it is a major part of the music industry! And yet, it seems rather odd to me that unless a person is 18, he or she cannot legally purchase pornography; but any young person, regardless of age, can go to any record store and purchase the same type of pornography in and on rock albums and nothing is said about it!

Pornography, nudity and all the rest are really nothing new, for we read in Exodus chapter 32, after God gave the Ten Commandments to Moses, he was returning to camp and heard and saw the people as they were singing and dancing in the nude around a golden calf that they were worshipping.

Imagine that! After the mighty miracles that freed them from slavery to the Egyptians and the opening of the Red Sea! They had lost hope in God and turned to idolatry, rejecting God's plan of salvation. That was the first "Woodstock"! America has been just as sinful after being just as blessed!

Faster Pussycat got their name inspired by a porno movie by Russ Meyer called, *Faster Pussycat*, a movie the group brags they have seen over and over, which depicts violence to women. Porno is the truest form of the destruction of love and the glorification of hate known to man! It's hellish long-term effects are just now beginning to be seen! There are many contributing factors to rape, incest, and other sexual crimes and sexual perversions in our land, but I believe that pornography, whether in movies, books, or music is *the major factor* to these growing problems! Think about this:

•Nearly 900 theaters show X-rated films and more than 15,000 "adult" bookstores and video stores offer pornographic material, outnumbering McDonald's restaurants in the U.S. by a margin of at least three to one.

•Each year, nearly 100 full-length pornographic films provide estimated annual box office sales of $50,000,000!!

•About 1.2 million children are exploited through child pornography and prostitution.

•Approximately 70% of pornographic magazines sold eventually end up in the hands of minors.[10]

But in the realm of rock music, how common is porno? Take a trip to your local record store and see for yourself! Such albums as **Scorpions** *Lovedrive*, **Be-Bop Deluxe** *Sunburst Finish*, **Supertramp** *Indelibly Stamped*, **Wilding/Bonus** *Pleasure Signals*, **Boxer** *Below The Belt*, **Pioneers** *Feel The Rhythm*, and hundreds more show nude women right on the album cover, not to mention the many other explicit album covers like those of the group **Ohio Players**. Other groups seem to save the porno for the inside...such as **Queen's** album *Jazz*, which had a pull-out poster of naked women in a bicycle race! Another example was the very controversial album, *Frankenchrist,* by the group **Dead Kennedys**. Included in the album was an untitled, fold-out poster by artist H. R. Giger. Commonly known as "Penis Landscape", the poster is a drawing of close ups of a series of ten cohabitating loins. This, as in all cases of pornography, goes hand in hand with exhibitionism and voyeurism.

Exhibitionism has been defined as a form of sexual deviation in which a person feels compelled to publicly expose themselves, whereas *Voyeurism* is the practice of one who seeks sexual arousal by secretly observing others undress or engage in sexual activity, also commonly known as a "peeping Tom". Both of these forms of sexual perversions are found often in the rock music industry.

Ratt, who get their name from a pornographic comic book, brought the voyeur mentality to thousands of their fans on the cover of the *Invasion Of Your Privacy* album. The album cover depicts a well-built teenage girl who is in her bedroom, either taking her clothes off or just putting them on. Regardless, those who just look at the album are able to get the "peeping Tom" effect as we invade her privacy. The T-shirts that go with the *Invasion Of Your Privacy Tour* shows a person peeping through the key hole while viewing the same scene.

One group, who call themselves, **Voyeur**, have an album cover that simply shows a key hole to peep through.

I've asked this question often in our crusades, "If you knew there was a "peeping Tom" in this service tonight who would walk around your neighborhood at night and peep through bedroom and bathroom windows, hoping to find someone taking their clothes off, taking a shower or having sex, you would consider that person 'sick'. But what is the difference of that person sneaking around trying to see a nude body and those of you who will pay $4-$5 to go sit in some comfortable movie theater and watch someone take off their clothes, take a shower, or have sex?!" There is really no difference, except one is acceptable, the other is against the law! I believe TV and theater have made a bunch of voyeurs out of the American public!

Kim Carnes went to the top of the charts with her hit, "Voyeur", which plainly deals with the private obsession of a woman whose "video is her only saviour". The song goes on to say:

> "Voyeur, voyeur are you hot tonight? Dance,
> Dance, Dance, till it makes you feel good?
> Voyeur, voyeur, who you got tonight? Is
> love alive, or is it just locked inside..."

Psychologists claim that those who are involved in voyeurism and exhibitionism are generally those who have serious feelings of inadequacy, insecurity, and have difficulty in establishing healthy relationships with the opposite sex. How long will it take our society to see what we are doing to ourselves! We are killing our God-given right to enjoy sex! We have twisted and mangled it so much that we are now seeing the fruit of our own labor!

In the case of exhibitionism, it may come in many forms...
•Walking exposed in shopping malls, campuses, open areas.
•Leaving curtains "inadvertently" ajar in bedroom or bathroom.
•Driving or parking in a car with pants pulled down.
•Leaving the pants unzipped.
•Having a "strategic" hole in a pair of jeans or shorts.
•Wearing swimming trunks without liners.

As mentioned earlier, an exhibitionist is a person who feels compelled to publicly expose themselves. Such was the case of **Jim Morrison**, former lead singer of the **Doors**. After exposing himself to his audience in Texas, police arrested him. Since then, **Elton John, Prince**, and scores of others have "mooned" their audience and little is said.

Clothes were made to conceal our nakedness and seen as a type or picture of our salvation; the covering of our spiritual nakedness, sin. When Adam and Eve sinned in the garden, one of the first things they tried to do was to cover their nakedness by sewing fig leaves together. Afterwards, God slew an innocent animal and used its skin to make the first fur coats. From that time on, God's Word tells us to dress ourselves in *"modest apparel"* (1 Tim. 2:9) and warns us of the *"attaire of the harlot"* (Prov. 7:10) Again, clothes were made to conceal, but much of today's fashion is made to reveal!

Tina Turner, is a woman who knows the power of the mini-skirt and the power of exhibiting the body. Her exhibitionism comes through loud and clear on her song, "Private Dancer", a song that brought her back to the rock scene, dealing with private-booth nude dancers:

> "Well the men come in these places and the
> men are all the same. You don't look at their
> faces and you don't ask their name. You
> don't think of them as human, you don't
> think of them at all. You keep your mind on
> the money, keeping your eyes on the wall.
> I'm your private dancer, a dancer for money.

I'll do what you want me to do. I'm your
private dancer, a dancer for money, and any
old music will do."

Another song dealing with the subject of private dancers was **Madonna's** hit, "Open Your Heart". The video version brings you right into a peep show setting, complete with an assortment of leering males as **Madonna** strips. Of course, stripping down is nothing new to this "Boy Toy", as she calls herself. She has appeared nude in both *Playboy* and *Penthouse* magazines, as well as the movie, *A Certain Sacrifice*.

Samantha Fox is a perfect example of how sex can make a rock star out of you. Appearing a number of times in various "centerfold" pornographic magazines, she had no trouble using her flesh to make a hit. In her first big hit, which was entitled, "Touch Me", she likened herself "like a tramp in the night". There was a time when women were respected and called, "ladies"; but today the image of moral or decent has been replaced with the loose and profane! I'm reminded of the verse in Prov. 11:22:

> *"As a jewel of gold in a swine's snout, so is*
> *a fair woman which is without discretion."*

Since clothing pictures our salvation and the covering of sin, nudity is a form of rejection of salvation. This is pictured in the story found in Luke chapter 8, when **Jesus** encountered a man who was possessed with an unclean spirit. The Bible says in verse 27:

> *"And when he [Jesus] went forth to land,*
> *there met him out of the city a certain man,*
> *which had devils long time, and **ware no***
> ***clothes**, neither abode in any house, but in*
> *the tombs."*

Later, after **Jesus** cast the demons out of the man, the Bible says in verse 35:

> *"Then they went out to see what was done;*
> *and came to Jesus, and found the man, out of*
> *whom the devils were departed, sitting at the*
> *feet of Jesus, **clothed**, and in his right mind:*
> *and they were afraid."*

Getting right with God will show up by the way you dress! Stories are too numerous to name of missionaries who brought the gospel to areas where the tribes always lived in the nude, but when they became believers "something" told them to cover their bodies!

Many Christians have called this type of teaching, 'clothes line' preaching and other things to try and make fun. It's a shame to say this, but I find such compromise among many Christian ladies and teenage girls when it comes to godly dress. If women could get a small idea of how much their tight pants and short skirts affect men, maybe they wouldn't be so

234

carefree. Enough said about that.

<u>Oral Sex</u>

I guess I shouldn't have been shocked, but when a pastor recently asked me to address the subject of oral sex to his youth group, I asked him why. He told me, "John, I have had a number of kids from our youth group who have come to me with that question. I didn't realize how serious it was until one girl told me that she and her boyfriend had been having oral sex for months and had been reassured that it was O.K. by her mother because she couldn't get pregnant! But she says she felt dirty after doing it, and really deals with a lot of guilt" The sad thing was the girl's mother was also one of the youth counsellors at the church!

Some have even told me that oral sex is an alternative to intercourse, and allows one to remain a "virgin", so therefore is not wrong. From his album, *Dirty Mind*, **Prince** sings in the song "Head" about his successful enticement of a "virgin" as she gives him some "head". The loss of virginity involves more than the physical act of penetration; it involves a state of the spirit, soul, and body!

I remember doing a youth camp the year **Motley Crue** came out with their *Shout At The Devil* album. Since this church camp didn't allow the kids to bring rock music with them, I saw a lot of kids going through "withdrawal". One 14 year-old girl protested the fact that while she might not be able to bring her tapes, they could never take the songs from her mind. To prove her point, she sat down and by memory wrote the entire song, "Ten Seconds To Love". The song gives a rather graphic example of quick oral sex in an elevator, part of which says:

> "...Touch my gun, but don't pull my trigger.
> Let's make history in the elevator. Or lock
> the door, shine my pistol some more. Here I
> cum, just ten seconds more..."

I asked her if she had any idea what the song was about, and her unashamed answer quickly came back, "Sure, oral sex!" I knew my work was cut out for me that week. That is a perfect example of just how far-reaching the message is getting into even the young teens! Another example of just how popular the message is getting comes from **The Beastie Boys**, who produced a trash-filled album entitled, *Licence to Ill*. The album cover depicts a plane which has crashed with the words, "Eat Me", spelled backward on the tail of the plane. "Eat Me" is just another slang form for oral sex. In fact, **Judas Priest** has a song entitled, "Eat Me Alive", which leaves little to the imagination as it graphically describes forced oral sex at gun point.

> "Wrapped tight around me like a second
> flesh, hot skin. Cling to my body, as the
> ecstasy begins. Your wild vibrations got me
> shooting from the hip. Crazed and insatiable

let rip. Eat me alive. Sounds like an animal,
Panting to the beat. Groan in the pleasure
zone, gasping from the heat. Gut-wrenching
frenzy that deranges every joint. I'm gonna
force you at gun point to eat me alive."

The point of this section is not to deal with whether oral sex is permissable in a married situation, but to address it between those who are not married. One guy wanted to argue his right to engage in oral sex with his girlfriend simply on the fact that she couldn't get pregnant, "Besides that, we are Christians!", he said. My response was this, "Well, in that case, would it be O.K. for your mother to have oral sex with another man in the church simply because both are Christians and your mom can't get pregnant?" After thinking for a moment he said, "I never thought of it that way before."

<u>Bisexuality, Homosexuality</u>

The terms bisexual and homosexual are almost as normal today in America as baseball and apple pie! Bisexual meaning, "to be sexually attracted to both sexes", and homosexual meaning, "to be sexually attracted to one's own sex". Today we have the so-called "gay" community in a "sad" situation, with the **AIDS** virus as a major threat, killing thousands annually. **AIDS** (Acquired Immunity Deficiency Syndrome) actually started out as **GRIDS**, (Gay-Related Immune Deficiency Syndrome) but because of gay lobbyists, the term was changed to avoid suspicion to the gay lifestyle.

Freddie Mercury, the lead singer for **Queen,** (the street term for the man who plays the role of a woman in a homosexual couple) boasts of his lifestyle, but says, "AIDS has changed my life. I'm not as promiscuous as I used to be. I've adopted an intelligent approach to it. After all, I've already had a lot of lovers."[11] Queen's song, "We Are The Champions", has been used as an anthem for the Gay Rights Movement for years.

Jimi Somerville, from **Bronski Beat,** says concerning their songs promoting the "gay" lifestyle, "It's not deliberate, but there's not much more we can sing about. Gay politics is obviously one of the most important things in our lives."[12] Their *Age of Consent* album is totally around the topic of 'gay rights' all across the world. Listed on the record sleeve are the "Laws regarding minimum age for lawful homosexual relationships between males" along with the phone number for the *National Gay Task Force.*

When **Boy George** won the "Best New Artist" of 1983, he "praised the American TV audience for recognizing a good 'drag queen' when you seen one."[13] He had readily admitted he is bisexual, meaning he has sex with both men and women.[14] "What frightens people most is that I'm not confused about my sexuality, I've said I'm bi-sexual and thats enough of an explanation."[15]

David Diamond, one of **Berlin's** synthesists is also one of the very few openly gay musicians in rock. "I've been gay ever since I was old enough to want sex." He tells of one tour, "I think I'm more into one night stands than the rest of the group," Diamond laughs. "There was this one guy in Columbus, Ohio who had his tongue hanging out at Terri the whole set. I'm thinking, 'This guy's absolutely a pervert! He's absolutely, incredibly disgusting.' Then I went out to do my guitar solo, and he did it to me! And I thought, 'On second thought, I'm taking him home with me!'"[16]

Frankie Goes To Hollywood, with their hit song, "Relax", refer to the pleasure of extended sex by relaxing. "Relax...don't do it...when you gonna come..." The video ends with an orgy with **Holly Johnson**, the lead singer of the group going through the motions of anal-intercorse with another man. On their **Welcome To The Pleasure Dome** album, which depicts an animal orgy on the back cover and on the inside, a close-up shot of a male erection with sperm turning into hundreds of bi-sexual animals. This quote can be found on the record sleeve...

> "Manipulation of children's minds in the field of religion or politics would touch off a parental storm and a rash of congressional investigations. But in the world of commerce, children are fair game and legitimate prey."

David Bowie, who has admitted more than once to his bisexual lifestyle, has used rock to promote that concept to his audience. "I'm a great believer that of all the art forms, rock is the living art form. It's the living culture; it's the one thing that can actually move and change society."[17]

Aerosmith, from their *Permanent Vacation* album glorifies the bisexual scene in their hit, "Dude (Looks Like A Lady)". Another group called, **Scorpions**, sing "He's Women, She's A Man" off their *Hot & Heavy* album. **Michael Jackson** is a perfect example of what is known as "androgyny", the merging of male (aldro) and female (gyne) characteristics in one person. This gender-blending concept comes in various forms, sometimes known as Transvestism, which simply refers to a person who wears the clothing of the opposite sex, usually for the purpose of one's own sexual arousal.

Daryl Hall, lead singer from **Hall And Oats**,has boasted of his sexual encounters with younger boys, saying he really saw nothing wrong with that type of lifestyle.

Other groups such as **New York Dolls, Village People, Dead Or Alive, Sweet, Grace Jones, Poison**, give off the androgenic concept through their album/music.

AC/DC, a term used for bi-sexuality, had an album entitled, *Dirty Deeds Done Dirt Cheap*. The title cut off the album says...

> "If ya got a lady but you want her gone/But
> you ain't got the guts/She keeps naggin' you

> night and day/Enough to drive you nuts, pick
> up the phone/Leave her alone/It's time you
> made a stand/For a fee I'll be happy to be
> your back door man." (a term used referring
> to anal intercorse)

Think about that next time you **AC/DC** fans go around proudly wearing your **AC/DC** T-shirts!

<u>Sado/masochism</u>

Sadomasochism comes from two different words...Sadist (a person who receives pleasure from inflicting pain or abuse on others), and Masochist (a person who receives pleasure by either self-inflicted pain or through receiving pain or abuse from others). In most cases this includes beating, choking, whipping, and bondages with chains, leather, hand cuffs, etc.

Sado/masochism is the ultimate example of self-centered sex. The love and tenderness and gentleness that should be expressed in sex is completely absent in S&M. Such was the case in much publicizied "Preppy Murder Case", in which 19 year-old Robert Chambers, Jr. murdered his girlfriend, Jennifer Dawn Levin, 18, while engaging in what was refered to as "rough sex".

Iron Maiden, who get their name from a torture device, sing in their song, "22 Acacia Ave", a song about S&M prostitution:

241

> "...Beat her, mistreat her, do anything you
> please. Bite her, excite her, make her get
> down on her knees. Abuse her, misuse her,
> she can take all you got. Caress her, molest
> her, she always does what you want."

Duran Duran, who got their name from a character in the science fiction movie, *Barbarella*, live up to his actions. In the movie, Duran Duran would use a machine to have sex with women. The video for their hit song, "Reflex", includes the silhouettes of a naked man and women as they begin to kiss and caress one another; by the end of the video, the couple are beating each other with chains in an erotic S&M "love affair". Their video for the song, "Girls On Film", again shows their lack of respect for the female race. The un-cut version depicted women fighting and wrestling with heavy sexual messages of lesbianism along with out-right nudity.

Rob Halford, lead singer for the group, **Judas Priest**, is known for his sadomasochism. The studs, chains, spikes and leather is not just a show as he admitted, "Sexually I have always been to the fullest extent of the experience that S&M has to offer."[18]

Such groups as **Bitch** depict and glorify S&M right on their album covers. Their album, *Be My Slave*, shows a young girl dressed in a tight, leather S&M garment with a variety of torture devices laying around her.

John Cougar went to the tops of the charts with the song, "Hurts So Good", while singing to his girl he says, "Sometimes love don't feel like it should, make it hurt so good..."

Pretenders sang in their song, "Bad Boys Get Spanked", about S&M and even gave the sound effects of a whip in the background.

Rolling Stones have repeatedly sung about S&M. One album that got them into some trouble with some women groups was the *Black And Blue* album, with the original cover depicting a women tied and gaged.

Pat Benatar had strong overtones of S&M in her song, "Hit Me With Your Best Shot".

Van Halen has seemed to enjoy the concept of S&M for awhile. Their album, *Women And Children First* came with a pull-out poster, depicting **David Lee Roth** chained to a fence with skin-tight leather pants. He made mention that, "it's always been one of my sexual fantasies to be tied up".[19]

Eurythmics sang, "Sweet Dreams", about how "...some of them want to abuse you, some of them want to be abused..."

<u>Pedophilia</u>

A pedophiliac is a person who gains sexual gratification through sexual activities with children.

The child abuse problem is at such an epidemic stage in our country today that the government is at a loss for answers. While experts believe that only about 50% of child sexual abuse cases are ever reported, we are still seeing over 1,200,000 cases a year involving children who are being sexually exploited! According to one article, the number of reported child sexual abuse cases rose a staggering 850% between the years 1976 and 1983![20]

There are now organizations which openly advocate the sexual abuse of children, including over 280 magazines dedicated to "kiddie porn". The California-based *Rene Guyon Society*, which boasts of a membership of 8,500 people, uses the motto "sex by eight or it's too late"! *The North American Man/Boy Love Association*, which is active in eleven major cities, advocates that the age of consensual sexual activity between adults and children be abolished altogether![21] David Thorstad, head of NAMBLA states:

> "The ultimate goal of the gay liberation movement is the achievement of sexual freedom of all, not just equal rights for "lesbians and gay men", but also freedom of sexual expression for young people and children..."[22]

Scorpions album entitled, *Virgin Killer,* is strong enough just from the title, but what is worse is the original cover which unashamedly shows an actual photograph of a young girl, completely nude, with her legs spread! Another group called,

Blind Faith, has a similar album cover of a topless, little girl holding a dildo-shaped airplane in her hand.

Oingo Boingo sings a song about pedophilia in, "I Love Little Girls", which says,

> "I love little girls, they make me feel so good.
> I love little girls, they make me feel so
> bad...Isn't this fun, isn't this what life is all
> about. Isn't this a dream come true, isn't this
> a nightmare too. Uh oh, take a second take,
> Uh oh, it's a mistake. Uh oh, I'm in trouble,
> Uh oh, the little girl was just too little."

Beastiality

Beastiality is the bizarre practice of sexual intercourse with animals, which is mentioned in the scripture as a sin that requires the death penalty. (Lev. 18:23)

W.A.S.P. have an album entitled, *Live...Animal,* which shows a woman being sexually attacked by a dog. One song on the album is entitled, "Animal F—Like A Beast". According to the group, **W.A.S.P.** stands for We Are Sexual Perverts.[23]

Scorpio's album, *Animal Magnetism,* shows a man standing in front of a girl on her knees along with a dog with strong overtones of perverted sex.

Alan Parson Project's album, *Eve*, has a song entitled, "You Lie Down With Dogs", which deals with a woman having sex with anything male, even to the extent of saying, "You lie down with dogs and come up with fleas." The album cover depicts three women who apparently have been infected with VD.

A group who call themselves, **The Handsome Beasts**, have an album called, *Beastiality*, which shows a man hugged up to a large pig.

Necrophilia

Alice Cooper's two songs of sexual relationships with dead corpses, "I Love The Dead" and "Cold Ethel", shows the degree that some "artists" will take their perverted minds.

My Girfriend's Dead is the title of one of **Ian North's** albums. He is shown on both the front and back cover with a naked girl in bed whose skin has turned pale as she lies dead.

Other bizarre practices such as Urophilia (sexual stimulation from an interest in urine), and Corpophilia (sexual stimulation from excrement), are being sung about by groups such as the **Mentors** in their song, "Golden Showers", which is simply too sick to even quote.

The list could on and on. The sad truth is that man's mind has become so corrupt and so wicked there seems to be no end to the perversion and abuse of God's wonderful purpose for sex. **Jesus** said that the last days would become just as bad as the days of Noah when...

> *"...God saw that the wickedness of man was great in the earth, and that every imagination of the thoughts of his heart was on evil continually. And it repented the Lord that He had made man on the earth, and it grieved him at His heart."* (Gen. 6:5-6)

Many of these forms of sexually perverted practices, which were once considered to be extremely rare, are becoming more and more common, especially through the increased popularity of pornographic material that caters to and specializes in many of these perversions.
Psa.12:8 says:

> *"The wicked walk on every side, when the vilest men are exalted."*

It does appear that wickedness is on every side, but it is only because the vilest of men have been exalted! We need for God to bring us as a Nation back to a comprehension of the HOLINESS OF GOD!! That the fear of such hideous sin will cause us to fall on our faces before an awesome, holy, and pure Lord who can cleanse us pure! If you and I wait for rock stars, Hollywood, or the congress to set the moral standards back for sexuality, we will be waiting forever! The answer will never be found in the problem! As God's representatives on this planet, we are called to be the salt, a perservative that holds back the corruption.

Let me close this chapter by sharing this with one who might be reading this and isn't quite convinced that God has the best way. The devil promises you if you follow him you'll become rich and famous. Well, if that's so great, why do so many rich and famous people end up in divorce courts, mental wards, drug and alcohol hospitals, or why do so many rich and famous people take their own lives?

Paul wrote to the Corinthians, a people who knew much of sexual perversness, of the seriousness of immorality in 1 Cor. 6:9-10:

> *"Know ye not that **the unrighteous shall not** inherit the kingdom of God? Be not deceived: neither fornicators, nor idolaters, nor adulterers, nor effeminate, nor abusers of themselves with mankind, nor thieves, nor covetous, nor drunkards, nor revilers, nor extortioners, **shall inherit the kingdom of God.**"*

But thank God, it doesn't end there! There is hope in Christ! There is power in the BLOOD! For the very next verse, (v.11), gives us this hope...

> *"And such were some of you: but ye are washed, but ye are sanctified, but ye are justified in the name of the Lord Jesus, and by the Spirit of our God."*

Thank God for that fact! Some whom Paul was writing to and some who read this even now were like that, BUT...

•YOU ARE WASHED! Nothing can be compared to the feeling of being washed from the filth of sin! Even the world speaks of dirty jokes, dirty books, dirty movies, dirty pictures, dirty mouths, dirty minds, and on and on. But why does even the world call it dirty? Because that is how sexual sins make you feel...dirty! But you can be washed from your sins! How? 1 John 1:7:

> *"But if we walk in the light, as he is in the light, we have fellowship one with another, and the blood of Jesus Christ his Son cleanseth us from all sin."*

As the old hymn goes, "What can wash away my sin, nothing but the blood of Jesus. What can make me pure within, nothing but the blood of Jesus." Isaiah said it so clearly when he wrote God's Word in Isa. 1:18:

> *"Come now, and let us reason together, saith the Lord: though your sins be as scarlet, they shall be as white as snow; though they be red*

like crimson, they shall be as wool."

•BUT YE ARE SANCTIFIED! That might seem like a hard word to understand, but it simply means "to be separated from something, and to be separated **unto** something"...you can be seperated from your sin once and for all and separated unto God! This is God's will for your life as 1 Thess. 4:3 says:

> *"For this is the will of God, even **your** sanctification, that ye should abstain from fornication:"*

Your can be sanctified, set free from lust, perversion, and immorality for good! And God **desires** to do that for you! He doesn't want you to be a slave to sin, but He desires to set you free and make you His!! Your life of dishonor can be one of honor as 2 Tim. 2:21 says:

> *"If a man therefore purge himself from these,*
> *he shall be a vessel unto honour, sanctified,*
> *and meet for the master's use, and prepared*
> *unto every good work."*

Yes, God can take that which was unholy and makes it holy and puts it back into an unholy world and will keep it holy!

•BUT YE ARE JUSTIFIED! As a young boy in Sunday School, I asked my teacher what that word meant and he said something I'll never forget...To be justified means: Just-if-I'd never sinned! Just-If-I'd!!! The prisons may pardon a criminal, but they can never justify one. God not only can forgive and pardon, but He can wipe away all records of your past sins! He can make you as if you'd never sinned! That's the Good News of the gospel! Our sins are gone!

---

[1]The Toledo Blade, March 21, 1986, pg.6
[2]Hit Parader, Sept., 1987, pg.31
[3]Creem, May, 1987, pg.5
[4]Metal Creem Close-up, Sept. 1987, pg.14
[5]The Rock Yearbook, Vol.8, pg.53
[6]Everything you want to know about Cyndi Lauper, K.K. Willis, Jr., pg 84
[7]Rock Magazine, June, 1984, pg.36
[8]The Book Of Rock Lists, pg.486
[9]Sexual Behaviour In The Human Male, Kinsey
[10]Henry Boatwright, chairman of the U.S. Advisory Board for Social Concerns
[11]The Rock Yearbook, Vol.8, pg.50
[12]The Rock Yearkbook, volume 5, pg.164
[13]People, Apr.23, 1984, pg.94
[14]Dayton Journal Hearald, May 30, 1984
[15]Rolling Stone, June 7, 1984
[16]Rock Magazine, June, 1984, pg.36-37
[17]The Rock Yearbook, Vol.8, pg.50
[18]Rolling Stone, Sept.15, 1980, pg.14
[19]US, Feb. 3, 1981
[20]Child Abuse: What You Can Do About It, Angela R. Carl, pg.31
[21]The Case Against Pornography, Donald Wildmon, pg.61-62
[22]Gay Community News, Jan. 6, 1979, pg.5
[23]CIRCUS, Jan. 31, 1985

9

SUBLIMINAL MESSAGES

"Music is the most extraordinary medium. It's the only thing that goes right to both hemispheres of the brain simultaneously, bypassing our rational functions, affecting us in a very deep way."[1]
-Judy Collins, popular folk singer

The word, *subliminal,* is derived from the Latin, *sub,* "below" and *limen,* "threshold" and simply means something "below the threshold of the conscious or apprehension", therefore, subliminal messages are messages that are aimed toward the subconscious mind in hopes that one can be implanted with persuasive thoughts. This is, no doubt, one of the most controversial themes in rock and roll, because is it still not a 100% proven fact that subliminals can "make" you do something.

The basic teaching behind this belief is this...the mind can be divided into two spheres, **"the conscious and the subconscious mind"**, or "the objective and subjective mind". It is taught by some psychologists and psychiatrists that the conscious mind is the seat of your <u>reasoning</u>, and acts as the guide in your contact with your surroundings. It represents about 10% of your mind and is a product of what comes through the five senses of hearing, seeing, smelling, tasting, and touching. Whereas, the subconscious is believed to be the seat of <u>emotions</u>, along with the area that produces dreams and memory. It represents the other 90% of your mind. It is responsible for carrying out the process of circulation, breathing, digestion, as well as all other "unconscious" actions.

The conscious mind is believed to be responsible for the reasoning out of what one believes, while the subconscious mind accepts what is impressed upon it. And since the subconscious mind does not reason out whether something is good or bad, right or wrong, true or false, it is therefore believed that one can be "manipulated" or "brain-washed" by the by-passing of the conscious mind and the targeting of the subconscious mind. Dr. N. F. Dixon, a British psychologist, author of *Subliminal Perception*, wrote: "It may be impossible to resist instructions which are not consciously experienced. There would seem to be a close parallel between these phenomena and those associated with, on the one hand, post-hypnotic suggestion and, on the other, neurotic compulsive responses."

This, of course, is the premise on which much of today's psychology is based and is still just a "premise". Many will find Freudian-type teaching, along with other types of humanistic philosophy, tied into this concept. As far back as 400 B.C., the Greek philosopher, Democritus, wrote, "Much is perceptible which is not perceived by us." Plato and Aristotle in ancient times, and Montaigne and Leibniz more recently, mentioned subliminal communication. Schopenhauer, Nietzsche, Freud, Jung, and Rorschach were preoccupied by it. Not only is this a major basis for most psychology, but it is also tied into parapsychology...

I have a number of catalogs put out by various companies who are suppliers of subliminal tapes and have found most of them are into New Age Teaching, Eastern Mysticism and the Occult. Many tapes are produced to help one practice yoga and meditation, hypnosis, develop E.S.P., altered states of consciousness, and out-of-body experiences, along with some pseudo-Christian teachings such as healing with the mind, holistic health, mind over matter, positive thinking, etc.

However, it still demands our attention and consideration as Christians to look into this very popular form of "programing the mind". Whether or not subliminals work, one thing is for sure; many groups have used these methods in hopes of getting their message across, and we need to be careful, as 2 Cor. 2:11 says:

> *"Lest Satan should get an advantage of us:*
> *for we are not ignorant of his devices."*

We know for sure that our <u>minds</u> are a target for Satan, for

Paul said in 2 Cor. 4:4 that Satan,

> *"...the god of this world hath blinded **the minds** of them which believe not, lest the light of the glorious gospel of Christ, who is the image of God, should shine unto them."*

Satan will try to blind people's minds because they are the direct route to the spirit and soul of man. So for one to guard his heart, he must be careful to guard his mind. (see Prov.4:23) Go over the important scriptures listed below and see the importance placed on the mind...

<u>**We are told in scriptures...**</u>

*You are to love the Lord with *"all thy mind"* (Mt.22:37)

*That a demon-possessed man was delivered and was *"in his right mind"* (Mark 5:15)

*To not be of a *"doubtful mind"* (Lk. 12:29)

*To receive God's Word *"with all readiness of mind"* (Acts 17:11)

*To serve the Lord *"with all humility of mind"* (Acts 20:19)

*God gives some over *"to a reprobate mind"* (Rom.1:28)

*To *"be carnally **minded** is death"* and *"spiritually **minded** *is life and peace"* (Rom.8:6)

*That the *"carnal mind is enmity against God"* (Rom.8:7)

*To be transformed *"by the renewing of your mind"* (Rom.12:2)

*To *"have the mind of Christ"* (1 Cor. 2:16)

*That there are those whose *"minds were blinded"* (2 Cor.3:14)

*To be careful lest *"your minds should be corrupted from the simplicity that is in Christ"* (2 Cor.11:3)

*Not to fulfill *"the desire of the flesh and of the mind"* (Eph.2:3)

*Not to walk as others do *"in the vanity of their mind"* (Eph.4:17)

*To *"be renewed in the spirit of your mind"* (Eph.4:23)

*To esteem others *"in lowliness of mind"* (Phil.2:3)

*That before Christ comes into your life, you are *"alienated and enemies in your mind by wicked works"* (Col.1:21)

*That some can be *"vainly puffed up by his fleshly mind"* (Col.2:18)

*To put on *"humbleness of mind"* (Col.3:12)

*That we are not to be *"shaken in mind"* (2 Thess.2:2)

*That we are to avoid *"perverse disputing of men of corrupt minds"* (1 Tim.6:5)

*That God is the one who gives us a *"sound mind"* (2 Tim.1:7)

*That there are *"men of corrupt minds"* (2 Tim.3:8)

*That there are those whose *"mind and conscience is defiled"* (Titus 1:15)

*That God says, *"I will put my laws into their mind"* (Heb.8:10)

*That you are to look to Jesus *"lest ye be wearied and faint in your minds"* (Heb. 12:3)

*A *"double-minded man is unstable in all his ways"* (Jas.1:8)

*We need to purify the heart if we are *"double-minded"* (Jas.4:8)

*We are told to *"gird up the loins of your mind..."* (1 Pet.1:13)

*That by reading the Word it will *"stir up your pure minds by* *way of remembrance"* (2 Pet.3:1)

Now, in dealing with subliminals, one must understand that there are many different types of subliminals: visual, audio, high-speed, slow-speed, subsonic, ultrasonic, and backward masking, just to name a few.

Experiments in subliminals have gone back as far as the '50's with the famous, "Hungry? Eat Popcorn", phrase flashed on a movie screen at the rate of 1/3000 of a second with the tachistoscope. Most people understand that something that fast cannot be perceived on a conscious level, but the surprising results shocked even believers of the unconscious! The test showed a very noticable increase of 57.7% in popcorn sales![2]

Jimi Hendrix told LIFE magazine's reporter, Robin Richman, "But I can explain everything better through music. You hypnotize people to where they go right back to their natural state, which is pure posititve - like in childhood when you got natural highs. And when you get people at that weakest point, you can preach into the subconscious what we want to say."[3]

Rush has an album out entitled, *Hemispheres*, which shows a man dressed all in black standing on one side of a large brain. On the other side, or "hemisphere" of the brain is another man, (who is holding his hands out toward the pentagram the group uses as their logo) pointing his finger at the man in black. This, of course, is a very important concept when dealing with subliminals.

Most neurologists divide the brain into "right and left hemi-sphere", with the right hemisphere being the "subconscious mind". Work by the Nobel Prize-winning psychobiologist, Roger Sperry, and others suggest that the left hemisphere is better at verbal, logical, quantitative, and analytical thinking, whereas the right hemisphere is more visually and spatially adroit, more artistic, **musical**, emotional, and creative.[4]

High Speed

Inventor Hal Becker's "black box" is one type of a high-speed behavioral modifier. Becker's subliminal message machine holds U.S. patent No. 3,278,676. The "black box" works on a high-speed, low volume message which is mixed in with background music. The phrases used say such things as, "I am honest...I will not steal", repeated 9,000 times an hour. According to Time magazine, it helped an East Coast chain to cut their shoplifting incidents down 37%, during a 9-month trial period, which brought them a savings of $600,000![5] About 50 department stores in the U.S. and Canada had installed the device to reduce shoplifiting and employee theft by the time this article appeared in 1979. The "black box" is also being used by psychologists to help people lose weight, stop smoking, and overcome the fear of flying. Becker claimed in the article that he has turned down politicians and advertisers who wanted to hire him.

Cheap Trick, on their **Heaven Tonight** album, have a song entitled, "How are You", which uses the same type of programing, high-speed messages. The song says,

> "I heard your voice/I couldn't stand it/You know, you talk too much/You even scare my friends*/What's with you/The words you say/I know you're lying/You lie in bed, you lie, you lie."

At the *, one can hear a beeping sound. When that portion is recorded and slowed down 1/8 of the original speed you can clearly hear the entire Lord's Prayer quoted. But why? Well, think for a moment as you read back over the song...after talking about scaring off your friends, isn't it interesting that they subliminally implant the most common quotation from the Bible, **Jesus'** prayer?!?! And then, as if that wasn't enough, it "just so happens" that after the Lords' Prayer, the song "just so happens" to say it is a "LIE"!!! Other groups such as **Blue Oyster Cult** and **Bloodrock** have also used this same type of high-speed programming.

Howard Shevrin, professor of psychology and director of the *Psychotherapy Clinic* at the *University of Michigan* claims that in a series of experiments using over 100 people, he and other specialists were able to conclude that the mind can associate high-speed images with words. By flashing pictures of a bee at the rate of 1/1000 of a second, Shevrin asked his subjects to tell all the words that came to their mind. Such words as "bug", "sting", and "honey" were found to be the most consistent.[6]

Visual

An advertisment for Edge gel appeared in *Newsweek* magazine, Jan.7, 1985 on the inside of the back cover. The ad, which was all air-brushed, shows a face of a very happy and contented, smiling man with his creamy shaving gel covering his face. The ad tells us that it's "Not Your Ordinary Shave" and of course, once you look close enough, you'll find exactly what they mean. The painting has subliminals in the shaving cream. On both sides and on the top of the man's mouth are, subltly drawn in, three naked women. Under his chin area is what appears at first glance to be the Hawaiian mountains, but by looking a little closer, you can clearly see a naked woman in a very seductive position. This is just one of many types of subliminals that are used by advertisers in hopes of getting a sale.

Santana has an album out, simply entitled, *Santana*. The album cover, when first looked at, just seems to have a face of a roaring lion. But by taking the time to look closer, one can see that the artist who drew this "lion" had actually drawn a series of faces, some screaming, others praying, all hidden in the eyebrows, eyes, nose, whiskers, and other parts.

A rather interesting hidden message on an album cover was found on Michael Sembello's album, *Bossa Nova Hotel*. The album shows three men. One reading a comic book, the other two levitating about a foot off the ground while looking up toward a light shining on them. The hidden message gets real obvious once you take the time to look closely. Of the two men looking up, one is wearing swimming trunks and the other is wearing a lion cloth, found often on paintings of Christ on the cross. All one must do is get a family Bible and take a look at the artist's rendering and 99% of the time you will find a gash on his side below his heart. This was the result of the Roman spear thrust in his side after his death on the cross. Look once again at the album cover and you'll find a noticable gash on this man's side below his heart. "Just an accident?"...hardly...one of the songs off the album that was a hit was called, "Automatic Man". Throughout the whole song the phrase, "we are Diablo people, we are Diablo people", is repeated over and over. ("Diablo" is spanish for "Devil")

Low Volume/Hidden Lyrics

The **Rolling Stones** had an album entitled, *Their Satanic Majesties Request*. The album not only had a plastic 3-D cover, (costing an additonal $50,000), which subliminally hid the faces of all four **Beatles**, but also used a form of subliminal in the song, "Sing this all together and sees what happens". The song actually is a weird-sounding instrumental that apparently says nothing. But careful listening will reveal a tune is actually being played, and at the end of the segment is a hard-breathing sound that is someone saying, "I hate you, I hate you, I hate you" The tune..."We wish you a merry Christmas".

The **Beatles** have a song entitled, "I am the Walrus", which combines various subliminals while ending the song with a chant, "Oom pah, oom pah, oom pah, oom pah" which slowly blends into "Smoke pot, smoke pot, everybody smoke pot, smoke pot, smoke pot, everybody smoke pot..."

The group **Pink Floyd** had a very successful album entitled, *Animals,* which incorporated a subliminal in the song, "Sheep". Carefully listening to the song, one can faintly hear talking in the background as the organ is playing with the sounds of sheep billowing. The words being spoken are a perverted form of the 23rd Psalm, actually found in the Book of Shadows, a handbook for the Satanic Bible. I've played this song hundreds of times before thousands of people telling them to listen and see if they can hear what is being said. In every case, most people pick up something, but they claim they cannot understand it. I then show the actual words right off the record sleeve while playing it again, and then most people are able to clearly understand what is being said. The only difference was by seeing what they were hearing, it was much easier to comprehend what was being said.

This is a very important thing to realize...by seeing the words, it really does "sound" clearer to the ear. How many times have you said, "I can't understand what they are saying.", but once the words are pointed out to you, or if you have the words in front of you while you are listening to the song, the words actually appear clearer, and you are able to understand. The only difference is, now "consciously" you are able to see what you had already "unconsciously" heard; either way, the mind *was* able to pick it up.

The group **Quiet Riot** went to the #1 position with their song, "Cum On Feel The Noize". In the middle of the chorus, a line is repeated over and over saying, "Cum on feel the noise, girl rock your boys..." At a certain place in the song, the second time the chorus is repeated, half the band will say the "F" word so that it mixes in without too many people catching it. They later admitted doing the same thing in their live concerts.

Backward Masking

Backward Masking simply means, "masking" or "hiding" something in a song, backwards.

I remember as a high school student hearing about backward masking for the first time. It was playing off the Beatle's, *Sergeant Pepper's Lonely Hearts Club Band* album. The class was doing a study on the so-called 'Paul is dead' craze. The **Beatles** were believed to be the first to use backward masking. **John Lennon** claimed he "discovered" the technique after winding his tape the wrong way in 1966, and used it on the song, "Rain". From that point on, backward messages could be found on a number of the Beatles songs as well as and Lennon's solo albums. After Lennon's death, **Yoko**

Ono claimed, "We both understood that working on a subliminal level was very important."[7]

On the back of **Motley Crue's** album, *Shout At The Devil,* can be found these words: "CAUTION, THIS RECORD MAY CONTAIN BACKWARD MESSAGES", and of course it does! **Nikki Sixx** from the band says concerning using manipulation of youth:

> "The one thing I got from Hitler was the idea
> of the Nazi youth. I believe in the Motley
> youth. The youth of today are the leaders of
> tomorrow. They're young, **they can be brain-
> washed and programed.**"[8]

<u>To me, backward masking can only be explained logically three ways:</u>

1. Those that are done on purpose. This is done through the technique of simply recording something, then dubbing it into a portion of the song. Bruce Helmink, chief recording engineer for Amerisound Studios in Columbus, Ohio, comments: "Backward masking does exist, but is very rare. At studio rates, it's very expensive because of the technical trouble involved in doing it well enough so that you can't recognize it when played forwards."[9]

2. Those that are pure phonetic coincidence. This is being as fair as one can be, giving some of these guys the benefit of the doubt. There could be some backward-masked messages that are pure coincidence. Because the english langage is made up of phonics that can form words when spoken backwards, it is entirely possible that a couple of words in a song playing backwards could say something and make sense. But, for complete sentences to make sense forward and also backwards, I have to think that this is more than coincidence. If these are just coincidence, why don't they say things like, "Eat your vegetables.", "Obey your parents.", "Clean your room."?! This leads me to the final explaination...

3. Those that are from a supernatural influence. In studying the topic of backward masking, I have found some rather interesting connections in doing things backwards and the occult. In the encyclopedia series called, **Man, Myth & Magic**, under the heading of *Inverted Symbols*, the authors wrote,

> "Symbols which are upside down, backwards or the wrong way round, usually connected with evil; inverted crucifixes or other Christian symbols are used in black magic because they deny God and the accepted order of things, and state disorder, abnormality and evil; prayers are sometimes said backwards in Black Mass and it was long believed that demons write backwards."

It is common knowledge, as already stated, that in the Black

Mass, the Lord's Prayer will be recited backwards. A group who call themselves, **Christian Death**, actually do just that on their *Only Theatre Of Pain* album. More than once in the *Satanic Bible*, Anton LaVey mentions that *evil* spelled backward is *live*. Matter of fact, **Black Sabbath** has an album entitled, *Live Evil,* showing the backward spelling.

<u>Some examples of intentional backward masking include...</u>

"Revolution #9"
Beatles, *The White Album*

<u>Forward:</u> "Number nine, number nine, number nine..."
<u>Backward:</u> "Turn me on dead man, turn me on dead man"

"I'm so tired"
Beatles, *The White Album*

<u>Forward:</u> Following the song, there is an number of unintelligible words.
<u>Backward:</u> "Paul is dead now, miss him, miss him, miss him."

"...And The Gods Made Love."
Jimi Hendrix, *Electric Ladyland*

<u>Forward:</u> A slow motion recording with some unintelligible

words.
Backward: "Yes...OK...one more time."

"Darling Nikki"
Prince, *Purple Rain*

Forward: An number of unintelligible words at the end of the
song talking about his sexual experience with "Niki".
Backward: "Hello, how are you? I'm fine, cause I know the
*Lord is cumming soon, cumming soon, cumming soon. Ha,
ha, ha, ha, ha..."

(Prince has many times stated he is the "Lord" of the sexual
revolution. For example, another song on the *Purple Rain*
album, called "I would die 4 U", Prince declares, "I'm your
messiah, and I would die for you.". This is one example of the
fulfillment of 2 Peter 3:3-4, which tells us *"scoffers, walking
after their own lusts"* would mock the second coming of
Christ.)

"Gotta Find A Way (to understand)"
Bloodrock, *Bloodrock*

Forward: An number of unintelligible words.
Backward: "Anyone who is stupid enough to play this record
backwards deserves what they're about to hear...(then fades
out as the person continues talking)

"The Devil"
The Brothers Johnson, *Look Out For #1*

<u>Forward:</u> An number of unintelligible words at the beginning of the song.
<u>Backward:</u> "Your mother sucks c—— in hell, give us your a—"

"Heavy Metal Poisoning"
Styx, *Kilroy Was Here*

<u>Forward:</u> An number of unintelligible words at the beginning of the song.
<u>Backward:</u> The Latin motto encircling the "Great Seal" on the back of the dollar bill, *"Annuit Coeptis. Novus Ordo Seclorum."*, which translates into english, *"Announcing The Birth. New Secular Order"*.

"The Damned"
The Plasmatics, *Coup De' Tat*

<u>Forward:</u> An number of unintelligible words spoken by Wendy O. Williams at the end of the song.
<u>Backward:</u> "Consensus programing is dangerous to your health, the brainwashed do not know they are brainwashed."

"Goodbye Blue Sky"
Pink Floyd, *The Wall*

<u>Forward:</u> An number of unintelligible words.
<u>Backward:</u> "Congratulations, you've just discovered the secret message. Please send your answer to 'Old Pink', care of 'Funny Farm', Chelford..."

"Fire on High"
Electric Light Orchestra, *Face the Music*

<u>Forward:</u> An number of unintelligible words at the beginning of the song.
<u>Backward:</u> "The music is reversible, but time is not. Turn back! Turn back! Turn back!"

"Strange Magic"
Electric Light Orchestra, *Face the Music*

<u>Forward:</u> At the end of the song, it fades into what appears to say, "All for all, we are magic, all for all, we are magic."
<u>Backward:</u> The above phrase is actually, "Face the mighty waterfall, face the mighty waterfall" backward.

"In League With Satan"
Venom, *Welcome to Hell*

<u>Forward:</u> An number of unintelligible words.
<u>Backward:</u> "It is better to reign in hell, than to serve in heaven. For I'm in league with Satan. You're gonna burn in Hell. I want your soul."

<u>The following examples are not done purposely...</u>

"Eldorado"
Electric Light Orchestra, *Eldorado*

<u>Forward:</u> "Here it comes/Another lonely day/Playing their game/I'll sail away on a voyage of no return, to see, if eternal life is meant to be."
<u>Backward:</u> "He is the nasty one, Christ, you're *infernal/ Though it is said/we're dead men/Everyone that does have the mark will live."

(*infernal means "damnable, hellish, diabolical, accursed, awful, horrendous, terrible, etc.)

"Another One Bites The Dust"
Queen, *The Game*

<u>Forward:</u> Repeatedly, "another one bites the dust"
<u>Backward:</u> "suppose to smoke marijuana, suppose to smoke marijuana, it's fun to smoke marijuana"

"You Took The Words Right Out Of My Mouth"
Meatloaf, *Bat Out Of Hell*

<u>Forward:</u> An eerie conversation between a man and woman before the song actually begins.
<u>Backward:</u> "Satan...see him follow you...Satan, see him follow you."

"Snowblind"
Styx, *Paradise Theater*

<u>Forward:</u> In the middle of the song, "I tried so hard to make it so."
<u>Backward:</u> "Oh Satan, use our voices."

(On their live album they deny that they used backward masking on the song, although, even on the live version, the song says that backwards.)

"Running With The Devil"
Van Halen, *Van Halen*

<u>Forward:</u> In the middle of a song talking about being on the road as a rock band, "...no love you call real..."
<u>Backward:</u> "Oh, he loves me, my Lucifer."

"Who Can It Be Now"
Men At Work, *Business As Usual*

<u>Forward:</u> The line "Who can it be now.." repeated over and over talking about someone he is trying to get away from.
<u>Backward:</u> "All I need is Satan."

"Tops"
The Rolling Stones, *Tattoo You*

<u>Forward:</u> "Take your chance now baby, I'm starving for the rest of your sweet love and life."
<u>Backward:</u> "I love you, said the devil...that's right."

"Hotel California"
Eagles, *Hotel California*

<u>Forward:</u> The whole song is talking about the First Church of Satan, "As she stood in the door way, I heard the mission bell. I was thinking to myself, this could be heaven or this could be hell. Then she lit up a candle, and she showed me the way. There were voices down the corridor, I thought I heard them say...Welcome to the Hotel California."
<u>Backward:</u> "Yes reverse, Yes reverse, Yes reverse...Yes, Satan had help...had organized his own religion...It was delicious...He cooks it in a vat, he fixed it for his son, whom he gives away."

"Consider Me Gone"
Sting, *The Dream Of The Blue Turtles*

<u>Forward:</u> A song about a suicidal depressant, "History reaks of the wrong we have done..."
<u>Backward:</u> "Hey Lucifer, hey Lucifer...he rewrote sin."

"A Child Is Coming"
Jefferson Starship, *Blows Against The Empire*

<u>Forward:</u> A song talking about a child getting ready to come and make the world a better place to live in. The chorus line repeatedly says, "It's getting better...It's getting better...It's getting better"
<u>Backward:</u> "Son of Satan...Son of Satan...Son of Satan..."

"The Battle Of Evermore"
Led Zeppelin, *Led Zeppelin IV*

Foward: "The pain of war cannot exceed the woes of aftermath"
Backward: "I am the *Bible, please spit on me...so funny."

(*It seems rather interesting that "The Battle Of Evermore" would attack the Bible because that seems to be 'the battle of evermore'; to destroy the Bible!!)

"Stairway to Heaven"
Led Zeppelin, *Led Zeppelin IV*

This song is considered by many to be the greatest rock song of all time. A song written by **Jimmy Page** and **Robert Plant.** Supposedly written in less than 15 minutes. **Plant** claimed while writing the song "...someone pushed my pen for me..."[10].

<u>Forward:</u> "It's just a spring clean for the mayqueen. Yes, there are two paths you can go by, but in the long run, there's still time to change the road you're on. And it make me wonder." <u>Backward</u>: "There is no escaping it...Oh, it's my sweet Satan...the one whose little path will make me sad, whose power is Satan...he will give you, give you 666."

<u>Forward:</u> "Your stairway lies on the whispering wind" <u>Backward:</u> "I will sing because I live with Satan."

It is worthy to note here that the house **Jimmy Page** lives in is the home of the late satanist, Aleister Crowley. This was the home that **John Bonham** died in. **Page** claims, "Yes, it was owned by Aleister Crowley. But there were two or three owners before Crowley moved into it. It was also a church that was burned to the ground with the congregation in it. And that's the site of the house. Strange things have happened in that house that had nothing to do with Crowley. The bad vibes were already there. A man was beheaded there, and sometimes you can hear his head rolling down...Of course, after Crowley there have been suicides, people carted off to mental hospitals..."[11]

A very important key to the answer of the why of backward masking might be with this group. **Jimmy Page** has deeply studied into the black arts. He has owned an occult book store for a number of years called the *Equinox*, named after Crowley's journal. Of course, one cannot be a Crowley fan without being aware of his large book, *Magick*, a most detailed writing on the subject of black magic. This book was copywritten in 1920. In Appendix VII, Crowley gives his disciples some practical experiments in the studies of the black arts...

(a) Let him learn to write backwards, with either hand.
(b) Let him learn to walk backwards.
(c) Let him constantly watch, if convenient, cinematograph films, and **listen to phonograph records, reversed,** and let him so accustom himself to these that they appear natural and appreciable as a whole.
(d) Let him practise speaking backwards: thus for 'I am He' let him say, 'Eh ma I'.
(e) Let him learn to read backwards. In this it is difficult to avoid cheating one's self, as an expert reader sees a sentence at a glance. Let his disciple read aloud to him backwards, slowly at first, then more quickly.
(f) Of his own ingenium, let him devise other methods.

Remember this book was written in the early 1900's, way before anyone ever heard of rock and roll, or even backward masking! But even then Crowley was given some form of revelation to a spirit world that would be found 50 years later.

In the movie, *The Exorcist,* a scene is shown where a priest is attempting to cast a demon out of a girl. After turning on a tape recorder, the priest began to talk to the spirits in the little girl. The demons not only spoke in a deep man's voice, but was able to speak various languages. When the priest began to throw 'holy water' on the little girl, the demons tossed her about and screamed out words that made no sense. Later, the priest takes the recording to a friend who informs him, "This is English in reverse", and with the tape playing backwards, the voices of those demons were heard clearly. This of course, was a Hollywood version of demon powers, but could very possibly explain how some of these messages get on the songs.

Another movie about this was the recent movie, *Trick Or Treat,* a story about a young man who finds out that by playing his record backwards, he can communicate with his favorite rock star who had died during a satanic ritual. The movie depicted demonic forces coming through these backward messages.

"Kiss, Kiss, Kiss"
John Lennon, *Double Fantasy*

<u>Forward:</u> Yoko Ono speaking Japanese words, (translated,

"Hold me, hold me"), then the song starts with "Kiss, kiss, kiss, kiss me love/Just one kiss, kiss will do."
<u>Backward:</u> "Come in 666...666 from Satan...", then Yoko's Japanese words backward, "We shot John Lennon, we shot John Lennon, *I shot John Lennon."

It is certainly an odd "coincidence" that those are almost the exact same words **Mark David Chapman** said after shooting **John Lennon** to death on Dec.8, 1980!!! **Chapman** was a **John Lennon** fanatic. He owned all his records, knew all his songs, would often sign his name as 'John Lennon'; he even married a Japanese girl who looked like **Yoko Ono**, Lennon's wife. *People Magazine* quoted Chapman about killing Lennon, "It was almost as if I was on some kind of special mission that I could not avoid"[12] When you study all the things that led up to the killing of Lennon, it does seem more than just a normal homicide. Chapman flew all the way from Hawaii, stayed in an expensive hotel that night, signed out the next morning as 'John Lennon'. The next night he stayed at the YMCA near the Dakota, where Lennon lived. The next day, Chapman waited out in front of Dakota, along with a handful of other Lennon fans hoping to get an autograph. That afternoon around 4 p.m., Lennon and Yoko were on their way to a recording studio, but stopped long enough to signs some autographs. Chapman handed him the Double Fantasy album and Lennon signed it, "John Lennon-1980". That evening, Lennon and Yoko worked on the songs, "Walking On Thin Ice", with one line talking about taking a chance like "rolling a dice" and "It Happened", with a line "...it happened when we least expected it...". At about 10:50 p.m., Lennon and Ono were dropped off in front of their apartment, which they very rarely ever requested, and before they made it into the building, John was shot to death by "a fan", Mark Chapman. Interesting enough, the man who was originally going to play the part of 'John Lennon' in the television movie, "John and Yoko-A Love Story" was rejected because his real name was Mark Chapman.[13]

"When Electricity Came To Arkansas"
Black Oak Arkansas, *Raunch and Roll*

Forward: An number of unintelligible words that make no sense being spoken during the middle of the song, mixed with screaming and groans.
Backward: "Satan, Satan, Satan, he is God, he is God, he is God...(followed by a hideous laughing)"

No doubt, this is one of the most chilling examples of backward masking I've ever heard. **Harvey Jett**, the former lead guitartist for the group (now a preacher of the gospel) told me that the concert was performed before thousands of fans in Seattle, Washington. He said that the band would do this in alot of their concerts which would "flip everybody out". It wasn't until a number of years after **Harvey** got saved that he found out that their "weird words" were actually praising Satan! He did not even know what backward masking was at the time of this recording!!! **Harvey** claims that even **Jim**

Dandy, whose voice is heard above the others, did not even think that the Indian spirit he was calling on, "NATAS" would come out "SATAN" when played backwards!! I believe this one example helps prove that many of these groups are being used as "pawns" by Satan!

Dr. Israel Goldiamond, psychology professor at the University of Chicago, points out that the way in which sound and speech work make it very difficult to intentionally say something forwards which will make sense when played backwards. When you talk, you push air through your throat and use the muscles in your mouth and vocal chords to vary the pitches, tones, volume, and rhythm. Says Dr. Goldiamond, "Words are not spoken one at a time, you speak in bursts of several words between breaths, with valleys and hills in the sound energy levels coming out of your mouth. The meaning of sound is what we put into it, intelligibility comes out of the code a listener applies. It is only 'English' because we have all agreed that certain combinations of sounds and rhythms mean certain things. The effort it would take to say something in English which would mean one thing forwards and another backwards is incredible."[14]

How can one be affected by things backwards? It is a fact that the brain does things backwards automatically...

As you are looking at this page, the image will pass through the lens of your eyes and will be reversed so that you actually "see" it up-side-down. The brain takes the image and instantly reverses it again so that it appears right-side-up. So, in essence, the brain constantly reverses things.

One study concerning backward perception involves a professor of philosophy at the University of Wisconsin, Andrew Levine. This man is one of few in recorded history who has the unique ability of speaking fluently backwards. As fast as you can talk to him, he can simultaneously speak the exact words phonetically backwards. In other words, one could record Levine speaking backwards and reverse the recording and it would sound like "normal" talking. No real answers have been discovered as to how Levine is able to do this, but speech specialist Ray Kent claims, "When Professor Levine can translate backwards a word like refrigerator immediately, it suggests that he has in his brain some elementary speech units which enable him to begin to reverse words without having to stop and imagine each word or having to write the words down. For Levine it's like reading something reflected in a mirror."[15] Possible explanations include people who have this ability are able to tap into the "right hemisphere" or their "creative brain" and unscamble the backward words and bring them to the "left hemisphere" on a conscious level. If this is true, it could also be possible that the brain "unscambles" in all of us, except most do not have the ability to consciously perceive it.

Dyslexia is a common learning disability that is believed to be the result of biological defects in the brain between the right and left hemispheres. Dyslexics are not mentally retarded.

Most have average or superior intelligence; some are geniuses. Albert Einstein, Thomas Edison, Woodrow Wilson, French sculptor Auguste Rodin, and Hans Christian Andersen (who had to dictate his stories) all were dyslexic to some extent. Dyslexics frequently write certain numbers and letters backward, particularly b and d, p and q. Some never learn the difference between their left and right.

Dr. Samuel T. Orton, the neurologist and psychiatrist who stimulated interest in dyslexia in the U.S., suggests that it results when one of the two hemispheres of the brain failed to gain dominance over the other. At Beth Israel Hospital in Boston in 1979, Dr Albert Galaburda and Dr. Thomas Kemper examined the brain of a 20-year-old dyslexic killed in an accident. Routine autopsy studies showed nothing unusual, but examination under an electron microscope revealed an abnormal layering of certain nerve cells and tiny bits of gray matter where white matter should be in the left brain. The finding has been confirmed in three more autopsies.[16]

It has been found in studies that many people can memorize much more effectively when they reverse the sequence. For example, my brother-in-law has a "photographic memory". His trick is to take the number and repeat it in his mind backwards. He is able to recall phone numbers, addresses, and even license plates from his childhood, and he is in his 30's!

The scriptures have a great deal to say about our minds and the need to beware of what we feed our minds on...

In Deut.6:6-8, God instructed parents concerning child training:

> *"And these words, which I command thee*
> *this day, shall be in thine heart: And thou*
> *shalt teach them diligently unto thy children,*
> *and shalt talk of them when thou sittest in*
> *thine house, and when thou walkest by the*
> *way, and when thou liest down, and when*
> *thou risest up. And thou shalt bind them for*
> *a sign upon thine hand, and they shall be as*
> *frontlets between thine eyes. And thou shalt*
> *write them upon the posts of thy house, and*
> *on thy gates."*

I had the great opportunity to go on a Holy Land tour a few
years ago and saw that the Jewish men still had the practice of
wearing phylacteries (*phylax*, "watchman"; *phylokterion*, "a
safeguard"), which are two small black cases containing
portions of scripture. They are strapped on the left arm,
resting against the heart, and on the forehead, resting between
the eyes. It was symbolic of the fact that God's Word would
serve as the "watchman" or "a safeguard" against any attacks
on our heart and minds. Again, the word, subliminal, comes
from two latin words, *sub*, meaning "below", and *limen*,
meaning "threshold" or "lintel". It's important that every
Christian has his "lintel" or "doorpost" guarded with God's

Word!!! David said this in essence when he said, *"Thy Word have I hid in mine heart, that I might not sin against thee."* (Psa.119:11)

Phil.4:7 *"And the peace of God, which passeth all understanding, shall keep your hearts and minds through Christ Jesus."*

Isa.26:3 *"Thou wilt keep him in perfect peace, whose mind is stayed on thee: because he trusteth in thee."*

---

[1]News & Tribune, Jefferson City, Mo., March 6, 1983, pg.12-A
[2]Christianity Today, Jan.31, 1975
[3]Life Magazine, Oct.3, 1969
[4]Discover, April, 1985, pg.30
[5]Time, Sept.10, 1979, pg.71
[6]Psychology Today, April, 1980, pg.128
[7]Rolling Stone, Nov. 5-Dec. 10, 1987, pg.54
[8]Faces Magazine, Sept., 1984
[9]Cornerstone, Vol.11, Issue 62, pg.40
[10]Circus, July, 1975
[11]The Rolling Stone Interviews, 1967-1980, pg.317
[12]People Magazine
[13]Middletown Journal, July 25, 1985
[14]Cornerstone, Vol.11, Issue 62, pg.40
[15]People Magazine
[16]American Way, Apr.2, 1985, pg.87-91

SUICIDE

"...Suicide is the only way out..."
-Ozzy Osbourne, "Suicide Solution"

I guess I'll never forget this day...Carolyn and I were walking back out to the car after holding a Sunday Morning service in a northern state. A lady walked over to us, shook my hand and with a cold look said, "Brother Muncy, you came too late." After a few seconds of trying to figure out what she was saying, I asked, "What do you mean?" And just as cold as before she said, "You've come too late." Being totally confused as to what she meant I said, "I don't understand what you're trying to say." "Well, you are about a year too late. There was a boy who went to this church who needed to hear what you had to say this morning." She continued to tell me a story about a 15 or 16 year-old boy who came from a broken home who had been attending that church since he was about 12. He had a pretty hard life growing up and was known to be a trouble maker. He was really into rock music and especially the group, **The Who.** She said he had gotten to be more trouble than his Sunday School teacher could handle and was asked to stop coming to Sunday School. Shortly afterwards the young man's mother found him in his bedroom laying on the floor in his own blood with a bullet through his head. He had taken his own life. Next to his lifeless body was a note that read something like this...

"Mom, I have nothing else to live for. Nobody loves me. My favorite band, The Who, has just broke up, and now I have nothing to live for, so I'm going to kill myself and go to hell, cause I know the devil loves me."

Can you imagine the thoughts that were going through that mother's mind as she looked into the face of her dead son? But sad to say, as many as 2 million teenagers will attempt a similar act this year.[1] On the average, 16-17 teenagers will succeed in killing themselves on any given day. That's about one every hour and a half, and about 6,000 a year! This, of course, is a conservative count...

"The actual suicide rate is much higher than 6,000 per year, claims Mitch Anthony, executive director of the *National Suicide Help Center* in Rochester, Minn. "I would estimate it at more like 20,000. This is because many accidents — currently the leading cause of death among teenagers — are really suicides that are reported as accidents. I know of a woman whose son hung himself. Even as he hung by the rope, the police officer asked her if she wanted him to report it as an accident. I have interviewed funeral directors who have confirmed that many so-called accidents were really sui-cides."[2]

Suicide has become the #2 leading cause of death among young adults today in certain parts of the country[3], nation-wide it is the third leading cause of death among 15-24 year olds! In the last 20 years, the suicide rate among adolescents has skyrocketed by 300%.[4]

All these facts are causing shock across the nation. All the major TV networks, along with most major magazines and newspapers have devoted much time to the alarming growth in suicide among youth. Schools officials are constantly having to deal with the issue and, of course, many parents are searching for answers to "why".

What is behind this terrible plague? **Jesus** said about Satan,

> *"The thief cometh not, but for to steal, and to kill, and to destroy: I am come that they might have life, and that they might have it more abundantly."* (John 10:10)

No doubt when we get to the real root of the issue, we find the destroyer, Satan. He is the very *author of death*. We find that demons can cause people to become suicidal. In Mark 9:14-27, we read the account where a father brings his young son, possibly a teenager, to **Jesus** to be set free from a demon spirit. The demon spirit would cause this teenager to be thrown into fire or water *"to destroy him"* (v.22) or in other words; suicidal. Again in Mark 5:1-13, we read where **Jesus** cast "Legion" out of a man, and the spirits entered into about 2,000 swine, who in turn *"ran violently down a steep place into the sea...and were choked in the sea"* (v.13), killing all of them. Obviously, not everyone who commits suicide has a demon, but we know from these two examples that being demon-possed makes a person more likely to be suicidal.

We recently held a crusade at Wright State University where the sponsoring Pastor told me this sad story: He pulled into the driveway of the parsonage and noticed a parked car in the church parking lot. When he walked over to see if there was something he could do, he found a young man who had locked himself in the car with the intention of killing himself. The police were called, and as the Pastor attempted to try and talk the man out of suicide, he repeatedly cried, "They're trying to get me! They're trying to get me!" as he would swing at invisible people. After the police repeatedly tried to get him to unlock the door, they finally broke in through the car window to try and get the man, however, he took a knife and cut his neck and died in a matter of minutes. As the Police and the Pastor looked on, nothing could be done in time. Later the Pastor told me that he believed the young man's suicide was the result of a demonic attack!

Suicidal thoughts are not uncommon. Studies show most everyone has, at one time or an other, considered wanting to die. A recent *"Who's Who Among American High School Students"* survey found that 31% of 'A' or 'B' students had contemplated suicide.[5] Even Elijah and Job, and other great men in the Bible desired to stop living. But how does one explain the enormous growth in the number of young people killing themselves? What factors can be found which make a young person pull the trigger, jump from the window, or hang themselves to end their life?

I don't think we can put all the blame onto one particular thing, but no doubt the media as a whole has contributed a major role in glorifying death and suicide. And rock music is no stranger to the topics of death and suicide.

The following rock stars all died, victims of suicide...

•Johnny Ace (R&B vocalist, shot himself)
•Barney Bubbles (designer/artist of many rock album covers)
•Bobby Bloom (sang "Montego Bay", shot himself)
•Graham Bond (Magick, threw himself under a train)
•Ian Curtis (Joy Division, hung himself)
•Jeanine Deckers (recorded "Dominique" as the Singing Nun)
•Tom Evans (bass player for Badfinger, hung himself)
•Pete Ham (guitarist for Badfinger, hung himself)
•Donny Hathaway (Soul-pop singer, jumped to his death)
•Yogi Horton (drummer for Luther Vandross, jumped to his death)
•Terry Kath (Chicago guitarist, shot himself)
•Richard Manuel (The Band, hung himself)
•Phyllis Major (wife of Jackson Brown)
•Pete Meaden (The former manager for the Who, pills)

•**Joe Meek,** (rock producer, shot himself)
•**Phil Ochs** (singer/songwriter, hung himself)
•**Danny Rapp** (wrote "At The Hop", shot himself)
•**David Savoy, Jr.** (Manager of the group Husker Du)
•**Rory Storm** (with the Hurricanes, sleeping pills)
•**Larry Williams** (singer, shot himself)
•**Paul Williams** (The Temptations, shot himself)
•**Mary Woodson** (Al Green's girlfriend, shot herself)

Marianne Faithful, singer and former girlfriend of **Mick Jagger** attempted suicide in 1969. Who knows the many more attempts that never make the news.

All one must do is listen closely to the message of suicide in many songs put out by popular artists...

Elton John, who has a song entitled, "Think I'm Gonna Kill Myself" which says,

> "I'm getting bored being part of mankind. There's not alot to do no more, this race is a waste of time. People rushing everywhere, swarming around like flies. Think I'll buy a forty-four and give 'em all a surprise. Yeah, think I'm gonna kill myself, cause a little suicide."

Now tell me, my friend, what value can be found in such a song? Absolutely NONE!! But isn't it sad that guys like

Elton John seemingly sees nothing wrong with it! But...do these songs really cause people to commit suicide? Well, we cannot blame rock music for all our ills, but we must be open to the fact that the media, and especially, music, has a platform that IS SAYING something!!! Jerry Johnston, an expert in the area of suicide documents a case where, in March of 1982, 17-year old Alan Stubbs ran a hose from the exhaust into the family car. At approximately 4:00 A.M., Alan died while listening to "Somebody Saved My Life Tonight."[6] (Elton John's "Somebody Saved My Life Tonight" is about a depressed boy who tries to kill himself at 4:00 in the morning!!!!!!!)

Probably the most controversial of all songs regarding suicide is **Ozzy Osbourne's** song, "Suicide Solution" off the *Blizzard Of Oz* album. After referring to various ways one might commit suicide, such as wine, whiskey, and hanging, the song says, "...Suicide is the only way out...". The controversy became even more intense when the parents of a California teenager who shot himself in the head while listening to Suicide Solution, sued Ozzy.

Ozzy, of course, denied that the song was encouraging suicide, and claimed it was written about the late **Bon Scott** who died from too much alcohol, the "suicide solution". (Oddly enough, I have a photo of Ozzy in my files sitting in a chair with a gun to his head, which appeared in the August, '83 issue of *Hit Parader* magazine, a popular rock magazine.) A trial judge dismissed the lawsuit on grounds that the lyrics are protected by the First Amendment. Recent findings have disclosed the use of subliminals on the song which go even further against **Ozzy's** statement concerning the supposed innocence of "Suicide Solution". *The Institute For Bio-Acoustics Research* (IBAR) found a "masked message" on the song which says, "...get the gun and try it! Shoot, shoot, shoot..."

Another song that **Ozzy** sang, while he was with the group, **Black Sabbath**, was "Paranoid", which says,

> "Think I'll lose my mind, if I don't find
> something to gratify, can you help me? Oh,
> won't you blow my brains, Oh yeah! And so
> as you hear these words, that are in you now,
> if I state, I tell you to end your life, I wish I
> could mine; it's too late."

"Killing Yourself To Live" by **Black Sabbath** is full of negative statements concerning life...

"Die Young", also by **Black Sabbath**, gives the idea that life isn't worth living, so one should just "die young, die young, die young"...*RIP* magazine claimed, "While Black Sabbath reigned as the princes of doom music, more people probably committed suicide with Black Sabbath records on their turntables than the amount of all other heavy-metal bands combined."[7]

Other songs such as, "Die Young, Stay Pretty", by **Blondie** speak of dying while still young, so as to avoid losing your beauty...

"Death Can Be Fun", by the **Kamikaze Klones** speaks for itself, named after the suicidal kamikaze fighters during WW II...

"Don't Fear The Reaper", by **Blue Oyster Cult**, which speaks of a suicidal love-pact like Romeo and Juliet...

"Goodbye Cruel World", by **Pink Floyd**, speaks of one ending it all to get out of this mess the world is in...

Suicidal Tendencies, which have an album out showing a fan of the group wearing a T-shirt depicting someone blowing their brains out, have a song called, "Suicidal Failure", which says:

> "...I don't want to live. I don't know why. I
> don't have no reasons, I just want to die..."

"Devil's Child", by **Judas Priest**, speaks of young people who offer themselves as a "human sacrifice"...The group has a lawsuit over their heads involving an incident where two young men shot themselves in the head after listening to **Judas Priest** albums for hours.[8] Apparently, eighteen-year-old Raymond Belknap and his nineteen-year-old friend James Vance spent about five hours listening over and over again to the *Stained Class* album while smoking marijuana and drinking beer in Belknap's bedroom. During their afternoon together, they apparently made a suicide pact, according to a statement Vance later made to the Sparks, Nevada police. Armed with a sawed-off shotgun, the two later attempted to carry out the pact in a nearby church-school yard. Belknap died instantly after shooting himself in the head; Vance's suicide attempt left his face permanently disfigured.[9]

"Shoot To Thrill", a song by **AC/DC**, has been repeatedly quoted as documentation for suicidal thought which encourages the listener to pull the trigger for that ultimate thrill...

One group, called **Suicide**, has an album which shows a young person on the cover in a depressed state with no answer but suicide to consider.

CH3 have an album entitled, *Fear Of Life*, depicting a young man with a gun pointed at himself, evidently more afraid to live than die.

Blessed Death sings, "Take me blessed death. Give me blessed death. Free me blessed death. Save me blessed death."

"Still Life", by **Iron Maiden**, speaks about spirits trying to get this kid to drown himself with someone else...

"Consider me gone", sung by **Sting**, speaks of a man in hopeless despair with nothing but death to look forward to...

"Jump", a hit song by **Van Halen**, was written from an actual suicidal situation. **David Roth** claimed, "I was watching TV and there was some stud on top of the Arco Tower who was ready to punch out early and there was a crowd of people down 35 stories on the street and it occurred to me there's always at least one scum in the crowd who says: 'Go ahead and Jump'!"[10] (One line of the song repeatedly says, "You might as well jump...")

"Russian Roulette", is the title of one of **Accept's** albums with the cover depicting a young man with a gun in his hand as he challenges a friend to join him in the deadly, suicide game. I remember doing an assembly in Ohio for about 300 students at a small, rural high school. Through out the whole presentation, a number of kids were mocking me and making comments about my "stupid speech" on suicide. Little did anyone know that while I was speaking, there was a student who had stayed home that day to do the very thing I was speaking against. And while playing a "game" of Russian roulette he shot himself in the head. Not surprisingly, the next day no one was laughing or making fun because now it was a reality!

"Can't stand losing you", sung by **Police**, is about suicide. The song says:

> "I can't see the point in another day, for
> nobody listens to a word I say. You can call
> it lack of confidence, but to carry on living

> doesn't make no sense...You'll be sorry when
> I'm dead, all this guilt will be on your head.
> I guess you call it suicide, but I'm too full to
> swallow my pride..."

Eddie and the Hot Rods have their album covers depicting suicide; one by hanging, another by a gun to the head...

A "best of" album made up of various punk groups entitled, *Let's Die*, glorifies death and suicide right on the cover.

Now, just by naming these few examples, can you see the possibility that some rock music can be an encourager of suicide? Especially for teenagers, who are emotionally at a very fragile time in their lives. You see, sometimes all one needs to do something foolish is a little encouragement from the right source. And in this case, music can be that "right source"!! Put yourself in the shoes of a depressed teenager, having a hard time in school, afraid of a nuclear holocaust, or seeing your parents go through a divorce, and then imagine hearing one of your favorite groups encourage escape through suicide...even if it is a small factor, it still is too much.

But why do they do it...why do people kill themselves? Well, there would possibly be as many different reasons as there are suicides, but I have found 5 basic reasons for suicide. One thing is sure, as a young friend of mine said, **"Suicide is a permanent solution to a temporary problem!"** In studying the scripture, I came across five suicides, and each one represents a different reason why people take their lives...

(1) FEAR OF THE FUTURE...1 Sam.31:4

In this case, we find backslidden King Saul who is so afraid of what the future might hold, that he goes to a witch and tries to call the prophet Samuel from the dead, (a sin called, 'necromancy'; talking to the dead, forbidden in the scriptures). With a message of doom, the next day Saul takes his own life with his sword. He had been wounded in battle and was afraid that if the enemy found him, they would torture him. He would rather take his life than to even try and escape the battle with his wounds.

Many people today have the same fatalistic view of life...they are more afraid to live than they are to die. I have a newspaper clipping about a boyfriend and girlfriend who took their own lives. They left a note that they were doing this because they felt the world would not last much longer, and they would rather end it now than to have to face a nuclear explosion! That was over 4 years ago! What a waste! That's fatalism!

Suicide is not the fear of death, but the fear of life! During the depression in the late 1920's, many wealthy businessmen took their own lives because they didn't think they could face the future. Today, many young people see another possible depression, the threat of war, the bomb, and other fearful things, and decide it would be better to die now, than later. Jesus predicted this time would come in Luke 21:25-26:

> *"And there shall be signs in the sun, and in the moon, and in the stars; and upon the earth distress of nations, with perplexity; the sea and the waves roaring; Men's hearts failing them for fear, and for looking after those things which are coming on the earth..."*

Suicidal Tendencies, a very popular punk group, have a song called, "Memories of Tomorrow" which says:

> "...I'll kill myself. I'd rather die. If you could see the future, you'd know why..."

By the way, I can't remember ever speaking at a school, christian or secular, in the last year and a half that I haven't had some teenager ask me what I thought about their favorite group - **Suicidal Tendencies**.

One thing is for sure...I may not know what the future holds, but I know *Who* holds the future...and *He* holds my hand!! Young person, life is worth living even during the bad times!! You can face the future if you put your trust in **Jesus**! He promised to never leave or forsake us, and that He will be with us till the end of the world. (see Matt. 28:20; Heb.13:5)

If you are really concerned about your future, you would do well to think about your eternal future!! Suicide only makes your future worse!!! Because the scriptures plainly teach murderers will spend their future in an eternal hell, and suicide is the *murder* of oneself!!!

> *"But the fearful, and unbelieving, and the abominable, and murderers, and whoremongers, and sorcerers, and idolaters, and all liars, shall have their part in the lake which burneth with fire and brimstone: which is the second death." (Rev.21:8)*

and again in 1 Cor. 3:16-17 Paul plainly taught against suicide...

> *"Know ye not that ye are the temple of God, and that the Spirit of God dwelleth in you? If any man defile the temple of God, him shall God destroy; for the temple of God is holy, which temple ye are."*

(2)A POPULAR FAD...1 Sam. 31:5

The very next suicide in the Bible took place just moments after the first suicide. It was Saul's armour bearer who watched as Saul took his life, then he did the exact same thing! Without hesitation, he fell on his own sword and ended his life!

In Japan, an 18-year-old female pop star, **Yukiko Okada** committed suicide, and according to one report, as many as 34 young people took their own lives within weeks of her death.[11]

It's common knowledge that when someone commits suicide, usually it will be copied by someone else. A perfect example of this was in Plano, Texas where, during '83-'84, a rash of teenage suicides took place. One right after another. It was like the "domino-effect". Studies have shown that suicides many times fall in successions, especially after well-publicized stories. For example, not long ago, I held a meeting in the state of New Jersey where four teenagers took their lives. They parked their car in a garage and asphyxiated themselves. Each one left their death letters. Less than a week later, two teenage girls in Illinois did the exact same thing! And all across the nation, reports came in of teens who were parking their cars in garages and taking their lives. In one city we were in, a young girl set her clock for the middle of the night and went down to the garage and turned her parents car on and laid on the seat. In a short time she was dead, but because the garage was attached to the house, the fumes traveled into the house and the whole family died!!!

In some areas, a suicide-pact will be started when a group of friends agree to commit suicide. This, of course, is made to look like real devotion, much like the Romeo and Juliet story. Movies many times will inspire young lovers to die for each other. What a silly idea!!! Why not *live* and *enjoy* each other, than die and *never* see one another again!!!

On Feb. 4,1984, Robbie De La Vallicre hanged himself. He was 13 years-old. Police speculate that the movie he recently saw, "An Officer And A Gentleman", may have influenced his action. In Westchester community after the suicide of Robbie, there were six suicides by March of that year. The victims did not know each other — 4 of the 6 followed the copy cat pattern of death by hanging... "Officer and Gentleman" style.[12] Some see this fad as a chance for fame, to get your name in the paper. Think of it though...people are actually "dying" to be noticed!!

Listen to me, teenager, suicide is permanent!! Oh, you might be missed for awhile, people will no doubt grieve over your death, but soon the tears will be wiped away and not long afterwards people will go about their own business. The world will not stop turning simply because you died!! In a couple of years, you will just be a faint memory in the minds of a few loved ones! Remember this verse...

> *"For in death there is no remembrance of thee: in the grave who shall give thee thanks?"*
> (Psa.6:5)

Friend, don't do something stupid like suicide...*we need you here*...life is worth living! Forget the popular fad...it'll lose it's popularity like every other fad has!!! If you really want to be popular, give your all to **Jesus** and be a "World-Changer"!!!

(3) SELF-PITY...2 Sam.17:23

In this passage, we read of the end of a man's life whose last years were "hell on earth" because of his unforgiveness and hatred toward King David. His name was Ahithophel, and he was consumed with the desire to get even with the man who committed adultery with his granddaughter, Bathsheba! He had the perfect plans to "get back" to David, and was responsible for an planned overthrow. Later his plans were all rejected and he was driven to suicide!

Like Ahithophel, many people are consumed with unforgiveness and burn with hatred toward someone. Many times these people become so frustrated with their feelings, they will do something drastic like kill themselves, supposing this in itself will "get back" at whomsoever. *Suicide is the ultimate selfish act!!!* A young man kills himself to "get back" at his girlfriend who broke up with him. A young lady kills herself because her parents get a divorce. A couple of teenagers kill themselves because their parents won't let them date! I have a clipping from the local newspaper where a young man killed himself after his parents had refused to let him get plastic surgery so he would look like Michael Jackson!!!! Imagine that! Of course, all this is rooted in self-pity..."I can't have it my way, so I'll show them!"

The group mentioned earlier, **Suicidal Tendencies**, has another song called "Suicide's An Alternative/You'll Be Sorry", saying,

> "...Sick and tired, and no one cares; Sick of myself, don't wanna live; Sick of living, gonna die..."

Self-pity has caused countless thousands to live a life of misery!! So you've been hurt! So you lost your job! So they don't care! So you've had a hard life! **Join the crowd...we** *all* have things to complain about! But things can get much worse, eternally speaking, if you use suicide to solve your problems! Stop feeling sorry for yourself and start helping others with their problems!!! Visit a child-care unit in a hospital...visit an old-folks home...go to a place where people *really* are hurting!!! Get your eyes off yourself *and start being a blessing instead of a burden*!!!

(4) HOPELESSNESS...1 Kings 16:18

In this story, Zimri was a man who came to "the end of his rope"! It's odd how he killed himself...his world was caving in on him, so he goes into the house and literally burns it in on him! What a terrible way to die! But when you are without hope, you'll do alot of foolish things.

Solomon referred to this feeling of hopelessness in Ecc.2:17,

> *"Therefore **I** hated life; because the work*
> *that is wrought under the sun is grievous*
> *unto me: for all is vanity and vexation of*
> *spirit."*

We are living in what can be a depressing age! It's a hopeless society outside of God. My Pastor often said as I was growing up, "I don't see how unsaved people can make it without the Lord!" Sad to say, many don't...we hear of little children as young as 6, 7, and 8 years-old killing themselves. The depression that some kids go through is horrible! No doubt, one of the problems today is that children are being pushed into a grown-up world, too fast, which is full of trouble!

Of course, many kids get their outlook on life from many popular singers, who sing empty songs from an empty heart! One favorite among heavy metal lovers is the group, **Metallica**. On their album, "Ride the Lighting" is a song called, "Fade to Black", which carelessly states:

> "Life it seems will fade away, drifting further everyday. Getting lost within myself, nothing matters, no one else. I have lost the will to live, simply nothing more to give, there is nothing more for me, need the end to set me free"

I just got a clipping out of the paper with the story of a young man who committed suicide and used the words of that song in his death letter!

Rock and roll offers no hope, Nashville offers no hope, Hollywood offers no hope, and with all the world offers, it cannot offer hope...but, thanks be to God, as Christians, we have hope, and we are to be:

> *"...ready always to give an answer to every man that asketh you a reason OF THE HOPE*

THAT IS IN YOU..."
(1 Pet.3:15)

Of course, *that hope is Christ Jesus our Lord!!!* Another beautiful passage concerning this is Eph.2:12-14, which says,

> *"That at that time ye were without Christ, being aliens from the commonwealth of Israel, and strangers from the covenants of promise, having no hope, and without God in the world: But now in Christ Jesus ye who sometimes were far off are made nigh by the blood of Christ. For he is our peace..."*

Yes, there is hope!! That hope can only be found in the **Lord Jesus Christ!** If you listen to the hopeless, you'll end up hopeless! Tune your heart into what God is saying and what He has to offer you!

(5) SIN AND GUILT...Matt. 27:3-5

Probably the most well-known of all the suicides in the Bible is the suicide of Judas, a former disciple and treasurer of the **Lord Jesus**. After seeing his terrible sin, he went and hung himself and then fell headlong into the valley below, where his bowels gushed out. (Acts 1:18) **No suicide is as tragic as that of Judas Iscariot.** He had it made...he could have repented and spent a lifetime of service for God, preaching the Gospel and winning thousands to Christ! The Lord would have easily forgiven Judas, just as He did Peter!

Today, the name Judas is almost a curse...no one names their child, Judas. Not so much because he betrayed the Lord, but because of how he dealt with his terrible sin. No doubt, Satan, who had filled his heart to do this (Lk.22:3), also told him that he could never be forgiven. I want to go on record as saying Judas had hope, if he would have simply humbled himself and repented; his life would have been a tremendous testimony to the grace of God! I know some may disagree, but I believe Jesus meant it when He said, "*...him that cometh to me I will in no wise cast out.*" (John 6:37)

Black Sabbath has an old album called, *Master of Reality*, with a couple of songs that I usually close our rock seminars with. One song is called, "After Forever". When first read, the song appears to almost encourage the listener to come to God, but a close look at the words show the same message Satan fed Judas:

> "...I think it was true it was people like you
> that crucified Christ! I think it is sad the
> opinion you had was the only one voiced.
> Will you be so sure when your day is near,
> say you don't believe? You had the chance
> but you turned it down, now you can't re-
> trieve..."

My friend, that is a lie! My Bible tells me in 2 Pet. 3:9 that God is "*not willing that any should perish, but that all should come to repentance.*"!!!!!!!! It's not too late for you! If you still have breath in your body, God is being merciful to you! He doesn't want you to perish! Your enemy isn't God, it's SIN! Turn your back on your sin right now, repent from your heart, and He promises that He will not only forgive but also cleanse you from your sin...no guilt!!!

Think about it...when was the last time you heard a rock and roll song offer it's listener forgiveness? When was the last time you heard a rock and roll singer tell about being forgiven and set free from guilt? Well, they never will until they come in contact with the ROCK THAT DOESN'T ROLL...JESUS CHRIST!!!!

In closing this chapter, let me tell you about the first "Jail House Rock"...Acts 16 sets the stage for the story...

Paul and Silas were in Europe preaching the Gospel. As they were traveling through a small town called Phillippi, they were met by a young girl who was possessed with a demon that gave her the ability to be a fortune-teller. Paul cast the spirit out of her and that's when the trouble started! They were brought before the rulers of the city and beaten and then thrown into prison! A jailor was charged to keep them safely, so he threw them into an inner chamber of the prison. Well, about midnight, Paul and Silas were praying and singing when all of a sudden, an earthquake hit so that the foundations of the prison were shaken, causing the prison doors to open and the chains to be loosened. The jailor, who had been asleep, saw what had happened and, supposing that all the prisoners had escaped, drew his sword and was getting ready <u>to kill himself</u>, but Paul yelled and told the jailor not to take his life for they were all there. The jailor got a light and ran into their cell and fell on his knees and asked Paul and Silas, *"Sirs, what must I do to be saved?"* Paul gladly told the man, *"Believe on the **Lord Jesus Christ**, and thou shalt be saved, and thy house."* (Acts 16:11-34) Thank God that Paul saw the man before he committed suicide! He was saved and baptized that night along with his whole family!

The story can end the same way for you...maybe YOU have thought about killing yourself, thinking it was the only escape, but you have been reading this book and God is speaking to you. *Stop running* from His love and forgiveness that *He offers you freely*, and simply put your trust in the **Lord Jesus Christ**! Turn to the end of the book right now and read carefully God's Plan of Salvation, and receive **Jesus Christ as Lord** of your life!!!

<u>Additional Help</u>

<u>Warning Signs Of Suicide</u>

<u>Check for these symptoms...</u>
√Change in sleeping or eating patterns
√Sudden drop in grades, desire to quit school
√Severe neglect of personal appearance
√Abrupt changes in personality or behavior
√Verbal warnings of threats of suicide

√Previous suicide attempts
√Giving away special personal possessions
√A serious illness
√Divorce, loss of friends
√A relative, friend or acquaintance who committed suicide
√Leaves diaries, poems, letters, drawings to be found
√Suddenly appears peaceful during a crisis
√Withdraws from friends and family
√Death in the family
√A victim of child abuse, rape, or domestic violence
√Persistent boredom
√Sudden interest or preoccupation with death
√Carelessness, accident prone
√Feelings of hopelessness and insignificance

How To Prevent A Suicide

•Take direct and indirect threats seriously
•Ask, "Are you thinking of suicide?", then, "How would you do it?" (If they have a method, this is a serious sign!)
•Encourage the person to express their feelings
•Listen carefully
•Never belittle a person's problems
•Show the importance of life
•Pray for them while holding their hands
•Ask them to turn their life over to Christ and be saved
•Notify someone else of the situation — family, minister, etc.
•Rebuke Satan's hold on their minds

•Follow-up until complete victory is seen

---

[1]Dr. Seymour Perlin, board chairman of the National Youth Suicide Center in Washington, D.C. as quoted from Christianity Today, March 20, 1987, pg.19
[2]Christianity Today, March 20, 1987
[3]The Findlay Courier, July, 1985
[4]Youthworker, Spring, 1984, pg.12
[5]Associated Press, "Teens: Drugs, suicide major problems"
[6]"Why Suicide", Jerry Johnston, pg.71
[7]RIP, June, 1987, pg.40
[8]Blast, Aug.8, 1987, pg.18
[9]Rolling Stone, Dec. 1, 1988
[10]Creem, May, 1984, pg.36
[11]Rolling Stone, May, 1986, pg. 17
[12]NFD Journal, June, 1984, pg.54

_______________________________**11**
Occult

Some people honestly ask why I even think Satan would use rock music. First of all, I think it's obvious...a recent survey found that the average teenager listens to rock music about 4-6 hours a day! Satan would have a be a real dummy not to get his hands on it! But the real reason why I believe Satan is using rock music is because music is an area he has always been very much a part of. We know from two different passages of scriptures that Satan, also called Lucifer before his fall, actually used music...

First, in Isaiah.14:9-15, we read,

> *"Hell from beneath is moved for thee to meet*
> *thee at thy coming: it stirreth up the dead for*
> *thee, even all the chief ones of the earth; it*

> *hath raised up from their thrones all the kings of the nations. All they shall speak and say unto thee, Art thou also become weak as we? art thou become like unto us? Thy pomp is brought down to the grave, and **the noise of thy viols**: the worm is spread under thee, and the worms cover thee. **How art thou fallen from heaven, O Lucifer**, son of the morning! how art thou cut down to the ground, which didst weaken the nations! For thou hast said in thine heart, I will ascend into heaven, I will exalt my throne above the stars of God: I will sit also upon the mount of the congregation, in the sides of the north: I will ascend above the heights of the clouds; I will be like the most High. Yet thou shalt be brought down to hell, to the sides of the pit."*

Notice the phrase which I highlighted, **"*the noise of thy viols*"**. Here we find a reference to the noise of a musical instrument connected with Lucifer. Viols are a type of string instrument. We get the word, "violin", from this root word. Today, the **viol** can represent a wide range of musical instruments. Everything from the guitar to the piano uses strings, and with modern technology, even a computer chip can reproduce the sounds of hundreds of various stringed instruments. The orchestrated music that came from Lucifer was breathtaking in its sounds, for he was, no doubt, the greatest musician that God ever created, which we'll prove later.

Lucifer would use viols to play rich, soothing music in the presence of God around His throne, which would set the atmosphere for worship.

Viols are referred to three other times in the scriptures: (Isaiah 5:12, Amos 5:23; 6:5). Actually, each time that viols are mentioned, a negative connotation are given to them. Not that viols or any other string instrument is evil in and of itself, but for the purpose it was being used. Sad to say, Lucifer has taken a beautiful gift and used it to tear down rather to build up. The music that he played was a part of worship and praise to God, but today, some music is worshipping and praising something else...sex, money, drugs, violence, and a multitude of other gods.

This was basically the same type of music that was played by David that drove the demons from Saul in 1 Samuel 16:23 when he played the harp. Music can actually do this; it can *drive* demons away! And if it can do that, it only seems natural that some music can also *attract* demon powers! What determines this is the anointing of the Spirit of God and the heart of the one who is playing the instrument. The Bible repeatedly tells us to play music unto the Lord .

The second passage of scripture that refers to Lucifer connected with music is found in Ezekial 28:13-15:

"Thou hast been in Eden the garden of God;
every precious stone was thy covering, the

> *sardius, topaz, and the diamond, the beryl,
> the onyx, and the jasper, the sapphire, the
> emerald, and the carbuncle, and gold: the
> workmanship of thy tabrets and of thy pipes
> was prepared in thee in the day that thou
> wast created. Thou art the anointed cherub
> that covereth; and I have set thee so: thus
> wast upon the holy mountain of God; thou
> hast walked up and down in the midst of the
> stones of fire. Thou wast perfect in thy ways
> from the day that thou wast created, till
> iniquity was found in thee."*

Again we find Satan referred to before being cast out of heaven. He was a beautiful and anointed cherub covering the throne of God. All types of precious stones covered him while it also says he used musical instruments! A trip to my *Strong's Concordance* revealed the Hebrew word translated, *"workmanship"*, literally means his "working administration, his occupation or employment". In this case, it was the occupation or working administration of Lucifer to use tabrets and pipes...two musical instruments as the chief musician in heaven!

The first instrument, **tabrets**, is the root word from which we get our word, "tambourine". It is referring to a small drum or any type of percussion instrument. Some people see anything that has rhythm or a beat as something evil, but it is clear from this verse, that even in heaven, God gave Lucifer not only the anointed ability, but also the instruments to produce rhythm! Now, I will be the first to tell you that Satan has perverted this music, but I also know that the Bible encourages praising the Lord on percussion instruments, such as found in Psalms 150! A small study in the scriptures will show over 30 verses that encourage the use of rhythm, used with cymbals, bells, tambourines, and clapping! The point is, though, that Lucifer was in heaven playing music with rhythm before *the very throne of God*. This was a time of great rejoicing around the throne...

> *"When the morning stars* sang together,*
> *and all the sons of God shouted for joy?"*
> (Job 38:7)

(* Some teach that many of the references to stars in the scriptures are actually angels. See Rev.12:4)

The next musical instrument mentioned were, **pipes**. Being plural, it refers to all types of wind instruments, which no doubt blended various tones and pitches, giving off a full range of harmonious sounds. From this, we get all types of brass, trumpets, cornets, flutes, and organ's sounds that are very common place still today. Here, again, we find instruments that in and of themselves are not evil, but can be used to worship the Lord. Paul gave some good advice here...

> *"And even things without life giving sound,*
> *whether pipe or harp, except they give a dis-*

> *tinction in the sounds, how shall it be known what is piped or harped? For if the trumpet give an uncertain sound, who shall prepare himself to the battle?"* (1 Corinthians 14:7-8)

So we see that from the body of Lucifer came a tremendous unity of melody (pipes), harmony, (viols) and rhythm (tabrets) which blended together in such perfection that it would just naturally cause one to be lifted up to the very heart of God. Understand, that even though this angel used music, it actually began out of the heart of God. God is the creator of music! Music has the unique ability to lift one's spirit into a state of worship; it can help soften your heart, or fill you with feelings of emotion and aid you in expression of "joy unspeakable"!

Now, one can only imagine the magnificent, commanding charisma that would penetrate your soul and spirit as you would listen to this splendid creation called, Lucifer. His music was perfect, never out of tune or even off beat! He was referred to as "perfect in thy ways" and God has never said that about anyone else. His name, Lucifer means, "the shining one". Ezekial 28:12 says he was, "perfect in beauty", but this became his downfall. (All who have been blessed with talents and beauty read this carefully!) He became lifted up with pride and soon began to desire a share in the worship that he was giving. Before long, he wanted to dethrone God and be worshipped himself. This is when the first rebellion began, and it has continued even unto this time.

The thing that is significant here is how music has played such an important part in *rebellion*. The music that Lucifer played *became* the vehicle he uses now to bring worship to himself and his system. He has been successful in using and perverting a God-given talent to draw others away from God. Today, we have a number of tremendously talented musicians that have fallen in the very same trap Satan fell into...Pride of one's own beauty and ability! If you are blessed with talent and beauty, give glory to God! Use your talent and beauty to praise **Jesus**!

Just as Lucifer, the "shinning one" became Satan, the "arch enemy of God"; in the same way, many beautiful, talented musicians have also become enemies and aliens of our great God and Saviour, the **Lord Jesus Christ**. So much of today's music is anti-Christ in its contents. Many groups will even go so far as to vocally blaspheme **Jesus**! Ask them why and they really don't know...just a gimmick maybe? Hardly! There is a spirit that works in them! Paul talked about it in Ephesians 2:2,

> *"Wherein in time past ye walked according to the course of this world, according to the prince of the power of the air, the spirit that now worketh in the children of disobedience:"*

One example that comes to mind, is **Bruce Springsteen**, who "was once asked at Catholic school to draw a picture of **Jesus**

— and handed in a drawing of Christ crucified on a guitar!"[2] Sad to say, many are using music to mock Christ instead of praise Him!

This is where the occult comes in. The word, *"occult"* actually means, "hidden, secretive". Much of the draw of the occult world is from the fact it is so secretive! As the saying goes, 'curiosity killed the cat'! So many people are sucked into the practices of the occult simply because they are curious and they don't want to be "in the dark", but that is the very thing that puts them in the dark: looking into the occult, into the unknown. Some of the biggest selling movies are occult-type movies. The following movies are all-time tops in box office sells...

The Exorcist (1973), $89,000,000.
Gremlins (1984), $79,000,000.
Poltergeist (1982), $38,700,000.
The Amityville Horror (1979), $35,000,000.
The Shining (1980), $30,900,000.[3]

This only goes to show the expense that people will pay to look into the supernatural and demonic! Not to mention the tens of millions spent on the *Friday the 13th* and the *Nightmare on Elm Street* series!

Many boast of the fact that they are not aware of such movies, but we, as Christians, are not to be "ignorant of Satan's devices", but we are to strip away the gloss of Satan's kingdom and expose it for what it is! Ephesians 5:11 says,

> *"And have no fellowship with the unfruitful*
> *works of darkness, but rather **reprove** them."*

That word, *reprove*, simply means "to tell a fault, to rebuke". We are told not to fellowship or participate with the darkness, but rebuke it and openly oppose and expose it! Notice carefully, it didn't say, "ignore it"...it says, "reprove it"!

Recently we had a pastor call and inform us that our crusade to be held in his area was cancelled. His reason was that after talking to some of the people in the church, they felt that our ministry was bringing this teaching into the church and, (these are his very words) "Christians should be ignorant of the things of the world". Now I guess that sounds real holy, or spiritual but it's neither! Just the opposite is true! 2 Corinthians 2:11 says,

> *"Lest Satan should get an advantage of us:*
> *for we are not ignorant of his devices."*

Another church cancelled us after the Pastor and his associate came to one of our crusades. His complaint was, even though he knew the youth were involved in most of the rock groups and attended most of the horror movies, that our message brought it out in the open! (That's exactly what we are suppose to be doing...exposing darkness!)

While we are trying to hide it from ourselves, the occult is seeing a real revival among the youth today! For no other reason, this alone should be enough to alarm us! Look at the average rock concert today; grossing into the millions of dollars per night in huge auditoriums and stadiums across this nation! Thousands and thousands of teenagers will stand in line for hours to get a good seat! Then with hands in the air, as their favorite group hits the stage, screams and cheers can be heard from miles away! What a loss! What a tragedy! For on those stages stand confused, lonely and often times, stoned out of their minds, entertainers who are being used as pawns by Satan to deceive and lie about life! But the master of deception has painted it to seem so attractive. He should, for he knows the power of music!

Some will think I'm referring only to some hard core or heavy metal band who blare out obscenities and sing about worshipping the devil. While obviously I'm not excluding them, I'm actually referring to any group, be it a "satanic" group or not, that glorifies the occult in its many forms. When we refer to the occult, we mean more than just satan worship. That is just one small part of the occult world. Satan is not so much interested that you worship him, as much as he is that you <u>don't</u> worship God!! Anything that can draw you away from God is what he is concerned about! Be it "innocent" astrology or sacrificing babies!

The Bible lays out nine forbidden occult practices in Deut. 18:9-12. These nine practices were called, *"abominations"* by

God. By calling them abominations, God says these are the most "detestable, loathsome, disgusting" things that mankind could ever do. God hates these practices because of what they do to all humanity. They are trafficking in demon powers! They are one-way tickets to Hell!

God gave these commands to people who had served as slaves in Egypt for about 400 years. They were the chosen people of God. They had become bound and enslaved by a nation of idol worshippers. During this time, Egypt was one of the most powerful nations on the earth. Tragically, they were deeply immersed in idolatry and occult practices. They worshipped the planets, the stars, the moon, the sun, the river, snakes, bugs, and almost anything imaginable. They were the great pyramid builders, and they are still admired for their workmanship in their tombs and embalming, but they believed in reincarnation. They would not honor the God of the Bible.

Once God delivered his people out of pagan-stricken Egypt, He commanded them not to join in with any other nation, because of these same pagan practices, but to worship only Him. Sad to say, Israel did not obey God. Psa. 106:34-39 tells us...

> *"They did not destroy the nations, concerning whom the Lord commanded them: But were mingled among the heathen, and learned their works. And they served their idols: which were a snare unto them. Yea,*

> *they sacrificed their sons and their daughters unto devils, And shed innocent blood, even the blood of their sons and of their daughters, whom they sacrificed unto the idols of Canaan: and the land was polluted with blood. Thus were they defiled with their own works, and went a whoring with their own inventions. Therefore was the wrath of the Lord kindled against his people, insomuch that he abhorred his own inheritance. And he gave them into the hand of the heathen; and they that hated them ruled over them."*

What was the reason for Israel's failure to stand against their enemies? They *"were mingled among the heathen, and learned their works"*! God plainly told them not to do this! Read this carefully, Deut. 18:9-14; there are nine of them:

> *"When thou art come into the land which the Lord thy God giveth thee, thou shalt not learn to do after the abominations of those nations. There shall not be found among you any one that 1) maketh his son or his daughter to pass through the fire, or that 2) useth divination, or 3) an observer of times, or 4) an enchanter, or 5) a witch, or 6) a charmer, or 7) a consulter with familiar spirits, or 8) a wizard, or 9) a necromancer. For all that*

do these things are an abomination unto the Lord: and because of these abominations the Lord thy God doth drive them out from before thee. Thou shalt be perfect with the Lord thy God. For these nations, which thou shalt possess, hearkened unto observers of times, and unto diviners: but as for thee, the Lord thy God hath not suffered thee so to do."

Just as Israel disobeyed God and were given over to their enemies, I fear that America is following the same steps. We must turn from these practices and return to our God!! Now let's take each of these nine practices and expose them for what they are...

PASSING THEIR CHILDREN THROUGH THE FIRE

This was a most wicked practice of nearly every pagan religion. Child sacrifice. They would literally take their children and pass them through the fire to dedicate themselves to their idol god! Over and over God pronounced His judgement on this hideous practice. There are many verses found in the Word of God making a clear stand against this. Here are just a few...

Lev.18:21 *"And thou shalt not let any of thy seed pass through the fire to Molech."*

Deut.12:30-31 *"Take heed to thyself that thou be not snared by following them, after that they be destroyed from before thee; and that thou inquire not after their gods, saying, How did these nations serve their gods? even so will I do likewise. Thou shalt not do so unto the Lord thy God: for every abomination to the Lord, which he hateth, have they done unto their gods; for even their sons and their daughters they have burnt in the fire to their gods."*

<u>Jer.19:4-5</u> "Because they have forsaken me, and have estranged this place, and have burned incense in it unto other gods, who neither they nor their fathers have known, nor the kings of Judah, and have filled this place with the blood of innocents; They have built also the high places of Baal, **to burn their sons with fire for burnt offerings unto Baal,** which I commanded not, nor spake it, neither came it into my mind."

<u>Jer.32:34-35</u> *"But they set their abominations in the house, which is called by my name, to defile it. And they built the high places of Baal, which are in the valley of the son of Hinnom, to cause their sons and their daughters to pass through the fire unto Molech; which I commanded them not, neither came it into my mind, that they should do this abomination, to cause Judah to sin."*

Molech was a pagan god, which was shaped in such a way that its stomach could hold fire. Its arms were outstretched over the stomach area so that the intense heat from the fire would make the arms literally glow. With the music blaring in the background, mothers and fathers would bring their baby to the priests and in turn he would usually cut out the heart and throw the body through the arms and into the stomach of Molech. This was practiced so much that the Bible said *"the land was polluted with blood"* (Psa.106:38)

I've heard people say, "But, John, we don't do such gross things today.!" I will admit we may not be taking our children and physically throwing them into the arms of a pagan idol god, but we are killing one baby every 20 seconds in America in the name of abortion! They're being burned alive in their mothers' stomach with saline solutions! One and a half million babies are killed every year in this "God-fearing" country! Lord, forgive us!!!!!

But besides abortion, there are studies that are showing an alarming number of child abuse cases linked to the occult. Gregory Simpson, a pediatrician from Carson, Calif. who also teaches at *Martin Luther King Hospital* in Los Angeles, claimed after extensive research, "The conclusion I reached is that satanic abuse of small children does exist, and it's something that needs to be dealt with by the medical community."[4] *The Kansas City Times* reported, "Former satanic cult members and those who have worked with cult victims, including counselor Jacquie Balodis and Larry Dunn, a Washington state deputy sheriff, say it's possible that devil worshipers sacrifice 50,000 humans a year, mainly transients, runaways and babies conceived solely for the purpose of sacrifice. That figure would be more than twice the number of murders reported by police agencies to the FBI in 1986."[5]

But besides all that, we are sacrificing our children **mentally** and **spiritually** everyday! The difference between many of us today, and those of Jeremiah's day, is that we have the added, so-called "convenience" of TV, radio, movies and books that are taking the souls of our youth! We are passing our youth through the fires of demon gods every time their young minds and spirits are subjected to perverted movies and satanic rock!

KISS says it plainly in one of their songs, "God of Thunder":

> "...the spell you're under will **slowly** rob you
> of your virgin soul...I command you to kneel
> before the god of thunder and the god of rock
> and rock..."

Our children are being bombarded with occult-type games, toys, cartoons, comic books, movies, video games, music, which all just claim to be innocent entertainment in the name of 'fun'. One such example would be the *Dungeons and Dragons* series. A fantasy role playing game that has been named many, many times as a determining factor for suicides and homicides among young men and women. The Bible says plainly that we are to guard our thoughts, and that we are even to bring every imagination into obedience to Christ. (see Phil.4:8; 2 Cor.10:5) It is very interesting that the original cover to the *Dungeons and Dragons Players Handbook* has

Molech on it, there with his open arms ready to receive the next sacrifice!!!

DIVINATION

The word, divination, refers to fortune-telling through the means of some object. It is claiming to have divine insight into the future. Divination can be done with crystal balls, tea leaves, Ouija Boards, palms, numbers, cards, dice, dowsing rods, stars, planets, the entrails of animals, salt, water, fire, moles on the body, letters in a name, dreams, and on and on. Regardless of its' form, the Bible forbids this, and calls it an abomination!

The Bible refers to one story in Acts chapter 16 of a teenage girl who was "possessed with a spirit of divination" (v.16) which reveals the fact that this power is given through demon power.

The following are just a few examples of divination encouraged through some popular rock groups...

1) <u>Crystal Balls</u>

There are many groups who readily show their confidence in divination through crystal balls by placing them right on their album covers...

Styx has an album entitled, *Crystal Ball*, which shows someone holding a crystal ball and seeing a dancer though it. They sing from the title cut:

> "I used to like to walk the straight and nar-
> row* line, I used to think that everything was
> fine. Sometimes I'd sit and gaze for days
> through sleepless dreams, all alone and
> trapped in time. I wonder what tomorrow
> has in mind for me. Or am I even in it's mind
> at all. Perhaps I'll get a chance to look ahead
> and see, as soon as I find myself a Crystal
> Ball."

(*an obvious reference to the straight and narrow way that Jesus said one *must* follow to have eternal life. Matt. 7:13-14)

Kenny Loggins is holding a crystal ball for all to see on his *Keep The Fire* album. Fire and crystal balls are both parts of white witchcraft.

Journey, on their album *Look Into The Future*, has the group levitating about a foot off the ground while they gather around the crystal ball. The record sleeve depicts the group in various shots playing with a crystal ball. Another one of their albums entitled, *Escape*, shows a scarab beetle smashing out of a crystal ball.

The group, Heart, has an album entitled *Little Queen*, which shows on the back side of the cover one of the girls from the group holding out her hand with a crystal ball. Some titles of their songs on the album include "Magic Man" and "Devil Delight".

Michael Cassidy has an album entitled, *Nature's Secret*, which shows a large crystal ball revealing a man sitting under a tree.

Spectres is the name of **Blue Oyster Cult's** album which has the band sitting around a table with a crystal ball in the bottom left-hand corner of the album. On the back cover, a member of the group is in astral projection, symbolized by a ray coming from his eyes.

Yoko Ono, the wife of **John Lennon**, is seen holding a crystal ball on the front cover of her *Starpeace* album. She also has a story entitled, "Crystal Ball", which I first read in a New Age magazine.

Rockwell has the album, *Genie*, which shows him standing behind a glowing crystal ball.

Fleetwood Mac had a very successful album entitled, *Rumours*, which shows **Stevie Nicks** looking into the crystal ball. The image inside the crystal ball is from a previous Fleetwood Mac album showing two members of the band playing with a crystal ball.

Dio, on the *Scared Heart* album, promotes the crystal ball.

The album shows someone holding the crystal ball with a dragon appearing inside. His promotional pictures for the album showed him sitting with a crystal ball.

Asia has an album showing a dragon. It is coming up out of the sea holding a crystal ball. It's very interesting to note that the dragon is a Biblical picture of Satan. Rev.12:7-9 says:

> *"And there was war in heaven: Michael and his angels fought against the dragon; and the dragon fought and his angels, And prevailed not; neither was their place found anymore in heaven. And the great dragon was cast out, that old serpent, called the **Devil**, and **Satan**, which deceiveth the whole world; he was cast out into the earth, and his angels were cast out with him."*

Point Of Know Return is the title of the **Kansas** album depicting a crystal ball with a dragon swimming around it.

Another group who promotes the dragon with crystal balls is **Jefferson Starship**, now known as, **Starship**. Their *Spitfire* album shows a woman on the back of a dragon holding the crystal ball in its clawed fist.

Grace Slick, lead singer for **Starship**, has a solo album out entitled, *Dreams*. The album shows her levitating another woman (who happens to be herself) with a crystal ball at her feet. On the back side of the album, she has disappeared, leaving the levitating woman and the crystal ball with a bright light shining from it. The record sleeve shows a close-up shot of the crystal ball with a snake wrapped around it.

2) <u>Tarot Cards</u>

Many groups promote divination through tarot cards, the black magic deck of cards that claims to show your future.

Renaissance has an album entitled, "Turn Of The Cards", which shows a hand holding a set of tarot cards. Life, according to the tarot cards, is just a 'turn of the cards'; based totally on fate.

Tim Bogert is depicted on his *Master's Brew* album as a witch stirring up his potion with a black cat and a bunch of levitating tarot cards.

Rainbow, the group **Richie Blackmore** put together, has an album entitled, *Rising,* with the song, "Tarot Woman", about a witch using tarot cards.

Tarot Suite is the title of a band whose whole album is dedicated to the reading of tarot cards. The inside of the album jacket reveals how the following of cards tell a story of one's life.

Blue Oyster Cult has an album entitled, *Agents Of Fortune,* which shows a magician holding tarot cards. The ones he is holding were designed by Aleister Crowley. Pointing to another occult symbol, the cards are held to say, "He who comes against this power shall be destroyed."

Triumph has an album out entitled *The Sport Of The Kings*, which plainly shows a number of tarot cards from *The Rider Tarot Deck*, the most popular tarot cards pack sold in America.

Led Zepplin's album which became known as the *Stairway To Heaven* album, has a very interesting design on the inside of the record cover when opened up. It shows a man dressed in a long, flowing robe holding a lantern in his hand, overlooking a small village. Also found at the foot of this steep, rocky hill is a person attempting to climb up, while a goat standing alone, looks on. Many people have tried to figure this illustration out. Some have even said this illustrates God at the top of the hill and a young person climbing the stairway to God or Heaven. Actually, this image is taken right off tarot card #9. Anyone who has studied the group **Led Zepplin**, will readily admit **Jimmy Page's** involvement in the black arts. He has repeatedly admitted his fascination with the occult. But without knowing this, all one must do is read the credit lines on the record sleeve itself and find these words...

"Inside illustration: The Hermit"

This is actually the name of a card from the black magic tarot

334

card deck. The hermit pictured on the card and also on the inside of the album is actually a Druid priest who is holding a lantern with the six-pointed star, known as the hexagram. (the hexagram must be present to place a "hex" or a curse on something) The Druids were the originators of the occult holiday known today as, "Halloween". Their practices on the last day of October included human sacrifices, as well as other very demonic activities. The *Houses Of The Holy* album by **Led Zepplin** shows little, naked children climbing up a hill with a strange glow over the other side. When that album is opened, it reveals a man holding one of those children up as a human sacrifice.

I just closed a crusade at a church not too far from Dayton, Ohio and was able to get into a high school to speak at an assembly. The first time I walked into that school I was totally shocked. Some of the students were given a project to paint different rock logos and album covers right on the walls of the school. Throughout the school, huge paintings could be found that depicted some of the most popular rock groups around. But the one that shocked me the most was the painting of the inside illustration from the Stairway to Heaven album, complete with the druid and all. It was painted on the first ledge of the stairway that hundreds of teenagers walked up and down everyday! Shortly after talking to one of the students who had painted it, who had just given her heart to the Lord in one of our crusades, she along with some others, were able to convince the school to have it removed from the wall...Praise God!

OBSERVER OF TIMES

This particular biblically forbidden practice deals with not only the observance of certain occultic holidays and sabbats, but also deals with following of zodiacs, astrology, stargazing, biorhythm charts, horoscopes, etc.

A group called, **Omen,** get their name from the practice of observing of signs and times to predict the future. (There is also a movie series out called, "The Omen", which deals with the Anti-Christ.)

One group calls themselves, **Samhain,** named after the god of death the druids honored on the last day of the Celtic calendar, which today is known as Halloween. [6] Halloween, according to the Satanic Bible, is the second most important holiday to the satanist.[7] One very popular heavy metal group calls themselves, **Helloween,** again named in honor of this satanic holiday.

The druids also are believed to be the ones responsible for the construction of Stonehenge. The unique design of these huge, rock-pillars are supposedly in perfect alignment with the zodiac.

Various groups sing about Stonehenge and others boast of their faith in it...

Ten Years After had an album entitled *Stonehenge*, not only depicting it on the outside, but when opened, it revealed the entire layout of Stonehenge.

Areosmith's album, *Rock In A Hard Place*, shows Stonehenge right on the front cover.

The Association had an album which depicted the complete Stonehenge design by making the letters of the band to form on the moon.

Graham Bond produced an album entitled, *Holy Magick*, also dedicated to the druid religion and showing an actual celebration at Stonehenge. Bond, who was very deeply involved in black magic, ended up taking his own life by throwing himself in front of a speeding train. It took a couple of days to find all of his body.

The Bee Gee's album, *E.S.P.*, shows the group standing around a rock formation similar to those of Stonehenge. E.S.P. is an obvious practice of consulters with familiar spirits, which we'll deal with a little later.

Many groups will place astrological signs right on their album covers. These are easy to spot, having the twelve signs either in symbolic form or actual drawings.

Grim Reaper has an album entitled, *See You In Hell*, which shows the death reaper on the back of the album with the zodiac around him.

The group, **Earth, Wind, and Fire,** give their astrological signs along with their birthday on many of their albums.

The Boogie Boys, a rappin' group, have an album out entitled, *Zodiac,* which shows the entire zodiac chart right on the front cover. Their song, "Fly Girl", deals with the girls they date according to their astrological signs.

The Fifth Dimension's very successful album, *Age Of Aquarius,* not only is based on a new-age form of the occult, but actually shows the astrological signs each member of the band was born under. The title cut deals with an age to come where, "peace will guide our planets and love will steer the stars." This is believed by many to have been fulfilled August of 1987 during the "harmonic convergence" ushering the Age Of Aquarius, named after one sign of the zodiac.

The group, **Yes,** also joined in with the Aquarian Age from their album, *Big Generator,* with the song, "Holy Lamb (Song For The Harmonic Convergence)".

<u>AN ENCHANTER</u>

An enchanter is a person who cast spells with words and is also referred to as a soothsayer.

Wendy O. Williams, from the group, **Plasmatics,** is standing in front of an upside down pentagram on the *Metal Priestess* album. On one of the songs entitled, "Doom Song", she actually casts a spell by saying:

> "Sanctify this place, protect us from evil, behold the power of the night, shine that we may see the light, curse the filthy hypocrites, crawl into their beds at night, ooze from slimy depths below, scream into their frozen brains, work thy wretched wrath, remove all obstacles from our path. I command that these things of which I speak will come to be."

Some even claim that certain groups will hire witch covens to place a "blessing" on the record so that it will be a successful seller.

Also look up the following verses for further references on the subject of enchantment...

Exodus 7:11,22
Exodus 8:7,11
Leviticus 19:26
Numbers 23:23
Numbers 24:1
Deuteronomy.18:10
2 Kings.17:17
2 Kings 21:6
2 Chronicles 33:6
Ecclesiastes.10:11

Isaiah 47:9,12
Jeremiah 27:9

A WITCH

A witch is a person who uses sorcery, magic, and enchantment. It's very tragic that today we have such a weird view of witches. The cartoons of an ugly old woman with a hairy chin and a wart on her nose, flying on a broom has given the impression that bad witches are ugly ones, while everyone knows the "good witch of the East" is beautiful. Simply put, according to the Bible, there is no such thing as a "good witch"!

Stevie Nicks, singer for **Fleetwood Mac** has copy written most of her songs under the name "Welch Witch Music". The live version of the hit song, "Rhiannon", is introduced by Nicks as a "song about a welsh witch". She has a solo album called, *Bella Donna*, named after a drug used in witchcraft potions. The bottom left hand corner plainly shows a crystal ball. Her other solo album, *Rock A Lite*, has a crystal ball in the bottom right-hand corner. Her 1983 tour book, *The Wild Heart Tour*, opens with this statement..."She can't read music. She believes in angels, witches and magic wands. Can this be a serious songwriter? You bet!" She claims her favorite holiday is Halloween and that she enjoys dressing up as a witch.[8]

Stiv Bator, formerly of the **Dead Boys,** now with the **Lords**

Of The New Church, claims he is "well-read in the area of Rosicrucian texts, and has researched and consorted with Wiccans (witches) since moving to England". His 'new religion' amounts to an embrace of paganism, as practiced by the Druids and the Celts".[9]

Other groups such as **Coven, White Witch,** etc. are named after the forbidden practice of witchcraft. A coven is made up of 13 witches. Authorities have estimated there were approximately 10,000 covens in the 1946, 48,000 by 1976, and 135,000 by 1985.[10]

Under Old Testament standards, being a witch was punishable by death! (See Exodus 22:18)

In Galatians 5:19-21, Paul lists 17 works of the flesh and says:

> *"Now the works of the flesh are manifest,*
> *which are these...witchcraft...of the which I*
> *tell you before, as I have also told you in time*
> *past, that they which do such things shall*
> *not inherit the kingdom of God."*

Those who practice witchcraft are preparing their own place in hell!
Also look up the following verses for further reference on the subject of witchcraft...

Deuteronomy 18:10

1 Samuel 15:23
2 Kings 9:22
2 Chronicles 33:6
Micah 5:12
Nahum 3:4

A CHARMER

This practice refers to casting of spells or putting things under a spell by the use of some device or an amulet. We have all seen the snake charmer, and the hypnotist with his swinging disk, and almost everyone has heard of 'good luck charms', but these are among the forbidden practices named here. Many of the symbols you see on album covers or around the necks of rock stars are actually **charms...**

1) <u>Crescent Moon and Star</u>

The crescent moon and star, representing worship to the queen of heaven, the sex goddess. In Jer. 7:17-18, God speaks to Jeremiah about this very thing...

> *"Seest thou not what they do in the cities of*
> *Judah and in the streets of Jerusalem? The*
> *children gather wood, and the fathers kindle*
> *the fire, and the women knead their dough, **to***
> ***make cakes to the queen of heaven, and to***
> *pour out drink offerings unto other gods, that*
> *they may provoke me to anger."*

From Dake's Annotated Bible comes this footnote on those verses:

> "Cakes were made of honey, fine flour, and other ingredients and shaped like the moon to which they were offered. Phoenicians called the moon, Ashtoreth, or Astarte, the wife of Baal or Molech, who was called the king of heaven. The male and female pair of deities symbolized the generative powers of nature; hence, the introduction of prostitution in connection with such worship. The Babylonians worshipped the goddess as Mylitta (generative). The moon became the symbol of female productiveness, and all women converts were supposed to submit to immorality in this worship, at least one time."[11]

A perfect example of this carrying on through to today's music is from **Donna Summer's** album, *Four Seasons Of Love*. The album shows Donna Summer seductively dressed and laying across a crescent moon mixed in with stars. She was known for years as the "sex goddess of rock music".

Her male counter part now is **Prince**. His *1999* album not only shows the 1 in the title *1999* as an erected male sex organ, but also shows a crescent moon and star formed from the letter C in the name, Prince.

Most Bible commentators I've read believe that the ornaments referred to in Isaiah 3:18 and Judges 8:21 were crescent-shaped ornaments worn around the neck in honor of Astarte.

Most of the posters and photos from rock magazines will show **John Bon Jovi** wearing the crescent moon and star around his neck. No one will deny the fact that sensuality seems to be a major message from **Bon Jovi.**

This symbol can be found on the upper-right hand corner of the Ouija Board, a so-called 'game' of divination.

Duran Duran's album, *Seven And The Ragged Tiger*, also has the crescent moon and star on the upper right-hand corner of the album cover.

Linda Ronstadt's album, *Hasten Down The Wind*, shows her on the front cover plainly wearing the crescent moon and star.

All you have to do is keep your eyes open, and you'll notice the many times palm readers, psychics, astrologers, and magicians will advertise with a crescent moon and star. I have over a dozen slides I show in our seminars of various occult book stores and palm readers across the country who use the crescent and star.

The Globe Min Mag #715, those little books at the check out stand in most grocery stores, shows a wizard looking into a crystal ball with a cape, complete with crescent moon and stars.

Even the Walt Disney movie, *The Sorcerer's Apprentice*, has Mickey using the wizard's "magic hat" that grants him magic powers. The design on the hat is the crescent moon and star. Many toys will have this symbol on them. The unicorn and pegasus from the "My Little Pony" series has the crescent moon and star. Even one of the 13 Care Bears (interesting number) has the crescent moon and star.

2) <u>The Ankh Cross, Scarab Beetles and Winged Disks</u>

The ankh cross (a cross with a loop at the top), **scarab beetle**, and the **winged disk** (a round object with falcon wings spreading out around it) are all Egyptians symbols of reincarnated life. They can be found on the Egyptian tombs dated back over 4,500 years ago. It was believed by the Egyptians that these symbols would help bring their dead back to life.

They are easily bought at most department stores in the jewelry department. They are often called the 'life cross'.

KISS on their *Lick It Up* album shows one of the guys from the group wearing the ankh cross.

The group called, **The Cult**, have an album entitled, *Love*, which shows the winged disk on the album cover, and the record sleeve reveals one member of the band wearing the ankh cross.

Aerosmith's album, *Get Your Wings*, shows the group sitting under their logo, which happens to be a winged disk. Their album, *Rock In A Hard Place*, not only has the winged disk mixed in with a pentagram and a pyramid, but also pictured on the front cover is a scene from Stonehenge.

Iron Maiden's album, *Powerslave*, is full of depictions of pyramids, winged disks, and scarab beetles on both the front and the back of the album.

Journey's album, *Evolution*, shows the winged disk, while their other albums depict the scarab beetle. Their album, *Escape*, shows a scarab beetle smashing through a crystal ball.

Blue Oyster Cult's album, *Fire Of Unknown Origin*, shows a coven of witches (13) wearing their hooded robes, while the leader has a pentagram on his robe and a scarab on his forehead.

Smokey Robinson is pictured on his *Essar* album leaning on a carving of the winged disk, with an Egyptian statue behind him.

Judas Priest's album, *Sin After Sin*, shows a temple prostitute sitting on the steps of a pagan temple during full moon, and there is a skull carved into the wall with glowing eyes and a winged disk underneath.

Nazareth's album, *No Mean City*, shows a demonic creature holding two switch blades with a belt buckle depicting a winged disk made from a human skull.

3) <u>The Hexagram</u>

The hexagram (a six pointed star), is the black magic symbol used to help cast a 'hex' or a 'spell' and has been confused with the so-called Star of David.

It can be found in the lantern of the druid high priest inside the **Led Zepplin** *Stairway to Heaven* album.

The hexagram is found on the back of the **Black Sabbath** album, *Born Again*. This album has a baby made to look like a demon on the front cover.

I have a book written by O. J. Graham, entitled, *The Six Pointed Star*. It is written entirely about the history of the so-called Star of David. Anyone who has seen the Israeli flag will know that it has a blue hexagram. This author, who is a Jewish journalist, trances the hexagram back to pagan religion. He further documents the fact that the true Jewish symbol is the manovah, the seven golden candlesticks, and each time Israel backslid, they would turn to pagan religions, including the occult. This is an interesting thought when you consider the fact that Israel as a nation has rejected Jesus as their Messiah. Some call the six-pointed star the "Seal of Solomon". Anyone studying the life of Solomon will remember how Solomon became involved in all the pagan religions of his many wives at the end of his days.

Jesus spoke to the church of Philadelphia in Rev.3:9 and said:

> *"Behold, I will make them of the synagogue*
> *of Satan, which say they are Jews, and are*
> *not, but do lie; behold, I will make them to*
> *come and worship before thy feet, and to*
> *know that I have loved thee."*

Isn't it interesting that the verse refers to ones from "the synagogue" or the church of Satan claiming to be Jews, knowing today that many Satanists use a symbol that is believed to be a Jewish symbol.

Recently, much controversy came from the makers of Count Chocula, the cereal for kids. It seems that some people were offended by the picture of Dracula on the front cover wearing a six-pointed star. "Officials of the Golden Valley based food company agreed that a medallion on Dracula's chest could represent the star, which is a symbol of Judaism. The picture is taken from Bela Lugosi's role in "House of Dracula," a 1931 film."[12] Even the movie industry knew, before Israel became a nation in 1948, that the six-pointed star was associated with the occult!

4) <u>The Lightning Bolt</u>

The lightning bolt (also called the power 'S'), represents the fall of Satan according to Luke 10:18, which says:

> *"And he [Jesus] said unto them, I beheld Satan as lightning fall from heaven."*

The Electric Lucifer is the title of an album done by **Bruce Haack.** The album shows an angelic being surrounded by various creatures with these words at the top of the album..."I do a lot with touch...let electricity flow through our bodies and touch each other and the electricity becomes sound." Two lightning bolts are coming toward Lucifer.

When *Look* magazine did an interview with Anton La Vey, the Pastor of the first church of Satan; they have a full page picture of La Vey wearing an inverted pentagram with a lightning bolt through the middle. I've seen a number of Satanic book stores that sell occult jewelry, and in every case, lightning bolts were being sold. Most rock magazines will have advertisements for necklaces and earrings which have all types of occult symbols, including the lightning bolt.

In the middle of the logo for **AC/DC** is found a large lightning bolt.

KISS uses the lightning bolt "S" for the last two letters in their name. This same design goes back to Hitler's SS team. The title page of a book by Reinhard Heydrich written in 1935 shows the SS, which was used in Rune Occultism.

Black Sabbath uses the lightning bolt very boldly on the cover of their *We Sold Our Soul For Rock 'N Roll* album. The inside of the album shows a woman lying dead in a casket, clinging to a cross.

ZZ Top, who used normal Z's until the *Eliminator* album came out. Now they even sell a lightning bolt key chain. One song off that *Eliminator* album was a big video success. It was called, "TV Dinners", and showed a man getting a TV dinner out of a microwave and placing it on top of an Ouija Board. Under the foil was a tiny demon, which would keep coming out and pointing next to the crescent moon and star on the Ouija Board.

Slayer uses the lightning bolt to form the letter S in the bands' name, which also forms an inverted pentagram.

Ozzy Osbournes' album, *Blizzard Of Oz*, has all the lyrics written on the record sleeve with lightning bolt S's. Even the copyright is ended with a lighting bolt.

Raven uses the lightning bolt above their name.

A recent ad in the paper for the *Time/Life* series, *The Enchanted World*, had a wizard with a outstretched hand. Around his hand was a box. Above the box was these words..."Draw the **lightning bolt** from the Wizard's hand and get a FREE desk top calculator." (Isn't that interesting!)

David Bowie's album, *Aladdin Sane*, shows him with a painted lightning bolt over his face.

Metallica not only has an album entitled, *Ride The Lightning*, but also has their band's logo made to appear as two lightning bolts. Their album, *Jump In The Fire*, shows a demonic creature in hell smiling while standing under the band's name, complete with lightning bolts.

5) <u>The 'Peace Sign'</u>

The up-side-down broken cross (the so-called 'peace sign'), is a part of the satanic rituals of mocking the cross of Christ by turning it upside down and breaking the arms downward.

Prince, from his *Sign O' The Times* album and tour, has brought back this '60's symbol. Others such as **Madonna** and **Cindy Lauper** can be found wearing this around their necks.

The group, **INXS,** had a very successful hit entitled, "Devil Inside". The 45-single was released with a drawing of a cartoon devil holding a pitch fork, in the background is up-side-down, broken cross.

6) <u>The Pentagram</u>

The pentagram (a five pointed star), has been used world-wide for centuries as the symbol of witchcraft with its five major points...Earth, Air, Fire, Water, Spirit. (This, of course, is where **Maurice White** from *Earth, Wind and Fire* got the title to his band.)

On the *Highway To Hell* album by **AC/DC**, **Bon Scott** is shown smiling and wearing the pentagram next to another member dressed up with horns and forked tail.

Richard Ramirez, also known as the 'Night Stalker', was the young man who was accused of the serial killings in California which got nationwide attention. He claimed inspiration for his killings from the "Night Prowler" song on the *Highway To Hell* album. After murdering his victims, he would paint a pentagram on the wall or table of the victim's home. In his trial, he held up his hand to the cameras and said, "Hail Satan". On his hand, he had drawn the pentagram.

Ringo Starr on his album, *Ringo The 4th*, is wearing a necklace that just so happens to have the pentagram on it.

Yngwie Malmsteen, the famous rock guitarist, wears a pentagram around his neck and admits his interest in the occult.

Richie Sambora, the guitarist for **Bon Jovi**, also wears a pentagram around his neck.

Venom uses the pentagram on their *From Hell To The Unknown* album. A man is seen with both types of pentagrams in his eyes while he holds out his hand, revealing another pentagram.

The group, **Rush**, has used the pentagram for years as their logo. Their *Archives* album shows a nude man holding his hands out toward the pentagram, gaining power from its force.

7) <u>The Inverted Pentagram</u>

The inverted pentagram (up-side-down, five pointed star), used worldwide as the symbol of Satan worship. Both the Satanic Bible and the Satanic Rituals depict the inverted pentagram on the front cover. Also found inside the inverted pentagram is the head of the goat, another symbol in satanism, even Jesus talked about dividing the sheep from the goats in Matt. 25:32-33.

Venom has used the inverted pentagram for years. Their album, *Welcome To Hell*, says these words on the back...

> "We're possessed by all that is evil. The
> death of you, God, we demand. We spit at the
> virgin you worship and sit at Lord Satan's
> left hand."

Celtic Frost's album, *Emperor's Return*, shows a half-snake, half-man wrapping itself around a partially naked woman, who has an inverted pentagram on her forehead and chest.

Such groups as **Motley Crue** boast of their use of the pentagram. They claim it has nothing to do with the devil. The fan club of Motley Crue is known as the "S.I.N." club, which stands for "Safety In Numbers". In various advertisements, their organization sells everything from T-shirts to underwear with inverted pentagrams. Their *Boys In Action Tour* T-shirt shows an inverted pentagram with a human skull under it, with blood pouring from its eye sockets. I thought it was interesting that they even sell wrist bands and head bands with the inverted pentagram. (The 'mark of the beast' is also to be placed on the forehead or hand! See Rev. 13)

Onslaught's album, *The Force*, depicts the inverted pentagram right on the front cover. Their album, *Power From Hell*, shows a demon materializing out of an inverted pentagram.

Running Wild has an album that shows a mad dog with an inverted pentagram carved into it's forehead.

BeBop Deluxe's album entitled, *Live! In the Air Age*, shows a robot walking away from its seat with a huge, inverted pentagram drawn on the wall.

The Plasmatics have **Wendy O. Williams**, the lead singer from the group, standing in front of an inverted pentagram on the *Metal Priestess* album.

Bathory has an album that shows a goat with red glowing eyes on the front and an inverted pentagram on the back.

Suicidal Tendencies has an album that shows various shirts of their fans wearing not only skulls, but also the inverted pentagram.

Slayer, on their album, *Show No Mercy*, shows a man wearing a goat head with a pentagram carved on it's forehead. He is holding a sword which is a part of a set of swords made to form an inverted pentagram. Instead of saying, "Side 1" and "Side 2", the album simply uses "6" and "66". The lead guitarist is playing with an inverted cross. Recently I read an magazine article written about **Slayer** entitled "Slayer, Hell Was Never So Much Fun!". The author ended the article saying, "If Slayer ever go to hell, they'd be the perfect house band. And I'll be right in the front row. After all, don't all the fun people go to hell, anyway?"[13]

The Rolling Stones album, *Goat's Head Soap*, shows an ectoplasmic formation of **Mick Jaggar** on the front cover, but also includes a picture of a decapitated goat head floating in a bloody cauldron.

8) The Satanic Salute

The Satanic Salute is used by scores of people. A sign that is made with the hand by raising the fist with the extended forefinger and pinkie. Also used, is the backward way of saying, "I love you", in sign language. This sign has been used for centuries as a sign 'to ward off the evil eye' and to give honor to the "horned hunter of the night".

All one must do is to take the time and see how many groups and artists use the satanic salute...

The *Marvel Comic* series, **Doctor Strange,** shows him giving the satanic salute on the upper left-hand corner of the comic book.

From *Dungeon and Dragon's* manuals comes **Elric,** shown giving the satanic salute. Also, on the D. & D. monthly magazine, *Dragon* #76, is found a wizard giving both forms of the satanic salute to release a girl from a huge octopus monster.

Recently, while doing some research in this symbol, I ran across an ancient picture of the Chinese bronze statue of Kwan Yin making the "Sign of the Horns" dating back before the time of Christ. Also, I found a carving of the Maya god, Ik Chuah, the black god of merchants and of coca, kneeling above Cizin, the god of death, giving the satanic salute. These symbols were being used hundreds of years ago. Some people would have us think that **Ronnie James Dio** made it up himself and that it means, "long live rock and roll"!

Blacklace on their *Unlaced* album, shows their female leader flashing the satanic salute.

The **Beatle's** album, *Yellow Submarine*, has **John Lennon** giving the satanic salute behind the head of **Paul McCartney**.

I have pictures from rock magazines with **Jon Bon Jovi, Cindy Lauper, L.L. Cool J.** and others giving the satanic salute.

KISS, on the *Love Gun* album, has **Gene Simmons** holding the satanic salute for all to see.

King Diamond is found constantly in photo sessions for rock magazines, flashing the satanic salute in the midst of inverted crosses, etc. For those who think it's just a form of advertisement, read this personal account from King Diamond, who claims to have had real experiences in the occult: "My interest in black magic came about totally by coincidence. There was something weird happening in my apartment. There was a glass rising from the table...and that was with other people there. I just couldn't explain it, but some invisible force had lifted the glass up in thin air. Then I started reading books about the occult. They all had this old-fashioned idea about black masses where you sacrifice pigs and drink their blood, stuff which is absolutely false. One day I saw a book called the Satanic Bible. The way the author saw the world and his philosophy was exactly the way I was living my life."[14] It's interesting that on back of the *Satanic Bible* and the *Satanic*

Rituals is Anton La Vey, and he is shown giving the satanic salute!

The **Beastie Boys** were interviewed shortly after their successful *License To Ill* album by *Spin* magazine. The magazine shows a two-page spread of them in live concert giving the satanic salute. Their video for the song, "She's On It", shows the whole group flashing the satanic salute.

Rick James is shown giving the satanic salute on the *Street Songs* album.

The group, **Frankie Goes To Hollywood**, has an album entitled, *Pleasure Dome*, which has a number of photos on the record sleeve, one of which shows the leader of the band flashing the satanic salute.

The record sleeve from **Cheap Trick's** album, *Dream Police*, shows one of the guys from the band giving the satanic salute.

Todd Rungren from the group, **Utopia**, is shown giving the satanic salute on the front cover of their *POV* album.

On the back side of the **Heart** album, *Private Audition*, both girls from the group are shown giving the satanic salute.

Many issues of various rock magazines, such as the Feb. 1986 issue of *Hit Parader*, will have **Ronnie James Dio** giving the satanic salute. His album, *The Last In Line*, shows the horned hunter of the night holding out his arms, giving the satanic salute. The record sleeve shows hundreds of Dio fans with banners depicting the satanic salute. The *Holy Diver* album shows the horned hunter of the night beating a priest with a chain, after throwing him into the water, during full moon.

Coven, a group who get their name right from the occult world, (meaning a witch gathering - usually 13), have an album entitled, *Blood On The Snow*. Depicted is the devil playing a viol, while flashing the satanic salute. Another one of their albums shows the band laying behind a black cat, with two members of the band giving the satanic salute. Their album, *Destroy Minds And Reap Souls*, shows the band in a full-blown, black mass complete with upside-down crosses, skulls, black candles, and a nude girl laying on an altar. Around her are people giving the satanic salute.

In one of our meetings in Kansas City, a young man brought in a whole case of tapes, records, T-shirts, mirrors, hats, pins, and posters to be destroyed. When he gave his life to **Jesus Christ**, he could not listen to, or be a part of the anti-Christ concept coming through much of his music. He was really into **Black Sabbath**. One of the hats he brought in came from the last concert of theirs that he had gone to. On that cap was a fist busting through the back of a cross, flashing the satanic salute. Their message was loud and clear...Satan is more powerful than the cross.

Black Sabbath, a group who got their name from the Boris

Karloff horror movie, *Black Sabbath*, have been one of the most successful "occult-type" bands in the history of rock 'n roll, starting back in late 1969. They have never tried to hide their satanic ideas, but have repeatedly boasted of their interests.

Ozzy Osbourne, former lead singer for **Black Sabbath**, attempted suicide by hanging himself when he was younger, but was found by his dad just in time. He claimed one of his favorite pastimes was visiting cemeteries. "I was always sitting in graveyards...I loved thinking about Satan..."[15] (Tragically, he may have an eternity to think about him.)

Tony Iommi's latest album entitled, *Seventh Star*, is based from the writings of **Nostradamus**. Iommi's wardrobe is comprised totally of black clothing. He is fascinated with black magic and is an avid reader of occult literature, along with being obsessed with Nostradamus, reincarnation, past lives meditation, and acupuncture. He declared, "We're into God," only to be countered by **Bill Ward** who stated, "But sometimes I feel Satan is God."[16]

9) <u>Pyramids</u>

A pyramid is considered by many to be a form of a charm. Many people wear them around their necks, place them under their beds, build them over gardens, place food under them, sit under them while meditating, etc. Many rock groups are heavily into the pyramid teaching, believing that the pyramids produce psychic energy to help the band perform better.

Ambrosia has an album that actually opens up into the shape of a pyramid. The listener is encouraged to allow the record to sit under the pyramid, to gain power before listening to it.

We were just recently in southern Illionis for a crusade in a small town where a young high school girl was using pyramids. She used a crystal pyramid under her bed to help bring her protection. The pyramid was covered with blood where she had daily cut her palm on the top of the pyramid and used her own blood in sacrifice. She had read many books on pyramid power and became bound by its power. We prayed she would come to the meetings, and on the second night she came and was saved! We have seen hundreds of people bring in their pyramid collections. In one crusade, a woman who owned an metaphysics book/health food store came and received Christ and brought in over a thousand dollars worth of pyramid materials.

Such groups as **Earth, Wind, and Fire** and **Utopia** have been known to perform under huge pyramids during their live concerts.

Teena Marie, referring to her *Starchild* album, says, "Starchild has to do with Egyptian pyramids. A lot of people don't know how they were built. Philosophers feel that extraterrestrials came down here from other places, built them and left the planet. And man still can't build a pyramid. I feel tied to this.

And I feel there are places, entities that I believe in."[17]

A CONSULTER WITH FAMILIAR SPIRITS

This is a person who will communicate with a spirit that seems familiar with the actions and voice of a dead person. It is actually a demonic impersonator. We find such a case in 1 Samuel 28:7-25, when Saul asked of the witch of Endor. (Also the name of the planet in the movie, "The Return of The Jedi") Verse 7 says:

> *"Then said Saul unto his servants, Seek me a woman that hath a familiar spirit, that I may go to her, and inquire of her."*

Saul, who earlier had forbidden this practice from Israel, went to this women hoping to get some direction on what to do. Since he had turned his back on God, he couldn't get any direction from God. Later we are told in 1 Chronicles 10:13:

> *"So Saul died for his transgression which he committed against the Lord, even against the word of the Lord, which he kept not, and also for asking counsel of one that had a familiar spirit, to inquire of it;"*

This passage makes it clear that Saul did not actually receive a message from dead Samuel, but it came from a **familiar spirit**; a demon impersonating the prophet Samuel. Some other things to consider...

*The witch claimed that she saw, "*gods ascending out of the earth*", (1 Samuel 28:13), "gods" being a term given to demon spirits throughout scripture.

*Saul did not see Samuel, but asked the women what she saw. She described to him "*An old man cometh up; and he is covered with a mantle. And Saul perceived that it was Samuel...*" (v.14) From the woman's description, he *believed* it was actually Samuel.

*Samuel would have never consented to appear before Saul since this was the forbidden practice of *necromancy*.

*The spirit that spoke to Saul said that he and his sons would die the next day and would "*be with me*" (v.19). This would leave no room for the fact that Saul had become an "*enemy*" of God (v.16) and would be confined to eternal torment, while Samuel was in paradise, a resting place for the people of God. (See Luke 16:19-26)

*Jesus made it clear in Luke 16:19-31 with the story of the rich man and Lazarus the beggar, that those who are dead cannot leave their place of abode, and if they would come back, it would have to be by being raised from the dead, not by spirit form. (Luke 16:30-31)

Julian Lennon, the son of John Lennon, claims in his song,

"Well, I Don't Know" that he has communicated with his dead father. In the song he literally asked this spirit to become a part of him!

A WIZARD

A wizard is one who gains knowledge through conjuring of spirits. Almost every time a wizard is mentioned is scripture, familiar spirits are also referred to.

Roy Wood, vocalist for **ELO** (Electric Light Orchestra), left the band to start his own band called, **Wizzard**.

Ever since the popular *Wizard Of Oz* movie came out in 1939, the concept of good and bad wizards and good and bad witches became a part of modern thinking; but according to the Bible, anyone who is practicing wizardry is committing an abomination! As mentioned earlier, both cartoons and toys have had a real impact in the acceptance of such practices as innocent. Satan is a master of deception and has no doubt been able to make real in-roads to many lives of precious young people through these means of covering the truth with attractive packages!

The scripture emphatically says in Lev. 19:31:

> *"Regard not them that have familiar spirits,*
> *neither seek after wizards, to be defiled by*
> *them: I am the Lord your God."*

Also look up the following verses for further references on the subject of wizards...

Leviticus 20:6,27
Deuteronomy 18:11
1 Samuel 28:3,9
2 Kings 21:6
2 Kings 23:24
2 Chronicles 33:6
Isaiah 8:19
Isaiah 19:3

A NECROMANCER

A *necromancer* is a person who consults the dead, many times in order to foretell the future. This was referred to earlier with the account of Saul trying to communicate with the dead prophet.

The group, **Rush**, has an album entitled, *Caress Of Steel*, which shows a necromancer on the front cover of the album. His hand is on a human skull, as he levitates a pyramid with a serpent at his feet. The last song on side one of the album is called the, "Necromancer".

On the back of **Yoko Ono's** album, *It's Alright*, there is a picture of Yoko and her son, Sean, standing in a park with a spirit form of **John Lennon** standing next to them. Various articles have been written about **Yoko's** attempts to contact

Lennon since his death in 1980. This is exactly what God was referring to when he forbid the practice of necromancy.

The whole concept of the *Star Wars* trilogy was based on the practice of necromancy. Luke Skywalker was in constant contact with dead Ben Kanobi who appeared to him during various important times giving him instructions. It's so sad to see how often we are entertained by practices which are abominable to God and never even catch it! Many cartoons on Saturday mornings also glorify these and many other occult practices.

The thing that breaks the heart of God in all this, is not that He is going to get hurt by people doing these things, but it's *you* He's concerned about! If you must run from God to find your future, you are open to all kinds of deception. In the end, you'll see that God was the One to ask. In Isaiah 47:9-15, God says:

> *"But these two things shall come to thee in a moment in one day, the loss of children, and widowhood: they shall come upon thee in their perfection for the multitude of thy sorceries, and for the great abundance of thine enchantments. For thou hast trusted in thy wickedness: thou hast said, None seeth me. Thy wisdom and thy knowledge, it hath perverted thee; and thou hast said in thine heart, I am, and none else beside me. There-*

366

fore shall evil come upon thee; thou shalt not know from whence it riseth: and mischief shall fall upon thee; thou shalt not be able to put it off: and desolation shall come upon thee suddenly, which thou shalt not know. Stand now with thine enchantments, and with the multitude of thy sorceries, wherein thou hast laboured from thy youth; if so be thou shalt be able to profit, if so be thou mayest prevail. Thou art wearied in the multitude of thy counsels. Let now the astrologers, the stargazers, the monthly prognosticators, stand up, and save thee from these things that shall come upon thee. Behold, they shall be as stubble; the fire shall burn them; they shall not deliver themselves from the power of the flame: there shall not be a coal to warm at, nor fire to sit before it. Thus shall they be unto thee with whom thou hast laboured, even thy merchants, from thy youth: they shall wander every one to his quarter; none shall save thee."

Now, what should you do if you have these things in your life? The Bible plainly states that you must do something!! In Deuteronomy 7:25-26, God tells us this:

"The graven images of their gods shall ye burn with fire: thou shalt not desire the

> *silver or gold that is on them, nor take it unto thee, lest thou be snared therein: for it is an abomination to the Lord thy God. Neither shalt thou bring an abomination into thine house, lest thou be a cursed thing like it: but thou shalt utterly detest it, and thou shalt utterly abhor it: for it is a cursed thing."*

Here, God plainly says if you have these things in your life or home, you have a curse upon you. A curse of Satanic power that *can* include everything from sickness, disease, and poverty to even famine and death. They are all listed in Deuteronomy 28:15-68 and you would do well to study it. Could this be one reason we have so many problems in our homes and churches today? I believe this is a major reason we are not seeing the power of God in full operation! We have brought these things into our own lives!

Jer.32:34 says:

> *"But they set their abominations in the house, which is called by my name, to defile it."*

To *defile* something is to make it "unclean and detestable". In Joshua 7, we read of a man named, Achan, who tried to hide the accursed things under his tent. God had instructed Joshua to tell the people not to take anything from the ruins of defeated Jericho. This city was overthrown because of it's sinfulness, and they were to burn the remains. Achan knowingly rebelled against the Lord's command and hid three items under his tent. Shortly afterwards, the children of Israel lost 36 men in a war against a small city. Joshua fell on his face before God asking why, after such a great victory over Jericho, that they lost the battle against the little city of Ai. The reply comes from the Lord in verses 10 through 13:

> *"And the Lord said unto Joshua, Get thee up; wherefore liest thou thus upon thy face? Israel hath sinned, and they have also transgressed my covenant which I commanded them: for they have even taken of the accursed thing, and have also stolen, and dissembled also, and they have put it even among their own stuff. Therefore the children of Israel could not stand before their enemies, but turned their backs before their enemies, because they were accursed: neither will I be with you any more, except ye destroy the accursed from among you. Up, Sanctify the people, and say, Sanctify yourselves against tomorrow: for thus saith the Lord God of Israel, There is an accursed thing in the midst of thee, O Israel: thou canst not stand before thine enemies, until ye take away the accursed thing from among you."*

Neither will you be able to stand before your "enemies" if you have the accursed things in your possession! Israel had to take drastic measures to correct the problem, but this would not have even come up if they would have obeyed the Lord!

In Acts 19, we read of a tremendous revival which broke out in Ephesus under the preaching of the apostle Paul. For two years this great move of God swept the occult-filled city of Ephesus, so much so that verses 18 through 20 says:

> *"And many that believed came, and confessed, and shewed their deeds. Many of them also which used curious arts brought their books together, and burned them before all men: and they counted the price of them, and found it fifty thousand pieces of silver. So mightily grew the word of God and prevailed."*

The Word of God can also prevail greatly in America if just Christians would do some spiritual "house cleaning" as these early believers did in Ephesus! In those days, to have a book said a lot. There was no such thing as a printing press that could run off thousands of copies, so they were all hand written. And you can imagine the cost of such an item. But when these people got their hearts right with God, money was not an issue; they burned their occult material. Of course, there was no such thing as a record player or a tape player, but I'm sure if there was, the occult records, tapes, and CDs, the videos, toys, charms, etc., would have been thrown in the fire as well. That should be enough example for us today to make just as strong a stand against the occult!

I challenge you to go through your home and see if you may be allowing Satan an opened door into your life through books, magazines, records, tapes, CDs, videos, toys, idols, pictures, statues, zodiacs, charms, paintings, or anything else that invites a curse in your home. To be safe, just ask yourself this question, "Would **Jesus** approve of this, would He listen or watch this, would He be a part of this activity?" If not, get rid of it! Clean house! Go all out to be a total, 100% Christian!! You've got to start somewhere!

[1]Circus, Jan.31, 1984, pg.70
[2]A Tribute to Springsteen, Vol. #1, pg.28
[3]USA Today, Oct. 31, 1986, USA Snapshots
[4]Middletown Journal, Jan.1, 1988
[5]The Kansas City Times, March 26, 1988
[6]See our booklet entitled, "Halloween...Is it a trick or is it a treat?"
[7]The Satanic Bible, pg.96
[8]Tiger Beat Rock, Feb., 1984, pg.40
[9]International Musician & Recording World, Summer, 1985, pg.42
[10]The National Sheriff, Feb.-Mar., 1987, pg. 40
[11]Dake's Annotated Reference Bible, pg.752, col. 4, letter p
[12]Springfield News, Act. 17, 1987
[13]Thrash Metal, Vol. 1, No. 1, pg.12
[14]Rock Beat, Fall, 1987, pg.17
[15]RIP, June, 1987, pg.58
[16]RIP, June, 1987, pg.42
[17]Bam Magazine, Aug.21, 1985, pg.21

What's A Parent To Do?

"The worst thing that good men can do
for evil to triumph is to do nothing."

After one of our services in a Mid-western state, a lady came over to me and asked if I was going to be dealing with **Bon Jovi** in any of our crusade that week. I told her, "Yes, the night I deal with Top-40 groups, I'll be talking about him." "Great! My 13-year old daughter just loves him. Is there anything wrong with him?" she asked. I returned my answer by asking her a question, "Does your daughter have any of his albums?" "Yea," the mother answered hesitantly, "she has his latest...I think it's called, *Slippery When Wet.*" "Well, I'm sure you know that the title of the album is *not* referring to road conditions," I said as I watched her face turn slightly red. "Well, Brother Muncy, what should I do, should I not let her listen to the record?" Again, I answered her by another question, "Have you ever listened to the songs on that album?" "No, I don't really like that kind of music." I quickly answered, "And yet, you bought the album for her, not even knowing what kind of message it is putting into your little daughter's heart?" With her head down, she asked, "But, what should I do?" I replied, "Well, sister, here is what I would suggest...go home tonight, go into your daughter's bedroom and get the album. With your 13-year old <u>sitting with you</u>, turn on the record player, find the song, "Social Disease", and lay the needle at the beginning of that song and listen...I think after listening to that, you'll know what to do." I wish I could have been there to see that mother's face when she played that song. I'm sure she was "blown away" as she heard the graphic sounds of **John Bon Jovi** and two other women moaning and groaning in a sex orgy before the song begins. It's a shame to say, but most parents would be totally shocked if they would take the time to listen to what their children are hearing through today's music!

A recent reprint of a letter from a rock fan to the rock group **Motley Crue** which appeared in the rock magazine *Circus* shows another result of some of the rock music. The letter read:

> "Since I became a Motley Crue fan my life
> has changed for the better. I have started to
> shout back at my mother and if she tells me
> to do something, I don't do it. If she tells me
> not to do something I do it. I have started
> drinking (Jack Daniels, of course), smoking,
> going to all-night parties and doing unmen-
> tionable things with my male 'friends'. Can
> you believe that just last year I made straight
> A's and was invited to be in the National
> Honor Society? Thanks to the Crue. I have

a new attitude toward life. So to Vince, Mick, Tommy and especially Nikki, thanks for making my life more fun. Someday Nikki, someday." Signed, Nikki Sixx Lover.[1]

What's a parent to do? Give up? Hide your head in the sand, and pretend this isn't really happening? Or maybe give in, as this mother writes in *Hit Parader* magazine:

"I have a teenaged daughter who is very much into heavy metal. Since my husband and I have always believed that she should be allowed to choose her own music — even if it differs from ours — we have never objected to her choice. Recently, a young man started lecturing her about joining a Fundamentalist church. He talked for about seven hours into the night. After allowing her to sleep for two hours, he took her to church with him. After spending all day listening to their philosophy, she was ready to join. The only thing that stopped her was the church's insistence that heavy metal was the "devil's music". They really picked on Motley Crue, who just happens to be her favorite group. Thinking of her ticket to the upcoming Motley Crue concert, she was able to resist. I'll be forever grateful to Motley Crue for saving my daughter from being "saved".[2]

Recently in the Ann Landers column was this article written by a mother from Madison, Wis. which was entitled...

<u>"Teen's Mother Upset By Concert"</u>

"Dear Ann: A few days ago, I took my 15-year-old daughter and three of her friends to a rock concert. I decided on the way out that instead of fighting the traffic both ways I would buy a ticket and stay and see the show.

"I consider myself fairly open-minded, but I was shocked senseless by what I saw and heard.

"The language of the kids around me was unreal. Every other word started with F or S. When one of the rock stars appeared in a G-string, the crowd went wild. That fellow was 99% naked.

"The audio was turned up, and the audience went crazy. My eardrums began to pop, but no one else seemed to mind; in fact, they loved it. Then the kids around me started to light up joints.

"People all over the place began to toss firecrackers. I swear, Ann Landers, I have never been so petrified in my life, not only for me but for every person in that building. There were broken bottles all over the place and several fights going on. The police were nowhere to be seen.

"I lost track of the number of people who had to be carried out. Some were unconscious. Others were hysterical. I saw two couples having sex right out in the open. Others were taking off their clothes all over the place.

"When the concert ended, there was an incredible stampede. I was afraid if I fell I would be stomped to death. I prayed for strength to stay on my feet.

"On the way home (still shaking), I told my daughter that she would not go to another rock show as long as she lived in my house, no matter how old she was. And I am going to stick to it.

"Here is some advice to every parent who is reading this. Don't ask your kid what goes on at these performances. Go see for yourself."[3]

That's some good advice that some of you parents need to consider! I'm amazed today that parents are so concerned about their children's education and yet think nothing of the things rock and roll is educating them in! The average mother will go to all expenses to be sure her little son or daughter has a well-balanced lunch, and yet gives no attention to the "poison" that is being fed into their young minds! I believe much of the blame for the condition of our young people must fall into the hands of Mom and Dad!

In one of our crusades in Kansas City, a young, cute, teenage girl came to me after the service and kept asking me questions about a certain rock singer who had become her idol. She had over $600 worth of records, posters, and other stuff just of this one guy! She was really struggling over the statement I had said that night about getting, "all that junk out of your life, and burn it!" With tears in her eyes, she told me, "I just can't give him up!" The more I talked to her, the more I saw a very empty girl starving for a man's affection, the kind who ends up getting used. I see it so many times, and it was true in her case; Dad was so busy with his job and other "important" things, that he spend little time with his kids. In this case, the Dad had even let his relationship with the Lord become secondary. He was a very "successful" businessman and his job was taking most of his time, requiring him to work 16-18 hours a day.

Night after night, this girl would come after the services and kept trying to convince me (herself, really) that no harm would come from her listening to this rock star. Even though she would admit that the songs were not very Christ-like, she was determined she could never give up this guy, she was in love with him! I told her, "Listen, this guy doesn't even know you exist! He wouldn't even walk across the street to spit on you! And **Jesus Christ** laid His life down for you and you would even give up this one guy for Him!" I could tell that even though this hurt her, she knew I was telling her the truth. That night her mother was there and I asked her to try and get her husband to come to the crusade. She assured me she would try, but seriously doubted he would come because of his job. A few nights later, the crusade closed. That teenage girl came almost every night of that two week crusade, but never did part with her "idol".

The next week we started another crusade only 20-30 miles away from the one in Kansas City. I was surprised when I looked out and saw the same girl, this time sitting with both parents in the meeting. That night we saw God do some powerful things, including that girl's Dad coming down to the altar and re-dedicating his life to Christ! A smile as big as I've ever seen was on that girl's face. Boy, was she happy! After the service was over, I looked around to try and find the family, but they had already left. But the next night, at least 30 minutes before service started, someone got me as I was walking into the church and said excitedly, "John, some teenager is here and wants to talk to you. She's got a bunch of records and posters and wants to destroy them." Sure enough, it was that same young teenage girl! But, it was like she was an entirely different person! She was so happy and excited about ripping up "this garbage"! She was showing me all the bad stuff about this guy. I stood there and just listened as she went on and on about how much better she felt since she took down her posters and pictures and brought in all the tapes and records! In the back of my mind I was wondering what made her change so suddenly, then it dawned on me...it was her DAD! He got right with God! And now he was trying to be the "man in her life"! She didn't need a rock star to admire, she could admire her Daddy! She didn't have to go crazy over some man who could care less about her. Once again, her Daddy was paying some attention to her and putting God back in his life!

That same week someone gave me this poem written by Joe Woody and I knew that God was saying something to me...

<u>"Who Is To Blame?"</u>

We read in the paper and hear on the air,
Of killing and stealing and crime everywhere.
We sigh and say as we notice this trend,
"This younger generation"— where will it end?

But can they be sure it's our fault alone?
Are they less guilty who place in our way
Too many things that lead us astray?
Too much money, too much idle time,
Too many movies of passion and crime.

Too many books, not fit to be read,
Too much evil in what we hear said.

> Too many children encouraged to roam,
> Too many parents who won't stay home.
>
> Kids don't make movies. We don't write the books.
> We don't make the liquor, we don't run the bars.
> We don't make the laws and we don't make the cars.
>
> We might take the drugs that muddle the brain,
> But they're sold by the older folks, greedy for gain.
> Delinquent teenagers. Oh, how they condemn
> The sins of a nation and blame it on them.
>
> By the laws of the blameless, the Savior made known
> Who is among us to cast the first stone?
> For in so many cases it's sad but it's true;
> The title, "delinquent", fits old folks, too!

How true! It's so easy to throw all the blame on to the kids, but the fact is that this generation is a product of you and me, we are the ones responsible for this generation!

In Psa. 78:5-8, David gives the godly formula for family living:

> *"For he established a testimony in Jacob,*
> *and appointed a law in Israel, which he*
> *commanded our fathers, that they should*
> *make them known to their children: That*
> *the generation to come might know them,*

> *even the children which should be born; who*
> *should arise and declare them to their*
> *children: That they might set their hope in*
> *God, and not forget the works of God, but*
> *keep his commandments: And might not be*
> *as their fathers, a stubborn and rebellious*
> *generation; a generation that set not their*
> *heart aright, and whose spirit was not stead-*
> *fast with God."*

It's not enough to bring children into the world, take them to church on Sunday, feed them three meals a day, and be sure they get proper education! God word says in Prov.22:6 to:

> *"Train up a child in the way he should go:*
> *and when he is old, he will not depart from*
> *it."*

The words, *"train up"* denotes more than just than telling your child the way he should go, but it actually means to "discipline by putting a throttle or a choker on them". Now, that may seem like child abuse to some, but the truth is, it would be more like child abuse if we let them do whatever they want! Children not only need to be disciplined in the way they should go, but they desire it! They want Mom and Dad to be involved in their lives. Of course, there has to be a continual allowance for the child to grow and develop as they get older. The time to begin is not when they're 17-years old! Former President Reagan said concerning parents part in all this...

> "...I often think the real heroes of today are
> the parents, trying to raise their children in an
> environment that seems to have grown more
> and more hostile to family life. Music and
> the media flood their children's world with
> glorifications of drugs and violence and
> perversity... and there's nothing they can do
> about it, they're told, because of the First
> Amendment..."[4]

Another thing that is an absolute necessity is to be consistent!
Don't say, "No", one time and, "Yes" the next time. Be consistent in your own life: don't tell your child he can't listen to rock music, while you're listening to "Kickin' Country"! We may not like to hear it, but as one Pastor friend said concerning child rearing, "When they are children, they'll do what you say, but when they are older, they'll do what you **do!**"

The television is another area of destruction for the home! Most "comedy" shows have become more against Christianity and the home than ever before. Most of today's T.V. programs are absolutely worthless!! To put it mildly, it is little more than glorified sin! Recent studies indicate American students watch an average of 23 hours of TV a week. By the time they're 70, they'll have spent a full seven years watching the tube! Each year children watch 14,000 sexual references (not counting commercials). Students also watch more than 2,000 beer and wine commercials each year.[5]

Don't be a hypocrite, Mom, by telling your kids that rock music is bad because of all the references to immorality, divorce, drugs, and drinking; while you're hooked on all those afternoon "soaps" dealing with the same things. I believe as long as parents continue listening to country and western music, and watching soap operas, and other forms of questionable television; they have little right to require their children to live any differently! Let me close this chapter with this...

"GOD'S ANSWER TO SOAPS!"

Written by John Muncy 11/83

Many do not realize that AS THE WORLD TURNS there are millions of YOUNG AND RESTLESS people who are on a SEARCH FOR TOMORROW, hoping to find some type of GUIDING LIGHT. You can go from just a small GENERAL HOSPITAL all the way to the very CAPITOL itself and find many who are living on the very EDGE OF NIGHT with no hope. But we know that RYAN'S HOPE or Jill's hope or "Whosoever's" hope comes from a LOVING God, Who desires to say to the entire world, "Come unto me ALL MY CHILDREN and I will give unto you ANOTHER LIFE! We, as Christians should remember that we have only ONE LIFE TO LIVE and that we should be using every one of the DAYS OF OUR LIVES telling others about Jesus and laying up treasures for ANOTHER WORLD!

A very appropriate verse right now would be Psalms 101:2-3:

> *"I will behave myself wisely in a perfect way. O when wilt thou come unto me? I will walk within my house with a perfect heart. I will set no wicked thing before mine eyes: I hate the work of them that turn aside; it shall not cleave to me."*

---

[1]AFA Journal, Sept., 1988, pg.14
[2]Hit Parader, May, 1988, pg. 24
[3]The Beacon Journal, Feb.7, 1988, pg. D6
[4]Express News, Oct. 10, 1985, pg. H-20
[5]NEA, Sept., 1988

13

The Most Important Chapter

After reading this book, maybe you sense there might be something missing in your life. Maybe you, like millions of others, tried turning to something to help you become "complete". For some it was drugs, sex, or alcohol; others turn to money, popularity, jobs; still others turn to religion, discipline, good deeds; while others turn to rock and roll!! Anything that could drown out that emptiness inside! But you'll never be able to fill it with anything else except one thing...the **Lord Jesus Christ!**

Jesus was called, **"The Rock"**, a long time before anybody even heard of rock and roll music! Rock music is just a counterfeit for the real Rock...**Jesus Christ!** If you want something to really stand on and believe in, well, **Jesus is the Rock that doesn't roll!** He is the **Solid Rock!**

Jesus told a story one time of two men who were building their own houses. One wanted to built as close to the beach as he could get, so he just built his house right on the sand. The other man built his on a firm foundation, a huge rock. Both had very nice houses, except one night, a terrible storm came and hit both houses hard. It doesn't take a whole lot of imagination to figure out the ending...the wise man, whose house was built on rock withstood the storm, while the foolish man's house was totally destroyed! We, too, are building our spiritual "houses", and when the storms of life hit, you'll either be standing on The Rock, or your life will be a disaster!

Maybe you are reading this and feel it's about time to start rebuilding your life...but this time on **Jesus!** I want you to read very carefully as I take you through God's Word on how you can experience peace with God and have your life on that **Solid Rock...**

There are a few things you must realize about what the Bible says about your condition...

1) You must realize that you are a sinner.

<u>Romans 3:23</u> "For all have sinned, and come short of the glory of God."

<u>1 John1:8,10</u> "If we say that we have no sin, we deceive ourselves, and the truth is not in us...If we say that we have not sinned, we make Him a liar, and His word is not in us."

<u>Isaiah 64:6</u> "...we are all as an unclean thing, and all our righteousness are are filthy rags."

2) You must realize you cannot save yourself.

<u>Proverbs 14:12</u> "There is a way which seemeth right unto a man, but the end thereof are the ways of death."

<u>John 14:6</u> "Jesus saith unto him, I am the way, the truth, and the life: no man cometh unto the Father, but by me."

<u>John 3:3</u> "...Except a man be born again, he cannot see the kingdom of God."

<u>Titus 3:5</u> "Not by works of righteousness which we have done, but according to His mercy he saved us..."

<u>Ephesians 2:8-9</u> "For by grace are ye saved through faith; and that not of yourselves: it is the gift of God: Not of works, lest any man should boast."

3) You must realize that Jesus came to give His Life in our place, to pay for the penalty of our sin.

<u>1 Timothy 1:15</u> "This is a faithful saying, and worthy of all acceptation, that Christ Jesus came into the world to save sinners; of whom I am chief."

<u>John 3:16-17</u> "For God so loved the world, that He gave His only begotten Son, that whosoever believeth in Him should not perish, but have everlasting life. For God sent not His Son into the world to condemn the world, but that the world through Him might be saved."

<u>Luke 19:10</u> "For the Son of man is come to seek and to save that which was lost."

<u>Romans 5:8</u> "But God commendeth his love toward us, in that, while we were yet sinners, Christ died for us."

4) You must turn from your sins with all your heart (repent)...

<u>Luke 13:3</u> "...except ye repent, ye shall all likewise perish."

<u>Acts 3:19</u> "Repent ye therefore, and be converted, that your sins may be blotted out..."

<u>Acts 8:22</u> "Repent therefore of this thy wickedness, and pray God, if perhaps the thought of thine heart may be forgiven thee."

<u>Isaiah 55:7</u> "Let the wicked forsake his way, and the unrighteous man his thoughts: and let him return unto the Lord, and He will have mercy upon him; and to our God, for He will abundantly pardon."

5) You must confess your sins to the Lord Jesus Christ...

<u>1 John 1:9</u> "If we confess our sins, He is faithful and just to forgive us our sins, and to cleanse us from all unrighteousness."

390

<u>Proverbs 28:13</u> "He that covereth his sins shall not prosper: but whoso confesseth and forsaketh them shall have mercy."

6) You must call upon the name of the Lord in sincere and earnest prayer...

<u>Isaiah 55:6</u> "Seek ye the Lord while He may be found, call ye upon Him while He is near."

<u>Jeremiah 33:3</u> "Call upon Me, and I will answer thee, and show thee great and mighty things, which thou knowest not."

<u>Acts 2:21</u> "And it shall come to pass, that whosoever shall call on the name of the Lord shall be saved."

7) Right now, by faith, receive Jesus Christ as your Lord and Saviour...

<u>Acts 16:31</u> "Believe on the Lord Jesus Christ, and thou shalt be saved..."

<u>John 1:12</u> "But as many as received Him, to them gave He power to become the sons of God, even to them that believe on his name."

<u>Mark 9:23</u> "...all things are possible to him that believeth."

<u>Hebrews 11:6</u> "But without faith it is impossible to please Him: for he that cometh to God must believe that He is, and

that He is a rewarder of them that diligently seek Him."

Mark 11:24 "Therefore I say unto you, What things soever ye desire, when ye pray, believe that ye receive them, and ye shall have them."

Romans 10:9-11 "That if thou shalt confess with thy mouth the Lord Jesus, and shalt believe in thine heart that God hath raised Him from the dead, thou shalt be saved. For with the heart man believeth unto righteousness; and with the mouth confession is made unto salvation. For the scripture saith, Whosoever believeth on Him shall not be ashamed."

So right now, as your heart is open to the Lord, why don't you pray a simple prayer something like this from your heart...

> "Dear God, I come to You as a sinner, confessing the fact that I have willingly sinned against You. I know I deserve punishment for my sins, but I believe that You sent Your only Begotten Son, the **Lord Jesus Christ** into the world, and that He died on the cross to pay the debt for sinners like me. I ask You, right now, to forgive me of all my sins and to come into my life as Lord and Saviour. I turn my back on sin and trust You to forgive and cleanse me from every single sin I've committed. I renounce Satan's power in my mind and in my life. From this day on, I will live for Him who died for me. Thank You,

Lord for forgiving me, help me live for You.
This I pray, and give You thanks, in Jesus
Name."

If you have sincerely turned your life over to the Lordship of Jesus Christ, you will desire to be as much like Jesus as possible. This *can*, and *will* be accomplished through the power of God's Spirit working in you! Ask God to fill you His Spirit! Walk in obedience to God's Word, the Bible! Read it every day! Spend quality time talking to God in prayer about every aspect of your life! Share your new life in Christ with others daily so they, too, will know the joy of Jesus! If I can be of any help in your spiritual growth, write me:

John Muncy
P.O. Box 377
Miamisburg, OH
45343

JESUS CARES MINISTRIES CASSETTE LIST

(Preached by Evangelist John Muncy)

Thank you for your interest in our tape ministry. Below is all the information that you will need to know when ordering our cassettes...

"SATAN'S MUSIC" Rock music and the occult! Some think it is a little ridiculous, others see it as a gimmick, but John takes a hard and honest look at the alarming occultism being promoted through many of today's secular rock groups. Since the average teenager listens to rock music between 4-8 hours a day, it is easy to understand why Satan would love to get his hands on it...and he has! Many will be shocked by this message.

Two 60-min. cassettes (suggested minimum price...$7.00)

*   *   *   *   *

"DRUGS, SEX, AND ROCK 'N ROLL" If there are two major themes that have been steadily found in rock music, it would have to be drugs and sex! At the same time these are the two major problems plaguing our Nation. In this series, John exposes the pressure placed on today's youth through the mass media of rock, and how it has influenced the growth of alcoholism, drug abuse, and sexual immorality. A much needed message for the adults as well as the youth!

Two 60-min. cassettes (suggested minimum price...$7.00)

*   *   *   *   *

"THE FALSE RELIGIONS OF ROCK AND ROLL" In the 60's, America saw a surge of new religions becoming a part of the rock industry. Slowly those "new philosophies" began to be more and more accepted until today thousands have been duped into believing what the Bible calls 'doctrines of devils'! John shows how entertainers from Michael Jackson to Judas Priest, John Denver to Elvis, Air Supply to the Rolling Stones all have one thing in common...false religion! Is it true that all religions lead to the same God? Jesus said NO!!!

Two 60-min. cassettes (suggested minimum price...$7.00)

*   *   *   *   *

"COUNTRY AND WESTERN MUSIC" Many parents yell at their children for listening to 'that filthy rock and roll,' while they are hooked on the 'kicking Country'!! No wonder young people have rebelled against the double standards! John calls this "3-D Music" (Drinking, Depression, and Divorce) and he pulls no punches on some of the most popular country artists today. Parts of this hard-hitting message will make you laugh, while other parts will make you boiling mad! Mom and Dad, this one is for you!

Two 60-min. cassettes (suggested minimum price...$7.00)

*   *   *   *   *

"THE CHRISTIAN ALTERNATIVE TO ROCK MUSIC" Are young people expected to stop listening to music just because the devil has perverted it? Can there be an alternative without compromising as a Christian? In this series, John shared from the Word of God what he calls "The 10 Commands For Christian Music." In this message, he gives scriptural guidelines that show us as believers the music that should be in our lives.

One 90-min. cassette (suggested minimum price...$4.00)

*   *   *   *   *

"THE DESTRUCTIVE FORCE IN ROCK MUSIC (VIOLENCE AND SUICIDE)" With the onslaught of demonic influence in much of today's rock, our nation is seeing a frightening rise in excessive violent music. Along with violence, our nation is seeing the problem of teenage suicide at an epidemic stage. John addresses these two crucial subjects in the light of many popular rock groups of today, and gives answers from God's Word. Also a very sobering cassette tape is played of a young man's final words to his mother right before committing suicide. John closes the message with a very positive answer from the Lord!

Two 60-min. cassettes (suggested minimum price...$7.00)

• • • • •

"HIDDEN MESSAGES IN ROCK MUSIC" An expanded and updated version of our most requested series on the use of subliminal messages and backward masking in rock music. John takes an honest look at the topic of subliminally-hidden messages found in many rock songs and album covers. Great detail is given to the "how" and "why" of these techniques, which have been proven to be an attack on the subconscious mind. Actual examples are played to clearly reveal various forms of subliminal messages and backward masking, as well as it's Satanic influence that is so subtly programming this generation. This tape series has been used to help lead literal thousands to Christ!!!

Three 60-min. cassettes (suggested minimum price...$10.00)

• • • • •

"WHAT'S WRONG WITH ROCK AND ROLL" (A radio interview) A live radio interview with John on the 50,000 watt AM station WLW in Cincinnati, Ohio. John shares his 10 reasons for preaching against secular rock. The lines were open for callers to voice their opinions and questions. Also during the interview, a disk jockey from one of Cincinnati's largest Rock Stations and a promoter from Polygram Record Company (one of the leading rock labels in the world) debate John's view. An interesting and sometimes heated conversation.

Two 60-min. cassettes (suggested minimum price...$7.00)

• • • • •

"THE SEXUAL THEMES OF TODAY'S ROCK MUSIC" Probably the most important message John has preached on rock music, simply because this is the most accepted of themes in our society today. When a Nation lets down its moral standards, nothing but destruction is in its path. Oddly enough, we continue our decline from God's ways to the ways of sensuality! Among the groups discussed are Duran Duran, Motley Crue, Chicago, Tina Turner, Sammy Hagar, Van Halen, Wham, Prince, Pointer Sisters, Billy Joel, Jacksons, Ratt, Madonna, Bruce Springsteen, The Cars, David Roth, Cindy Lauper, Beach Boys, Hall and Oats, and many more!!

Three 60-min. cassettes (suggested minimum price...$10.00)

• • • • •

"ROCK MUSIC IN BIBLE PROPHECY" A frightening look at how rock music is preparing this generation for the Anti-Christ! In this message, John shares an over-all view of the last days according to the scriptures, and then shows how young people are being fed lies about World Peace, World Government, and a World Leader. Many groups are even now encouraging their fans to mock Jesus Christ and take the 666! One very popular group calls this generation "the children of the beast!" Also new material on what pyramids, UFO's, and the back of the dollar bill have in common. Many Christians say this is their favorite message.

Two 60-min. cassettes (suggested minimum price...$7.00)

• • • • • •

"SATURDAY MORNING CARTOONS" Could it be possible that our little children are being introduced to the world of the occult through "innocent" cartoons? John exposes the sophisticated, glossed-over mass media of cartoons and its effect on the acceptance of such occult practices as: Spells, Crystal Balls, Fortune-telling, Witchcraft, Levitation, Telepathic Communication, Necromancy, Sorcery, Magic, Wizardry, Mind Reading, and more. A look at many of the more popular cartoons. A must for parents!

Two 60-min. cassettes (suggested minimum price...$7.00)

• • • • •

"OCCULT TOYS AND GAMES" Many psychologists say that toys are a direct reflection of our society. This is interesting when we see the increase of toys that are violent and occultic in nature. John gives a very enlightening message on some of the most popular toys and games including: The Masters of the Universe, The Princess of Power, My Little Pony, Care Bears, Smurfs, Rainbow Brite, and much more. Also discussion is given to the popular Dungeons and Dragons game. The message ends by showing Christian alternatives to occult toys. A very important message!

Two 60-min. cassettes (suggested minimum price...$7.00)

"CRESCENT MOONS AND UNICORNS...CUTE OR CULT?" What's behind the strange infatuation with unicorns, an ancient mythological deity? Why does the crescent moon and star show up on everything from the Ouija Board to Bon Jovi's necklace, from the "My Little Pony" Unicorns to one of Duran Duran's album? Why are many groups using the lightning bolt? In this most interesting series, John deals with the scriptural references to lightning, crescents and the unicorn and shows a very eye-opening parallel to the spirit of Anti-Christ with the "spirit of the unicorn," a beautiful creature of peace. A must for every Christian!

One 90-min. cassette (suggested minimum price...$4.00)

• • • • •

"THE 9 FORBIDDEN PRACTICES IN ROCK MUSIC" In Deut. 18:9-12, God lists nine things that He forbids His people to practice. Sad to say, thousands of Christians are involved in many of these very same practices on a daily basis! John takes a candid look at all nine and goes into detail what they mean and how many of them are being used in much of today's music, movies, and television programs. Hosea 4:6 tells us that God's people are "...destroyed for lack of knowledge...", so this series was designed to give knowledge and to help open eyes to the many deceptive ways Satan binds people.

Two 60-min. cassettes (suggested minimum price...$7.00)

• • • • •

ROCK MUSIC...A "STAIRWAY TO HEAVEN" OR A "HIGHWAY TO HELL"? A message that has been preached before literally thousands of people and has been used to win hundreds to Christ. John not only deals with the gradual acceptance of the satanic and perverted messages in rock music, but also address the churches' responsibility for not being the "salt of the world!" John shows how rock music is trying to fill the emptiness that young people are experiencing, and how they are actually being led to blaspheme their only hope...Jesus!

Two 60-min. cassettes (suggested minimum price...$7.00)

• • • • •

THE SOUL THAT WILL DESTROY YOUR SOUL! A long needed message that deals entirely with Black Artists. John preached this message before a church of over 1,000 black people in San Francisco, CA. No punches were pulled as he addressed the message of immorality being glorified in today's rhythm and blues, soul, and rappin' music. A mixture of humor and heavy duty preaching brings a tremendous response from the audience. After the message, the altars were full of young and old alike giving their all to Christ.

Three 60-min. cassettes (suggested minimum price...$10.00)

• • • • •

"SOULWINNING CRASH-COURSE" Nearly 4 hours of teaching on this very vital, but sadly neglected subject. John gives this informative teaching on how you can be effective in personal evangelism. Topics included are: Qualifications for Soul-Winners, The Use of Tracts, Looking for Opportunities, The Use of Scriptures, Altar Work, Dealing with Problems, Do's and Don'ts, Witnessing like Jesus did, Visiting the Sick and Shut-ins, also Religions and Cults, How to Handle Excuses, plus much more. Inspiring, Motivational, and Educational.

Four 60-min. cassettes (suggested minimum price...$13.00)

• • • • •

"ROCK MUSIC UP-DATE...PART TWO" This message is the audio portion of the video series "The Sexual Influences In Rock Music." In this series, John covers many of the latest groups and their message of immorality. John also goes into the background of rock music up to the present time, showing how the influence of poplar music is able to mold the minds of precious young people. 4 solid hours of Bible based teaching!

Four 60-min. cassettes (suggested minimum price...$13.00)

• • • • •

"THE AGE OF ROCK VERSES THE ROCK OF AGES" With such groups as Metallica and Guns 'n Roses coming to the tops of the charts, strong messages are being preached to the minds of millions of young people, and the messages are what the scripture call "vain philosophy." In this series, John exposes the deception coming through many of today's hard rock groups. The age of rock is presenting evolution and revolution, while the Rock of Ages is our only real solution!

One 90-min. cassette (suggested minimum price...$4.00)

• • • • •

"ROCK MUSIC AND NEW AGE DECEPTION" So much talk is given today concerning a movement that has had such reception among "the upper class" as well as "the lower class," a movement that claims to have a new Christ who will bring the world together in perfect peace, calling itself the "new age movement." Most record stores carry a section referred to as "New Age Music." From as far back as the hit song "Age of Aquarius" to the modern hit song "Man In The Mirror," John shows how the music has played an enormous role in the acceptance of New Age deception. What part does all this play in Bible Prophecy? And how has this deception lied to this generation? A must for every student of prophecy!

Two 60-min. cassettes (suggested minimum price...$7.00)

• • • • •

"THE HELLISH TRUTH ABOUT HORROR MOVIES" Literally millions of dollars are pumped into the movie industry today by young people who have become "blood thirsty" for the "slash and dash" horror type films. In this new message, John deals with such horror movies as Nightmare on Elm Street, Friday the 13th, Hell-Raiser, Psycho, Texas Chainsaw Massacre, and many others. As John goes through the audience, young people tell why they watch horror movies and what their feelings are concerning them, as John gives 5 reasons horror movies should be avoided. A badly needed message to a sadly needy generation!

Two 60-min. cassettes (suggested minimum price...$7.00)

• • • • •

We have a newsletter that we would love for you to receive free. It's called "The Cutting Edge" and sent out as the Lord provides. Each issue deals with various topics concerning what is happening in the world around us in the light of the Bible. Along with articles and personal insights from John and Carolyn, each issue contains pictures from the crusades and seminars, video and cassette tape offers, testimonies, and general up-dates on the ministry. If you would like to receive "The Cutting Edge," simply write and request to be placed on the mailing list. Please print your name, address, and zip code very neatly.

When ordering cassettes, please request them by title and enclose either a check or money order (U.S. Currency please) made out to: JESUS CARES MINISTRIES. If you can enclose something for postage and handling it would be greatly appreciated. JESUS CARES MINISTRIES is a Non-Profit Organization, all your gifts are tax-deductible. If you want a receipt, simply request it. IF you should get a defective tape, please return it with a note of explanation and we will correct the error. Be sure to print your name and address, including zip code, neatly to insure proper delivery. Allow 4-6 weeks for your material to arrive. Address all correspondence to:

JOHN MUNCY - P.O. BOX 377 - MIAMISBURG - OHIO - 45342

(THIS LIST WAS UP-DATED FROM 3/89)

* * * Order Form * * *

Title of Tape	Qty	Price
_______________________	___	_________
_______________________	___	_________
_______________________	___	_________
_______________________	___	_________
	Total	_________

To order tapes, make checks payable to:
Jesus Cares Ministries.
Mail to: Living Word Church, P.O. Box 377,
Miamisburg, OH 45342
(513) 424-3192

If you can enclose something for postage and handling, it would be greatly appreciated.

· ·

Order **THE ROLE OF ROCK** here!

Title	Qty	Price	Total
The Role of Rock	____	**$9.95**	_________
		Subtotal	_________
		5% Sales Tax (Ohio residents Only)	_________
		Shipping*	_________
		Grand Total	_________

*Shipping: $2.00 for first item, 50¢ for each additional item up to $4.00 maximum.

Make checks payable to Daring Publishing Group, Inc. Mail order to: Daring Publishing Group, Inc., P.O. Box 20050, Canton, OH 44701 or call 1-800-445-6321.

THE ROLE OF ROCK may also be ordered through Living Word Church at the above address and phone number.

Name ______________________________________

Address ____________________________________

City/State/Zip ______________________________

Phone Number ______________________________